5 Magic Paths to Making a Fortune in Real Estate

SECOND EDITION

JAMES E. A. LUMLEY

WILEY

John Wiley & Sons, Inc.

Published by John Wiley & Sons, Inc., Hoboken, New Jersey.
Published simultaneously in Canada.

For general information on our other products and services please contact our Customer Care Department within the United States at (800) 762-2974, outside the United States at (317) 572-3993 or fax (317) 572-4002.

Wiley also publishes its books in a variety of electronic formats. Some content that appears in print may not be available in electronic books. For more information about Wiley products, visit our web site at www.Wiley.com.

Library of Congress Cataloging-in-Publication Data:
Lumley, James E. A.
    Five magic paths to making a fortune in real estate / James Lumley.—2nd ed.
      p.   cm.
    Includes index.
    ISBN 0-471-54825-1
    1. Real estate investment—United States.   2. Real estate business—United States.
  I. Title: 5 magic paths to making a fortune in real estate. II. Title.
  HD255.L86   2004
  332.63'24—dc22   2003070172

10 9 8 7 6 5 4 3 2 1

CONTENTS

CHAPTER

10

Financing II: Help from the Seller **136**

CHAPTER
18 **Managing Your Property**   **266**

CHAPTER
19 **The Magic Formula for Success:**
Use Flexible Strategies   **279**

PREFACE

Five Magic Paths to Making a Fortune in Real Estate was written to help the beginning investor or anyone else interested in buying and selling real estate. The price of this book is modest compared to the cost of expensive courses and seminars, but the information here is straightforward and reliable. In this book, you're not going to be told you need to go in hock, sell your firstborn, or go to the limit on your credit cards in order to get started. You're not going to learn the latest technique to cram your deal down a seller's throat. Instead, you'll learn the basics of different ways of investing in property, the mechanics involved, methods of valuing property, how to negotiate a fair deal, and above all, how to make a profit.

There comes a time when we realize we've talked and dreamed about improving our financial position in life and never really put out any real effort to do so. That time came for me many years ago when I first attended courses on commercial and investment real estate sponsored by the National Association of Realtors—the NAR. I can still remember the legendary instructor Jay Levine energetically instructing the neophytes in—what seemed to us then—the esoterics of capitalization rates and discounted cash flow.

I bought my first apartment building in the late 1960s, and I owned outright or participated in ownership in a number of other buildings over the years. I also managed property. I've fixed property up and resold it, and I've wholesaled single-family houses. As a broker, I've helped investors lease/purchase and exchange property. In recent years I've consulted, encouraging and bringing others into the various aspects of the real estate business.

This book comes from my years of experience as well as that of many others who are actively practicing today the different techniques we'll explore in this book. All the examples used in the *Five*

Magic Paths are part of today's real estate world. So if you're looking to buy a two- or three-family house in which you'll live in one part while you rent out the rest, or if you want to fix up a house to resell, or simply find property to fix up for others, or lease a house to a tenant with an option to buy—all major strategies in today's market—then this book is for you.

In fact, the goal of this book is to walk you through the several processes. Here is the basic information you need to help you decide on which strategy or strategies you wish to practice, as well as a thorough explanation of how to put each strategy into action—how to buy at the right price, price repairs, value property, wholesale and lease/option property, and profit with the traditional buy-and-hold.

When I started out in those NAR courses, I made a promise to myself that I would reject the typical advice—never borrow, earn money at a 9-to-5 job, retire at 65—and follow a different path. What made the difference to me was the knowledge I was gaining through my studies. At the time, the NAR courses were all that was available, but they were enterprising and had a high degree of integrity and professionalism. These courses are still given and remain of the highest quality. Today we also have many other opportunities available for real estate education—seminars, books, conventions, and of course, the Internet. But knowledge on its own isn't enough. We must also have a positive attitude and an enthusiasm for what we're doing.

So if you're serious about real estate investing, you owe it to yourself to jump-start your efforts by reading about the major techniques used in real estate today as outlined in *Five Magic Paths.* You'll be happy you did.

James Lumley
Amherst, Massachusetts
E-mail: James@Lumley.com
Web page: www.JIMLUMLEY.com

ACKNOWLEDGMENTS

My thanks to Jay Levine, who as an instructor opened my eyes to the world of real estate investing; to David Huskin, who lent inspiration to my effort; to my editor at John Wiley & Sons, Michael J. Hamilton, whose guidance and encouragement led to the completion of this book; to the staff at Cape Cod Compositors, for their patience in the final editing; and to Margaret Roberta Dakin, for her constancy and careful reading. And, to my many clients who have used my services to buy and sell investment property.

INTRODUCTION

In the recent bestseller *The Millionaire Next Door,* by Thomas J. Stanley and William D. Danko (Atlanta: Longstreet Press, 1996), we learned that two-thirds of all millionaires in the United States are self-employed. Many of these people made their fortune in whole or in part by investing in real estate. In this book you will find out how you, too, can join this elite club.

Put simply, these are the "five magic paths" to building a fortune in real estate:

1. Buy, fix up, and sell single-family houses in need of repair.
2. Wholesale or "flip" properties to other investors.
3. Secure properties with lease/option for "rent-to-own" with tenant-buyers.
4. Buy and hold single-family houses.
5. Invest in apartment buildings and small commercial properties.

Are you working hard for little pay? Is your work unappreciated? Is your job not satisfying? Do you desire more gratifying work that would also bring in more money? Do you go into work each day feeling you'd like to tell your boss you can't stand it anymore? Maybe you or someone in your family has been downsized out of a job. Do you really deserve to be treated this way?

Maybe it's time to take charge of your future. Maybe you need to make some real money, pay off some debts, and have the lifestyle you and your family deserve.

Five Magic Paths to Making a Fortune in Real Estate describes five simple but proven real estate investment techniques, any one of which can make you well-off and change your life forever. Here you will gain an understanding and level of knowledge that will start you on the path to wealth. All you need to do is act.

The five "magic" techniques described in this book are the ways successful investors are currently, and have been for some time, making money in real estate. You may choose to use any one of the techniques or some combination of them, depending on the time you wish to devote. All offer a reliable way to continually generate cash—money that you could spend for your own needs, or reinvest.

After reading about the five approaches to property investing in *Five Magic Paths*, you can start off with the strategy with which you feel most comfortable. Learn them one at a time, and get to know how they fit together. All it takes is a little knowledge, the proper guidance, and a desire to succeed. By doing so you will be putting the odds of real estate success in your favor. Once you become adept at one technique, add another. In fact, here you will read about using more than one strategy at a time, increasing your profits when you do. Each strategy is a powerful tool, but when they are used in combination, these strategies can be extraordinarily successful.

The goals of this "magic five" program are to help you become more knowledgeable, to keep you in touch with new possibilities, and to expand your experience level so that you can take advantage of the opportunities that are right in front of you. As you've seen, real estate can help you build wealth in the future, and it can also help you improve your life today.

These "magic paths" aren't imaginings or unproved techniques. They are firmly established procedures in extensive use everywhere in the United States. They are the major ways in which individual investors approach real estate today. And—just to tantalize you—if you master these strategies, there are even more ways, each with its adherents, that we don't go into in this book. They include trading lease options, mortgage lending, mobile homes, buying discounted mortgages, and tax lien certificates—the list goes on and on.

Are you already baffled? I know I was when I first started out. But I was fortunate to have some wise mentors who took me under their wings and provided some guidance. I began with all the available Certified Commercial Investment Member (CCIM) courses sponsored by the educational arm of the National Association of Realtors, and they're still the best educational opportunities around.

The techniques I talk about in this book are the more popular ones that I've done exactly or some variation thereof at one time or another. Now let me remind you that you don't have to become an expert in all the methods presented here. In fact, it's better to specialize in one or two depending on the current activity and profit potential in your marketplace. By this I mean that if, for example, the small apartment buildings available for sale are being bought for prices that the new owner will have to take a loss on for several years before breaking even, then consider alternative strategies, and wait for rents to catch up with expectations. Similarly, if the older houses that need fixing up in your area are priced beyond reason, you might want to stay away until the market swings back in your favor. Or, for another example, perhaps you could lease a single-family home that the owner is having difficulty selling and re-lease it with an option to a tenant who wants to buy but needs more time to save up a down payment or repair credit so he or she can buy in a year or two. But if leases with options are seldom used in your market, or even over-used, it might be better to consider another strategy.

The choices seem endless. But when you look at your market—the properties available for you to buy, sell, or trade—your individual choice becomes clearer. What I would not recommend is attempting to apply all strategies at one time. Start by learning one—or two at the most—strategies that you feel will work best in your market.

Another reason why it's better not to jump around attempting a medley of techniques is that each one requires time, not only in terms of understanding a technique, but in getting the word around in your community that you provide a given kind of service—fixing up property, buying apartment buildings, or enabling others to rent to own. Each strategy, in other words, requires a different public presentation.

You may also be hampered by time constraints. If you have a full-time job, you will have to be careful to choose projects that you can fit into your schedule; perhaps, for example, you will find an opportunity to fix up a small property in which you can involve others in the work. Owning a group of apartments, on the other hand, can be a full-time job in itself unless you hire a competent property management firm.

Over time you may notice that market conditions have changed and decide that one of the other strategies would be more appropriate to the new conditions. That would be the opportunity to learn another strategy and see how it works for you. But one step at a time. Start small (even while you think big). Many investors begin by using the rent-to-own or lease/purchase techniques to build up some cash, then buy a fixer-upper to resell, and then, with a greater nest egg, secure a small apartment building.

Whatever technique you choose, go for the strategy that engages you, the one that you can get and stay excited about. Remember that if you apply the knowledge you'll gain here, you have the potential to become wealthy. If you're the best at what you do, the best is sure to come.

INTRODUCTION TO
THE SECOND EDITION

Since the founding of our country, through good times and bad, real estate values have edged higher. Real property has proven itself to be a sensible, steadfast, and lucrative investment. And, not surprisingly, due to modern mortgage financing it is an investment in which you don't need a lot of money to make money.

This book shows you the way to get started investing in real estate, even if you don't have a great deal of funds. Begin by reading this book—in whole or just the parts that interest you. Be mindful that not all of the techniques described here may work in your area. See what other successful investors have done and study the techniques they have used. Some of these investors have probably made a lot of money. Many of the techniques they used are described in this book. The techniques are not gimmicks; they are established ways investors have used for decades to make fortunes.

After you have read, decide on one or two of the techniques that you can put to work in the time you have available. Once you act on the right "opportunity," you will be on the path to financial freedom. Create wealth by taking control of your life and your choices. This book is really about investing in yourself!

At the beginning of the last century Thomas Edison said, "Opportunity is missed by most because it is dressed in overalls and looks like work." If we want to be successful in life, and if making money is part of the way we define that success, we need to embrace a good work ethic that includes a readiness to roll up our sleeves and plunge into a task that faces us. For real estate, that may mean, for example, researching operating expenses for a building you want to buy. It might be to confer with tradespeople on the work needed in a fixer-upper. It might mean that you and your spouse will clean out an apartment at the end of a tenant's stay. In real estate all these tasks are opportunities to insure a prosperous financial future. And that future starts with seeing opportunity the way Edison saw it. And do we see opportunity in real estate investing today? Perhaps never before have we seen such a range of opportunity.

Consider these facts:

■ *There is a shrinking housing inventory in the lower price ranges.* Much writing in the popular press is devoted to the scarcity of affordable housing. Many new families are forming who need houses as well as working singles who need homes now and will need larger ones when they form families of their own in the future.

■ *There is an unusually low number of rental vacancies.* With little vacancy landlords can keep properties rented for more money and for longer periods of time, thereby stabilizing investments. It is a supply-and-demand situation, with more renters than available rental housing.

■ *There is increasing demand for new housing in all price ranges.* It's not just the young who need housing. People work at home more and have more children; the concept of required homespace is becoming larger.

■ *Capital gains rates are near an all-time low.* The mere fact that capital gains exist, allowing lower rates on sales, is unlike the situation some years ago when many sales were taxed at ordinary income rates. And in fact, the new tax law passed in 2003 has lowered them even more.

■ *Homeowners can sell nearly tax-free every two years.* The current $500,000 ($250,000 for singles) exclusion on the sale of your personal residence can be repeated for every home in which you have resided for two of the last five years. Under the right circumstances (see Second Homes Taxing elsewhere), the exclusion is available for a second home. Note that the previous one-time exclusion of $125,000 after age 55 was phased out in 1997. Furthermore, if taxable gains exceed limits ($500,000/$250,000), convert the home to a rental and use Starker 1031 exchange (see elsewhere) to get a new property and defer the gain.

■ *Exchange provisions allow investors to defer capital gains.* Long-term investors may defer capital gains by exchanging equity into another property of equal or greater value. The favorable twist in recent years is to allow the investor to delay the actual identification and purchase of the next property.

■ *Lenders are anxious to loan funds.* Financing is available for nearly all home and investment purchases, including monies for fixer-uppers and non–owner occupied properties. Leverage (loan amount to cash down) percentages are historically high: 90 percent for many owner occupants, 75 to 80 percent for many investors. In fact, the opportunities for real estate funding are so abundant that you need to shop around more than in the past just to get the best deal.

■ *Home equity lending frees up money for investments.* Funds from a home equity loan can help beginning investors make a down payment on a new property or make needed capital improvements on existing property.

■ *Interest rates are near historic lows.* At no time in the last three decades have interest rates been so low. And although rates may not remain low, they are not likely to rise substantially either (see discussion elsewhere).

All these facts bode well for investing in real estate.

We cannot predict precisely what will happen in the foreseeable future. It does seem that many favorable factors as outlined above will support a lively investing climate. Will investing be as lucrative as the 1980s and 1990s? The dynamics are in place for a continuation of profitable investing. The key, however, is not to view the investing climate from a distance but to craft each deal carefully—and that's what this book is about—how to evaluate a property and make the right deal. Whether it's a fixer-upper, a lease/option, the purchase of a two- or three-family, or a larger multifamily, it's all about a particular property and the deal you make for it. And this book will help you make the best deal.

1

Five Magic Paths to Making a Fortune in Real Estate

For many people, real estate has been the investment of choice to become wealthy. In no other way can you consistently and safely make substantial amounts of money. In this first chapter we'll take a look at each of the five "magic paths" to use real estate to gain financial freedom. We'll also look at how these techniques work with one another. We'll talk about how you can get started with little or no money and with modest work in your spare time on a road paved with great profits for years—a road where you are your own boss, you make your own time schedule, and, as you master these skills, you prosper.

THE FIVE MAGIC WAYS TO WEALTH

The general benefits of real estate that can make you wealthy were discussed in the Introduction, so now we'll turn our attention to a brief view of each of the five techniques explored in this book and how you can be flexible enough to profit with each one.

   1. *Buy and fix up single-family houses for resale.* This is one of the greatest markets of all time. Nowhere else can the average investor start increasing wealth faster. Many of the skills needed are common-sense ones. First, you secure a property that is priced reasonably because it needs repair. Then, you manage or do these repairs yourself; and finally, you resell the property to a retail home buyer. Sound complex? Not at all. Because the single-family fixer-upper can be sold or rented to a huge market of buyers or renters, it's one of the most common real estate ventures. And you can find as much help as you need. If you work with a real estate agent, you'll discover his or her expertise in property values to be worthwhile. If you work with a carpenter or contractor, you will easily find out the expense of needed repairs. The fixer-upper is one investment opportunity that's win–win. It's ideal for getting started and generating cash, particularly for those investors who don't mind rolling up their sleeves and doing the necessary repairs themselves, at least to get started.

You start by looking for single-family properties that may be in distress but that do not require major repairs and that are low enough in price to permit a robust profit on resale. Two to four deals a year will earn you more than, for example, the average teacher's salary. One of the ways you will obtain property is through a lender, mortgage company, tax authority, or other lien holder that has foreclosed on a property. As foreclosures often need rehabilitating, they remain one of the best opportunities for acquiring fixer-upper properties. Since obtaining a foreclosed property is different than negotiating with a home seller, we address this separately. Here you will gain the special knowledge needed to make this area profitable.

2. *Buy or control property to wholesale or "flip" to another investor.* An alternative version to buying the fixer-upper, doing the work, and re-selling it is to secure the property by contract and assign your position in the contract to another who will close and do the work. This is called wholesaling or flipping. Wholesaling or flipping a property means that you sell a property, normally as is, very soon after you secure it by agreement. Some investors concentrate on wholesaling as a primary activity. You might take title and resell in a simultaneous closing—buy and sell at the same sitting—or sell before taking title.

Wholesaling is perfect if you don't want to take title on a property and follow through with the necessary amount of fixing up and waiting for a retail buyer to come along. It's also great if your skills lie in negotiating deals with owners, or time constraints work against your doing the necessary repair project. It's a great way to make a profit without spending a lot of time, tying up much cash, or triggering a mortgage commitment. You may not make as much profit wholesaling as if you took title and completed the repair work, but then for little effort your modest gain will be a significant profit in a deal that may require little down payment.

3. *Lease/option or "rent-to-own" property from a seller and contract future sale with a new tenant-purchaser.* In lease/optioning property you control a property by leasing it from a willing owner who gives you an option to purchase the property sometime in the future. Favorable lease terms such as low monthly cost, long duration, ability to sublease, and a reasonable purchase price in the future are all terms you want to negotiate. In a typical lease/option deal you become sublandlord and rent out your leased property—for a higher price than you pay to the owner—to a tenant committed to buy at some future time. To insure this purchase you receive from your tenant-buyer a down payment, and in turn you give a credit of the monthly rent toward the agreed-upon purchase price. Only at the future closing will your renter take title.

It's an advantage for this renter because it gives him or her a chance to build up equity in rent credit as well as time to save more down payment before taking title. The renter also gains any appreciation in the property. For you as an investor it allows a profit as you net the difference between the lease amount you pay the owner and the rent the tenant pays you, while further receiving a cash gain at the closing of the future sale. Although you may not gain as much profit in comparison to that of outright ownership, the deal is similar to wholesaling in that you are able to avoid making a large down payment or securing a mortgage. And you could sell or assign your position at any time. A lease/option can be attractive to a current owner who wants to get rid of the day-to-day responsibility of running the property while procuring a specific future sale.

A variation of the lease/option technique is only to negotiate an option—the right to buy at some future time—without passing this right on to a tenant. In this way, with limited risk to yourself, you control the appreciation of the property and have time to arrange for financing for a future close and/or find a buyer.

4. *Buy and hold single-family houses for long-term investment.* The first three "magic paths" deal with several short-term techniques of ownership and control. The fourth involves buying and holding the single-family home for a longer period. The buy-and-hold technique relies on the long-term appreciation of a property over a 3- to 20-year period. Here we examine the continuing renting and management of a single tenant in one property and how it differs from shorter-term techniques. Buying and holding a house that does not necessarily need rehabilitation but perhaps is worthwhile because of location or price can end up being a bargain as time increases its value. Many investors have used their investment skills to profit from long-term single-family rentals.

5. *Buy and hold multifamily apartment and small commercial properties.* You might stumble onto a six-unit apartment building or a small commercial building that may need fixing up (and what one does not?) and you decide to make the repairs and resell it right away. That's fine. Or, as you just read in the previous section, you might also decide to buy and hold a single-family property. That's okay, too. However, consider that the basic construction and design of an apartment (or commercial) building permits the continued use, and abuse, of nonowning tenants more than a single-family house normally built and designed for the presumably more considerate owner-occupant. True, over the years numerous investors have collected houses like postage stamps and rented them out for the long term. But, due to design and durability, the long-term investment has less risk if it's a building built specifically for tenants.

Therefore, an excellent way to start in long-term investing is to buy a duplex or another building of up to six or eight units. The chapters (14–17) on multiple units discuss income, expenses, and mortgage costs that must be considered to assure a positive cash flow. Benefits besides cash flow include equity buildup through appreciation, and amortization of debt. The risk includes making sure apartments stay rented and maintenance is not delayed. Here you will find what you need to know about the benefits of long-term property ownership and how to find, buy, and manage these properties profitably.

The techniques discussed in this book may be altered to fit the property activity in your area. You might fix up a single-family home to hold long-term. You might fix up an apartment building to sell. You might even combine techniques. You might buy a single-family home and exchange its equity into a small apartment building. You might add an option to a property you wish to lease and rerent.

You will achieve your maximum effectiveness by being flexible enough to use several of these techniques. But that doesn't mean you should start by mixing techniques together. Begin by focusing on one area. Perhaps you might wish to start in the area that interests you most. The next chapter will discuss buying, rehabbing, and reselling the fixer-upper; much of the information will support the techniques that follow. As a guide for success, you must study and learn what will work in your own market. You must locate and inspect property, negotiate with current owners, and arrange financing, lease, or option for what you wish to acquire or purchase.

NOW IT'S TIME TO MAKE REAL MONEY

Success can come from using any one of the five "magic" techniques, or a combination of several. The idea is not to jump from one technique to another indiscriminately, but to begin by focusing on one, to specialize in that area, and then add to your growing expertise by undertaking one of the other methods. However, too many good opportunities can come up at a moment's notice not to be able to take advantage of them. Therefore, you may need to be versatile enough to shift gears at any time into another mode. It certainly would not be unusual to have a lease/purchase in process when the chance comes up to buy a distressed single-family.

Now that we've said it's best to begin with one technique, we will also say that while it's true that specializing in one niche improves your expertise in that area, the opportunities available in any given property market may not be in your area. Besides, if openings in any one niche area were in abundance the competition would be fierce, driving up prices beyond reason. It's best to stay flexible and be prepared to learn another method—again, one method at a time—so that you can take advantage of varying opportunities.

If you work only in a narrow area, like buying and holding single-family houses, you will miss much of the picture because you are concentrating on a small part of real estate investing. Perhaps you should consider buying and selling without holding over a period of time, or becoming a landlord of a building designed for long-term use, such as an apartment building. Specifically, buy low and resell a few properties to build up some cash before holding a few, or sell with owner financing for a cash flow. Unless you have lots of money in the bank, don't think just of holding, but of buying and selling.

The bottom line is that while you will be learning and gaining experience, you will also be making money and building a financial base that will make you wealthy. And, yes, it may seem easier to hone your skills in a single area and develop such expertise there, but you want to be able to take advantage of whatever the case is in your market. It's a lot of work, particularly when you must anticipate several avenues of investment techniques, but it is rewarding.

GUIDELINES FOR GETTING STARTED

Here are some guidelines for choosing which method you might begin with:

1. Study your local market. The technique you use will be determined by the opportunities available. You have to work with what people want in your area. In Chapters 2–6 on fixer-uppers you will see more on measuring your local market.

2. Note what's going on in your regional economy. Will fixer-upper opportunities be better in a few years when the local manufacturing plant relocates? Or will apartment buildings rise in value, as more people are coming into your area than are leaving?

3. Try to find the technique that appeals to you, something that not only fits your market but fits you.

4. Note that some techniques require more money, at least to put down initially, than others. Specifically, the lease/option allows you to put little down to get the deal started, but the apartment building purchase may require 10% to 20% down unless you can finance it creatively.

5. Gauge the amount of time you have available to get started. And be aware of when that time is free. Generally, real estate allows you control over your time. You can probably manage and maintain a small apartment building in the evenings or on the weekends, but working on a fixer-upper may require some weekday time when tradespeople are available.

COMBINE TECHNIQUES TO ENSURE SUCCESS

First consider a basic axiom of real estate investing: When possible, have a secondary possibility for the property. For example, if you're buying a fixer-upper for resale as your primary investment, bear in mind its potential as a rental in case it does not sell right away for the amount you want. In other words, think "insurance": What alternative will you have as a fallback position to safeguard this investment? This has nothing to do with lacking confidence in your original intent; it's simply some preinvestment precautionary thinking that will make it easy for you to shift gears if you have misjudged the market.

So you must be prepared. That's why you need to be able to think on different levels and be willing to manage the investment in a different way if it turns out you need to do so to best maximize your profits. In the example of shifting a fixer-upper to a rental (at least temporarily), part of your consideration might be the property's suitability as a rental in terms of durability and location.

Another example of shifting techniques midstream would be a situation where you have a small apartment building that you were going to buy and hold, but because of the expense of needed improvements you would prefer to resell it soon for a modest profit and recoup capital funds. To have this as a viable alternative, you need to know beforehand the exact cost of repairs and know how much they will increase the value of the building in order to judge whether it is a good investment overall.

BEFORE YOU ROLL UP YOUR SLEEVES

A lot of us have managed to struggle through the ups and downs of real estate values of the past decade. Some say genius is a rising market. But many investors with knowledge and creativity can survive in any market by learning to distinguish lucky chances from solid investment techniques.

Note that profitable investing can be done anywhere in the nation. Even within well-to-do regions there are houses that are modestly priced. There is opportunity everywhere. You need never get discouraged! There are always fellow investors working through the same deals elsewhere. Be persistent and good deals will come your way. Remember, if you spend an hour a day looking for the right property, in a few weeks you might land a deal, and from there you can see how productive you will become if you do it consistently.

If you know what is going on in your local economy, you can take better advantage of the opportunities. Is the answer to specialize? Perhaps, but only if your market does not offer a wide-ranging opportunity to carry out more than one technique successfully. To be the most productive, you will use two if not three techniques in which you can succeed. Additionally, you must read and research all you can on creative real estate investing. Capability comes from knowledge and imagination!

TAKE SOME MEASUREMENTS OF YOUR MARKET

Before we leave our overview and go into details of our first strategy, take a moment and evaluate your own marketplace. Here are some characteristics you could investigate about your marketplace and the neighborhoods in which you will look for property:

- Establish the territorial area in which you will prospect for property.
- Determine territorial divisions of neighborhoods in which you will do business.
- In each neighborhood determine if the number of home sales as well as the value of their prices are rising or falling, and look at trends for the past several years.
- Look at the number of single-family houses in contrast to the number of multifamily dwelling units, and find whether the trend for the past several years is increasing or decreasing.
- For single-family houses, determine the ratio of tenants to owner-occupants, and the trend there for several years.
- Determine the profile of the typical buyer in each of the respective neighborhoods.

Don't let this list intimidate you. Investigating these characteristics isn't meant to be a demanding task. You probably already know much of the information. Whatever you don't know can be learned from local real estate agents, property appraisers, assessors, or other investors. A check at the county registry of deeds office may also be helpful. The purpose is for you to start gaining a sense of what's happening in real estate in your marketplace. This will start you thinking about whether the value of single-family properties is going up and whether the tenant mixture is moving toward owner-occupants—two important points in using the real estate techniques in this book.

MAGIC PATHS FAQs

Before you read about how to put the five "magic paths" to work, take a moment to look at these frequently asked questions.

Is this book designed for the experienced real estate investor?
Absolutely not. Although anyone with real estate experience could benefit by reviewing the material here, what is presented is primarily for the beginning investor.

Will these strategies work in my area?
Certainly. Although markets vary, opportunities abound in each area. The book contains a discussion on how to evaluate your local market for using the best strategy.

Do I create a lot of debt in real estate investing?
Not necessarily. Creating debt is not your goal. Just remember what debt you do take on is backed up by a tangible property that is worth more. And when these debts are paid off their value will have gone into your pocket.

Will all the techniques discussed in the book work?
Yes, they comprise the major techniques used to practice investing in real estate in the United States today. Although some have more popularity than others, none are minor or insignificant.

Do they involve "no-money-down" schemes?
Not at all. Some require more money than others. But often several techniques are used to build up cash reserves for their use elsewhere.

What is this so-called creative financing all about?
Creative financing is a catchall term that usually involves financing other than or beyond a traditional mortgage loan. When used in this book it refers to the seller's participation in secondary financing and the conservative use of a home equity loan.

Will using the techniques described here take much time?
Some take longer than others. You certainly don't need to give up your present work to get started with using several of the techniques. Securing and arranging the work on a fixer-upper can often be done easily on a part-time basis. Correspondingly, however, something like

the operation of several apartment buildings may take a larger commitment in time, unless professional management is used.

If I'm buying a single-family house or small apartment building do I have to swindle the seller?
Of course not. Great profits come from dealing fairly in the marketplace. Note that all prices come from comparable sales in the marketplace; even a damaged fixer-upper has a reason for its low price.

Is this book comprehensive and all I need to know?
No, your study of real estate should be lifelong. Although the techniques presented here are thorough and intended to get you started, each is its own field with a distinct fraternity of followers, books, courses, and gurus.

Are negotiations with sellers difficult?
Not at all. Even when you need to offer a seller less than what he or she is asking, a seller is generally persuaded by the factual material and comparable selling prices that you will gather regarding a property's value. You can make negotiating pleasant if the seller knows that you want to take some of the responsibility of the real estate problem off his or her shoulders. Note that you can often come near the seller's asking price if you name the terms; that makes it win–win for you both.

I'm not sure about my credit. How do I go about qualifying for a mortgage?
Two observations: First, consider that many investment properties, both single- and multifamily, are financed in whole or in part by the seller; second, many lenders base their mortgage decisions more on the value of the property and less on the borrower. Once you have real estate, regardless of how it's financed, you will have gone a long way to repairing any credit problem.

Do I need a real estate license?
Not to practice as an investor, you don't. In fact, having a license may compromise your investor status with the Internal Revenue Service (IRS), as well as be a hindrance in working with sales agents. Further, many sellers simply don't want to talk to brokers, so don't license yourself to become one. Note that wholesaling a property may feel like it requires a license, but even here you're selling a contract to buy a property over which you have a measure of control—and not for a fee, but for a markup, or difference in price.

Do I need to incorporate?
Generally, no. In fact, you will lose important tax advantages if you do. Incorporating is supposed to limit liability, but if individuals within a corporation act irresponsibly, the corporation will not shelter their liability. As far as liability for someone having an accident on your property goes, you should always cover yourself with the proper insurance, and liability insurance is relatively inexpensive. As for liability for the mortgage, even if you have a corporation you are likely to be required to sign personally on the mortgage. (In this regard, you should always make sure the mortgage is less than the value of the property.)

What are the main ways in which I will spend my time?
Oh, yes, I didn't tell you yet? It's not so much about bricks and mortar (although there may certainly be some of this). You will spend most of your time contacting people, and the second biggest investment of your time will go toward establishing value by investigating comparable sales.

Will it take persistence?
Yes, definitely. It will also take indefatigability, stamina, determination, purpose, grit, and, of course, pluck. Yes, lots of pluck.

In the next chapter, we'll begin setting out the way you make money with fixer-uppers.

2

Making Money
with Fixer-Uppers

In this chapter we'll look at the first choice of many property investors, the fixer-upper.

THE FIX-UP-AND-SELL STRATEGY

Here's why the fix-up-and-sell strategy is so popular today. First, the idea is to beat the ups and downs of the economic cycle. We, as investors, do that by getting in and out quickly. Second, because the property we wish to buy needs some work, many retail home buyers will not compete with us on price because they often choose a home that needs little or no work. This leads to our being able to buy our target properties at advantageous prices. Third, as long as we can determine what needs to be done and know what we can sell the property for when it's fixed up, we can lock in our profits.

The key advantage of this strategy is that you, the investor, aren't at the whim of inflating or deflating prices, or interest rate direction, or even fluctuating vacancy rates. As long as you know how much it will cost you to fix up the property and what it will sell for, you know what your profit will be. You are in control.

Like any task that is financially rewarding, it involves work and understanding. Diligence and patience will bring success, and with experience each success will lead to another.

At this point you may be asking yourself whether owning rental property over the long term is a bad strategy: Certainly not. As you will read in Chapters 13–17 on the buy-and-hold strategy, long-term profits exist in the ownership of both single-family and multifamily properties. If you buy low in the real estate cycle and sell high when it peaks, you can't lose. The timing of your purchase and sale must be in harmony with your local real estate cycle. It's like investing in the stock market. You buy when prices are low and nobody wants the stock, and sell when the market is hot.

What is the status of your local real estate market? The answer to this question will guide you in the timing of your rental purchases. In this book you will read how to determine the status of your local market.

Even though you might not have a huge pile of money, you will learn how to surround yourself with those who can assist you with your project: carpenters, skilled artisans, home inspectors, appraisers, and real estate agents. You will learn how to gain funding that will give you all the money you need to buy and rehabilitate your properties.

We'll also show you concrete examples of property inspections, detailed repair cost estimates, and how to negotiate the deal and then prepare a purchase offer.

The rehab business is not a get-rich-quick scheme. You will work hard for your profits by using your brain and, to whatever degree you choose, your hands.

BUYING A FIXER-UPPER

Once you've found a prospective buy, the first thing to do is to make an itemized list that will help you determine the cost of repairs. Next, you need to value the property. Since it might be difficult to find a similar property in a comparable unrepaired condition (so that you can compare prices), you will make your comparison based on what the property will be like when it's repaired or brought into the same condition as the other property. This also allows you to target your final selling price. Once you have a projected selling price, you subtract the cost of repairs, a minimum profit of 15% based on the final selling price, and overhead and selling costs of another 15%. The remaining amount gives you the maximum of what you can safely pay and still make a profit.

Here's an example of how it might work: You find a clunker that no potential home buyer has bought because it needs too much work and the present owner is asking too much money. You start with a thorough examination and find that repairs must be done on the roof and in the kitchen, that it will require a lot of painting, and so forth. Nothing major, but in all you estimate the repair cost to be $15,000. Next, you find several houses in the same neighborhood that have sold within the past year and are similar to your subject house—once the work is completed. The three houses most similar to your new to-be-fixed-up house average closely at $85,000. Now you subtract from this projected selling price 30% (profit, overhead, and selling costs), or $25,500, which leaves you with $59,500; subtract from that repair cost of $15,000 and you get $44,500. In other words, $44,500 is the most you should offer.

Comparable value as finished:	$85,000
Repairs needed:	−15,000
Profit, overhead, selling cost:	−25,500
Maximum "buy" price:	$44,500

Note that this is only a shorthand form of the overall process, and the prices may be a little low for most markets. Later in Chapter 5 we deal extensively with how you arrive at repair and value figures.

A property you can buy at a relatively low price, check the title for any liens, obtain accurate repair prices, get real-world comparables for its fixed-up condition, and prove to yourself that it's profitable after all costs and salable in a popular price range for your area—this is a property you should buy.

Let's take a look at another example before going on.

Now we'll get into a price range not uncommon to many markets. You find a property that you feel would be an excellent fixer-upper. The seller is asking $115,000 for the property. You check the fair market value for the property as if it were all fixed up against comparables in the $185,000 to $205,000 range for that neighborhood. To be conservative, you estimate it will sell for $190,000. Repairs will cost you $25,000. You assume closing costs to be around 6%.

With 10% off the projected selling price for overhead, your final estimate of costs is:

Property:	$115,000
Repairs:	25,000
Closing costs:	11,400 (6% of $190,000)
Overhead:	19,000 (10% of $190,000)
Subtotal:	$170,400
Projected price:	$190,000
Remaining amount as profit:	$19,600

In this example, should you carry the property longer than you estimate before selling it, you have sufficient overhead funds to pay the carrying costs. A profit of $19,600 is 10.3% of your projected selling price. And of course you can increase your profit if the seller is willing to take less—every dollar less he or she takes will be one dollar more in your pocket. Always negotiate on selling price as much as the seller will tolerate.

Note that one of the keys in working the fixer-upper market is that the price of the house once fixed up will fit into a range in which buyers are actively seeking homes in your area. Sometimes that range is lower than this example, sometimes higher. Generally most investors familiar with rehabbing recommend that one stay in the lower price ranges—upscale houses limit your market. But never go extremely low; you want to stay on the low side of the most active price range in your market. That's where the best profits are made.

SEEK FIXER-UPPERS IN ALL PRICE LEVELS

As indicated, many fixer-upper investors feel that you don't need to deal with expensive properties. The cheaper properties have the best possibility for higher profit. In an expensive property you are likely to tie up too much capital, ultimately hindering your goal of making profits. For example, what may seem like a great deal at $250,000 because it will take only another $15,000 to fix up may not be so great if it can't sell for substantially more. And if you must use an agent to sell it later, that commission cost may eat up too much of your profit. Unless it's located in Beverly Hills with a scenic view of the Hollywood Hills, you might be better off passing. Here are some of the reasons the action is better in less expensive properties:

1. Study the price action in your market. If there are more buyers in the first-time home market than any other, you'll have more possibilities for selling a smaller home than a larger, more expensive one.

2. First-time home buyers, although not normally inclined to participate in extensive work, may not be as fussy as buyers of expensive homes. They will accept more deferred maintenance and obsolete style problems because they are anxious to settle into their first property.

3. Homes in a lower price range generally need more work than expensive homes. This allows investor-buyers to increase their equity by the work they can do or arrange to have done.

4. More beneficial financing is available for first-time home buyers. Government programs and the modest amount of money required by a lower-cost home make lenders more comfortable with lower down payments. Again, this increases your pool of potential buyers.

5. If your fixer-upper fails to sell immediately you can usually rent it out for an amount to cover costs until the market improves.

Having given these points that indicate the advantages of buying and fixing up lower-priced property, don't be wedded to this as a rule. Let your market determine the best price range in which you will deal. You will want to consider those opportunities that become available. For example, if the primary home market in your area is in the more expensive homes, seek opportunities for this market. Just remember that, as a general rule, higher-priced homes cost too much in carrying costs and commissions to be profitable.

YOU MAY WISH TO LIVE IN YOUR INVESTMENT

It should be noted here that you may be planning to live in the house once it is fixed up. Favorable financing and an eagerness to own a property that happens to need some repair often provide a bargain for the investor who also happens to be looking for a home. Frequently in this book the fixer-upper that the investor tackles will require more effort than a house the first-time homeowner normally opts for. But in this case, the investor and home buyer are one. Just remember that major repairs often include health and safety risks for which local communities prohibit occupancy until corrected.

EIGHT-POINT CHECKLIST FOR MAKING MONEY WITH FIXER-UPPERS

Being familiar with your local economy and real estate market is a foundation for any of the techniques described in this book. If you know the price level at which property in your area is selling, you can instinctively recognize a good deal. Of course, with experience you will also come to know the general parameters of prices in which you can make the most money. However, even when you find something within your range, it doesn't mean you should slap down a deposit right away. You still need to follow these guidelines, which are explored in detail in subsequent chapters:

First, find the right property. There are many ways to do this. One way is to work with agents. Their formal obligation is to represent a seller but in doing so they must present the seller's property to all potential buyers. If you remain close to agents as a potential buyer for any and all properties that fit your criteria, they will let you know of potential good deals even before they get on the Multiple Listing Service (MLS) public market. Another way is to prospect directly for sellers. You can do this by canvassing neighborhoods for For Sale signs and searching the newspaper advertisements for sellers. All of these methods should be used to find possible deals. Your goal is to have a constant flow of property that fits your criteria.

Second, inspect the property. You need to make a comprehensive inspection of the physical characteristics. Pay particular attention to location, size, and general condition. From this information you can do a quick market analysis as to its value. Make a detailed list of needed repairs. Are they due to the owner's negligence or because of its age? Are there obsolescent features? The work may be as simple as general cleaning and repainting or as extreme as reroofing and upgrading kitchen and bathrooms or adding a dormer. The point here is that you need to have a good idea of what to expect—you don't want any unpleasant surprises, so be thorough.

Third, estimate repair costs. Investigate the cost of whatever needs to be done. Do this by expanding on your inspection list—determine what must be done, what is required by the local building inspector, and what you should do to make the property more marketable. Decide what you want to do to make it look better—the cosmetic repairs. Once you have a list of what should be done, price it out with carpenters and contractors, or subcontractors and handymen so you know exactly what your repair cost will be in order to determine the price you will offer.

Fourth, look at comparables. One of the key factors in your success in the fixer-upper market will be your ability to determine value of the property, not only going in but what you can sell it for after you've brought it into shape. You do this by finding property comparable to your subject property, imagining that the latter is all fixed up. Why not find comparables as the property is now, without work being done? Because you need to know your end price—that is, what it will sell for once the work is done. It may seem backward, but it's not. It directly targets your profit and allows you to lay out just what will happen in each stage of the deal.

Fifth, determine offering price. You do this by taking the estimate of final value, subtracting your profit (up to 20%), subtracting repair costs, and selling and overhead costs (another 8% to 15% respectively), and arriving at a must-not-go-above price. From there you wish to offer a downward amount, as your seller is likely to counter with one higher. Your offering price, then, is one that includes your profit after all expenses are taken care of, including the property.

Sixth, negotiate the deal. Negotiation is about getting the property at a price that includes your profit. Once you know what you can safely pay—the price that ensures your profit—make a workable offer, perhaps one that the seller is not likely to accept but close enough that it doesn't insult him or her and gives you an opportunity to go up. Later in Chapters 9 and 10 you will see examples of how to include financing and structuring to your benefit. Here, let it be enough to say you will need to negotiate with the seller or agent for several important factors beyond price, including financing, length of time before closing, and assignability if it may be your desire to wholesale the property to another. Have in mind several clauses (as we will detail later in Chapters 7 and 8) ready to go that protect you as a buyer. You can have a preprinted "offer to purchase" form when you are working with a seller directly, or you can just add the substance of the clauses on the agent's form.

Seventh, arrange financing. Obviously you will know in a general way how you will finance the purchase before you finalize the offer. You may have lined up a bank that has prequalified you for a mortgage. Or you may be asking the seller to carry the mortgage until the repairs are completed and the property resold. Or there may be third parties providing financing on a short-term basis. Whatever form financing takes, once you have agreed with the seller, you can complete the financing arrangements. Note that although you always want to ask the seller to carry back the mortgage for you, not all will be able to do so, and you don't want to lose a good deal if he or she can't. Therefore, if you can prequalify yourself with a conventional mortgage source, you will reduce running around at the last moment (more on this in Chapters 9 and 10, on financing). So know your options in advance and be prepared.

Eighth, close and take title. Formally take title to the property by closing the transaction correctly. Stay in touch with your attorney— and you should always use one—on exact figures. If you've done your homework, problems at the closing will be infrequent, but they can happen and you need to be prepared. Using a knowledgeable attorney, as well as having an accountant who can participate, can make for a smoother closing.

SOME BARGAINING IDEAS

When negotiating price, do you lead with your best offer first? Absolutely not! Always explore what the seller—or lender if it's a foreclosure from a bank—will take by offering a sum that is another 10% to 20% off. But remember, you've calculated the price you must not go above. And if you don't get your price, you can walk away, knowing someone else is going to short themselves some dollars along the way. Just keep making offers based on a formula that insures your profit.

You could start by asking what the seller's absolute bottom price would be if you offered all cash and a closing within 30 days. Don't be surprised if the price drops a lot when you ask this question. Don't mention a price first; wait for the seller (he or she who mentions price first, loses). Then you can put in your low offer and start negotiating.

Just like in the stock market, you should never fall in love with a stock or a property. Always look objectively. That's the only way you can arrive at accurate prices and make the numbers add up.

Make sure there's a clause in your contract that states you have

20 days to inspect and approve the property or the contract is null and void and any money you put down to bind the deal is returned to you. Further, just for safety's sake, you need a clause in your contract that states that the full liquidated damages—an amount encompassing all claims—for nonperformance are limited to your deposit.

With these two clauses you can search for an investor, research additional expenses, obtain financing for a full 20 days, and if you are not satisfied, you can send a registered letter stating that after a full inspection, you do not approve of the property, and you will get your deposit money back. Should the term of the contract expire on a 30-day closing and you find that you cannot perform, you lose only your earnest money.

And, of course, put a clause in the contract that you have the right to show the property to potential renters, appraisers, inspectors, or other investors given 24 hours' notice. You should also make the contract fully assignable should you decide to wholesale (more on wholesaling in Chapter 8). This clause can say, "This contract is fully assignable by either party." Or you could put the words "your name and/or assignee" where the purchaser signs. You can always say you're not sure if you want to purchase the property as an individual or in a partnership.

Note that when you wholesale, you assign the contract. Normally, you do not take title. When you assign a contract, you receive an assignment fee, in effect selling your position to a new buyer who steps into your shoes.

REHABBING: FREQUENTLY ASKED QUESTIONS

Do you need a lot of money to get started in rehabbing fixer-uppers?
Some money helps, but it's true you don't need a lot. You don't need as much as you might to put a down payment on an apartment building. Generally, you can plan for as much money as it takes, usually 20% or more, to buy the property in need of improvements. In most cases you will be getting financing for the sale as well as the repairs.

How much experience do you need to get started in fixer-uppers?
As long as you feel confident that you can do the sort of tasks described here—working with sellers to find property, inspecting and estimating the cost of repair, working with contractors, comparing the finished product with comparable sold properties, and following through to get the property sold—you will do well. It's very much a

hands-on activity, but not one for which you can train in school. It requires an assortment of skills—and a can-do attitude.

Bear in mind that the close alternative to fixer-uppers is wholesaling (Chapter 8), where you have to find the property and do the negotiating but pass it on to another investor who will actually buy, complete the repairs, and resell to a retail homeowner.

Are some markets better for rehabbing than others?
It does help to have around plenty of single-family houses in need of repair. Typically these are older homes that the owners have not kept up to the latest standards of consumer desirability. It doesn't mean these properties should be torn up or trashed, but rather that due to this need for renovation, a big price margin exists between what they are worth in their current state and what comparable homes in good repair all fixed up sell for.

In addition to the condition of the properties, it's important to ascertain the desire of new home buyers to buy the homes at retail in these respective neighborhoods. And the condition of the market in an individual neighborhood can change. An undesirable neighborhood may for regional or local economic conditions change to one of desirability. For example, if there is little building of new homes, the neighborhoods of existing homes will experience a renewed interest.

Often you will see a home buyer purchasing a house in need of repair. Don't look at these people as your competitors, because they help make the market for that neighborhood and bring in bank financing on distressed property. As a general rule most homeowners don't have the time, inclination, or skill to deal with a fixer-upper. Because of their other commitments, they usually need to have the home ready to live in.

Generally, several areas within each metropolitan area have whole neighborhoods in need of renovation.

What's the biggest error one can make when getting started?
Avoiding the research. Several key areas of rehab work require an investigation of repair cost, value analysis, and marketability. Your individual strategy must be to inspect the property yourself, with knowledgeable professionals, to ascertain what's needed for the repairs, and gather the repair costs from contractors or from your previous experience. And you must compare the property as it will be once the repairs are done to what is similar that has recently sold. If

you've done this latter comparability study carefully, your end game of selling should be the easiest part.

Once you've been through this process of understanding values a few times, it will be easier for you to gauge market value. But you should never make offhand estimates of values; they should be thoroughly researched based on current selling prices for truly comparable property.

The ability to determine what needs to be done and what it will cost combined with correctly valuing the finished property when done are the key elements for success in the fixer-upper rehab market. To ignore them invites failure.

Are special skills needed in remodeling and fixing up a house?
Yes, there are some, but you don't have to be the person to do the actual work. In fact, in your estimates of labor and material you always assume the work will be done by an outside repairperson. Many investors who specialize in the fixer-upper strategy rely entirely on professional contractors to do all the work. This allows them to concentrate on finding property and making accurate estimates of repair cost. They make their main object to get in and get out as fast as possible in order to minimize holding costs. Of course, if you are handy at repair work and you're just getting started, you may choose to do much of the work yourself.

It's common to parcel out some of the more complex work, such as plumbing or heating, to a professional while reserving for oneself less intricate tasks such as painting, minor carpentry, and landscaping. But just remember—you don't have to be handy to engage in the fixer-upper market.

Do you need to steal the property at an unusually low price to profit in fixer-uppers?
Not necessarily. Many properties that are distressed or damaged have plenty of room for you to buy them at the current fair value, do the necessary repairs, and resell them at a new market value. To put this in context, one of the reasons you as an investor are needed is that in most cases the final user of the property, the homeowner, is not able or inclined to buy such property and perform the repairs. Someone has to bring this property up to acceptable condition before it becomes desirable for the retail homeowner. You add considerable value when you bring a property from a poor condition to one that engages a home buyer.

What kind of properties do you target in the fixer-upper market?
Three qualifications are required of a fixer-upper property: The first is
that the property itself be in need of substantial enough repairs so
that the homeowner is not likely to buy it in its present condition;
second, that these repairs keep the price relatively low; and third, the
seller must be motivated enough to make a good deal. A seller could
be motivated by his or her need to move, a death in the family, or a
divorce—all "have to" reasons for selling.

How do you get financing for a property in need of significant repair?
Generally, banks don't like to finance properties in distressed condition. Therefore, the deal has to be presented to them in such a way
that they see that they are really financing the property as it will be
fixed up. This usually involves the bank's scrutiny of your repair figures, including acknowledgment of building code violations and how
they will be fixed, and the facts of the comparable properties matching the subject property.

In other words, you make the deal approximate a new construction loan with which banks are familiar. Note that often this financing approach requires that the work be done by qualified contractors
who have submitted written estimates, and not by unskilled hands.

Should you not be able to get bank financing at all, you may
need to finance it yourself with the aid of a home equity loan or with
the help of the seller, both of which are discussed in Chapters 9 and
10. Since a loan of this nature is short-term, usually less than a year,
it should be easily obtained.

Consider establishing a line of credit with a commercial bank that
specializes in short-term business loans. A commercial bank that loans
money to restaurants is often delighted to grant a short-term loan
where the underlying asset is real estate (that's why they call it "real").

You may need to use a private mortgage lender who specializes
in offering loans for both purchase and rehab. This would often allow
you to use little of your own money in the deal. Taking in a partner
or another investor can also help make the financing work.

What kind of interest rates am I going to pay for any financing?
Expect to pay a higher interest rate than you would on your own
home. For you, as well as the lender, this is a commercial transaction
for which higher interest rates are normally charged. However, it is
only for a short time, because as soon as the house is fixed up, perhaps even sooner, it is offered for sale. It is not unusual for the entire

period of the loan to be only six to eight months before the property is resold.

Note that you have accounted for the interest rate cost in your overhead and holding amount subtracted from the final selling price.

Do I need to be rehabbing full-time to succeed?
Not at all, although that may be your goal. In order to get started you only need the time to find the property and negotiate with the seller. This can all be done part-time. Further, you will likely have outside workers do the needed repairs and a sales agent to find the final buyer. In fact, if you're like many other fixer-upper investors, you'll always use outside inspectors, repairpeople, and sales agents, and use the balance of your time to find more deals.

Once you have secured an agreement with the seller, you may decide to wholesale the property to another investor. This further reduces the time you need to complete a deal.

In the following several chapters we'll continue to present a step-by-step guide to finding, buying, reselling, and cashing in on fixer-upper houses.

3

Finding the Fixer-Upper Bargain

When you begin to look for bargain houses, you may be overwhelmed by all the different possibilities: vacant houses, For Sale by Owner signs, newspaper advertising—just where do you start looking for the best rehab properties? In this chapter we'll look into ways to find the right property and the right seller.

MINING FOR GOLD: TARGET A NEIGHBORHOOD

One of the best ways to find sellers is to mine a target neighborhood for "gold." You could start by picking a neighborhood where there is an increasing number of owner-occupants, as opposed to an increasing number of tenants—and also where prices are growing. Or perhaps you already have prospects who would buy homes in a blue-collar neighborhood you know of, and perhaps the price range in this neighborhood is typical of your community at large. What would be ideal in your subject neighborhood is a large group of homes that are relatively similar in value, with a measure of cultural diversity and a solid economic base.

As you read the list in the first chapter, you are looking not only at your overall community, but also at selected neighborhoods within the community. And although several neighborhoods in your community may fit your criteria, you need to be flexible, as relative prices are always changing. You can start by making a list of neighborhoods; then break them down by major streets so that when you ride through each one you can reference the locations of possible fixer-uppers. Here are some attributes that have served fixer-upper investors—but be cautioned: You must adapt to your local sales and price levels within your marketplace.

1. A neighborhood where the values are rising and the houses appear to be well-kept.
2. Homes that are 30 to 40 years old, with a few showing some signs of wear.
3. Reasonably maintained lawns and landscaping.
4. Some, but not extensive, new construction.
5. Primarily owner-occupied homes, with minimal apartments.
6. Signs of children playing and well-groomed animals.
7. Yards with swimming pools and recreational boats.
8. Neighborhoods populated by different races.

You should avoid neighborhoods where most of the homes are rented out. Your goal is to buy, fix up, and sell, not buy and rent out (unless you choose that technique, as described later in Chapter 13). If you buy and rent out in a declining neighborhood, you could end up holding the property for a long time. Also avoid neighborhoods where a number of houses are vacant and boarded up. It is an indication of a declining neighborhood, as are debris, unregistered cars in yards, and unclean streets.

Older neighborhoods where there is a fair amount of resale activity are good targets. You could find out about this sales activity at the Registry of Deeds, or from the Realtors' MLS. Since you are in the business of buying, fixing up, and reselling, and are not looking for a home to meet your own needs, you can be more objective about what you are seeking.

Drive through neighborhoods. Train yourself to look for houses that might be likely purchases. These might include vacant houses, houses with For Sale signs, either by owner or by agent. Some of the best candidates may not even be offered for sale. You may notice houses in disrepair, or simply older ones with obvious deferred maintenance.

You can also look for absentee owners of neglected or abandoned houses. And check the tax rolls at the assessor's office to find out the identity of any out-of-town owners of such property in the neighborhood. Track down these owners. Pursue leads by knocking on doors.

Don't be afraid to get out and talk to some of the people who live in the neighborhood to get a sense of what kind of place it is to live in. Is there any crime? What are the concerns of the residents? Drive through the neighborhood on the weekend or in early evening when many people are home and pursuing activities. This can give you a sense of what life is like in that neighborhood.

Now that some middle-class, middle-price-range neighborhoods have been outlined for you to explore, does that mean seeking out a middle-of-the-road house? Not at all. You want to find the beat-up derelict in the midst of houses in better condition. If we're a bit stringent about what you should look for, it's because of the greater margin of profit available from fixing up a beast versus taking on a property that needs only a little work.

FIND SELLERS WITH NEGLECTED PROPERTIES

Remember, when you are touring a neighborhood you are not looking for the fine and fancy buildings. You want the tough ones—not just because they might be available at a lower price, or because the seller might be very motivated, but because of the difference between the present state of such a property and that of the homes around it. The larger this difference, the more potential you have to make a profit.

So when you're driving around with your cards (or notebook) and camera, focus on For Sale by Owner (FSBO) signs, and write down any telephone numbers and addresses. Note other properties that might be for sale. Or, you may stop and ask if you see people around. You're not going to barge in and say, "Your home really looks lousy and neglected. Do you want to sell cheap?" If you reach an owner, you're simply going to say, "I was looking for a house for sale in the neighborhood—do you know of any?" Maybe the owner just needs to know someone might be interested. It might start him or her thinking. If it seems of little interest, the owner still may lead you to someone who is responsive to selling. You can at least leave your card and keep a record of your contact—an interest in selling may develop in the future.

Also, going up to the front door of a house, even though you find it is vacant, will give you a quick idea of its age and condition. The condition of the yard may say a lot about how the house is inside. Now or in the future such a place may turn into a profit. If no one else wants the place, it'll be inexpensive and likely to have a huge allowance for profit. The tougher the shape, the better potential.

For those properties that look possible but don't have an FSBO sign in the yard, go to your tax assessor's office and look them up. Nobody even needs to know you're investigating them. At the assessor's office it's quiet and discrete. Contact the owners. If you can reach them and they are motivated, you're in luck. If you can't find them, ask the lender what happened and check out any possible liens at the courthouse.

You may not want to live in one of these distressed houses yourself, but you'll find them a low-cost gold mine of profit. For that reason go out and tour different neighborhoods, keep changing your route, and make lists and more lists. The information you write down may lead you to some great deals.

SCREEN THE SELLER'S MOTIVATION— USING THE TELEPHONE TO ADVANTAGE

Use the telephone as a low-cost marketing tool and a way to gather information. In the initial telephone conversation, screen the seller to determine if it's worth spending the time inspecting the house and property. Ask questions to determine the seller's motivation. After you've identified yourself and your interest, and determined whether the owner has any corresponding interest, you can then move on to questions of price and negotiation. In this way you separate the productive leads from the ones that will go nowhere. You can easily tell if you've got a prospect who meets your guidelines. You know what you're looking for and how you wish to buy it. These questions are for testing the seller's motivation; they are not necessarily scrutinizing how firm the seller's price is.

Not infrequently, the firmer in price people say they are, the more they will negotiate in the end. This is because they are insecure about price and feel they have to defend it. Besides, when you do make your offer, it may be nowhere near what the owner wants. The key is that if he or she wants to sell, you're likely to make a deal. Ultimately, that motivation will make or break the deal. Also, because of your knowledge of the local market, once you have an idea what the seller will take you are likely to know if that price is a good deal, or if it's even in the ballpark.

You still have to do the legwork, but one of the reasons to know value is to work smarter, not harder. The real negotiating will come later, after you know the cost of repairs and have estimated the value when completed. For now your questions are acting like a filter to separate the possible from the impossible. The questions are also inquiring into the motivation of the seller. When you arrive at a point where you feel the owner is interested and ready to negotiate, ask whether he or she has substantial equity and thus may be in a position to carry the mortgage. Owner financing can be the best deal you make. If he or she has little or no equity, you may use the buy-and-hold strategy where you hold the house for several years, benefiting as the value increases. The answers to these questions help you start planning for the actual purchase.

It helps to know why they're selling. Is their motivation other than profit? Is there a divorce? Transfer? Estate? If the reason to sell is a necessity, it's better for you than if they are just trying to make a profit. If they seem really driven to sell, start getting some details on the property. What is it they've got to sell? Number of rooms? Bedrooms? Baths? Fireplaces? Amenities? Type of heat? Lot size? The basics.

Next, ask about the condition of the building. Sellers may not be the most objective people to describe what needs to be done but their answers may surprise you. At least it starts them realizing that condition is important. You can probably get an idea whether the repairs needed are cosmetic or structural. Does the basement fill up with water? Are there any problems that keep occurring? You are never going to know the exact answers to these questions until you inspect the property, but this talk with the seller does give you an overview of what lies ahead.

And, of course, think about the location and ask relevant questions. Is it near any harmful industrial plants? What's the neighborhood like? Is shopping nearby? Although the final answers lie in your inspection, the seller's answers will give you a sense of how a resident (a very subjective one) sees it.

Bear in mind that at this stage you're just collecting information. Your questions prepare you to move forward with or reject the deal.

Develop your own approach. But the best style is to have no style at all. You never want to seem like a professional who is going to take advantage of people. You want to find good deals, but at the same time you don't want to deceive someone.

If sellers seem appropriately motivated, let them know that you will be glad to come out and see the property. If they can be flexible in what they are asking, you will likely make an offer. It will work to your advantage if they know you will be seeking a discount right up front. Without mentioning any figures, you are trying to gauge if they will take a 30% to 40% discount. If they know you will be offering less than the asking price and are still willing to show you the property, it may be worth going to meet with them and view the property carefully.

WAYS TO FIND SELLERS

The challenge to you is less about finding property to buy than about finding a seller who is serious about selling. To get yourself linked to this seller, you've got to cast a wide net. Let's consider eight ways you find sellers:

1. *Hand out business cards.* You can start by getting a business card. It doesn't have to be fancy or have elegant graphics all over it. In fact, it's better if you don't come across as an enterprising professional. Keep a modest profile. Remember, you've got to deal with people and their problems at their level, and many of the sellers you'll be dealing with are distressed by their need to sell. Your card only needs to say (again, in simple language everybody can understand) "I Buy Houses"—of course, with your name and telephone number included. Unless you work out of a formal office, you don't need an address on the card. An address will just get people dropping by when you're not there. Besides, you want to talk on the telephone with sellers to gauge their motivation before you meet with them. You might want to add "Any Condition"; this helps convey that you are drawn to the tougher properties—which you are. Use these cards constantly; get them out to all the places and people you visit. You never know when someone might know someone who knows someone. . . . Everyone is a prospect or a potential source for a referral. Most of your cards will be thrown out, but you can make thousands of dollars on the ones that are kept.

2. *Run classified advertisements.* One proof of motivation is when sellers call you, especially when those sellers have exhausted other avenues of selling, such as brokers. The seller is ready to bargain and may have to settle for a discount. Keep your ad simple, like your business card. And remember, you never want to give the impression you're about to make a lot of money off them. Perhaps you will—but to do that you've got to start by solving their problem. Your advertisement could read, "I buy houses and make quick closings—for cash, any condition." Include your phone number. Not every call will be worthwhile. In fact, you want to follow up only with sellers who are eager to act. When you find one, you can set up a meeting at the property.

3. *Call "seller" advertisements.* For many experienced rehabbers, one of the favorite places to study is the newspaper—particularly the real estate or home section. Owners who wish to sell their own property often place an advertisement in the classified section of the local newspaper. One reason for doing this is that properties with problems tend to be difficult for real estate agents to sell in their primarily retail marketplace. Although the agents can sell them at a discount, owners of distressed property often feel they can do better by selling their property themselves. Newspaper advertisements offer a variety of possibilities—from "lease/purchase" to "estate sale" to "needs work" to "take over payments"—all workable deals if you know the ways described in this book. Some large newspapers have Internet web sites with properties listed by MLS and FSBO that can be searched by price, number of rooms, school district, or town name. If you are interested in a property, you have only to call the listed agent or owner.

4. *Find For Sale by Owner signs.* Homemade FSBO signs posted in the front yard or on the building are an excellent source of leads. Call the number. If one is not written down, that's even better as it allows you to march up to the front door and meet the owner. Because they are often unreadable from the street they may not generate a lot of calls for the owner. This works to your advantage when yours is one of the few calls the owner does get. Every time you go out and tour the neighborhoods look for property with FSBO signs.

5. *Pay and gain referrals.* Pay people to refer property to you. It will help you tremendously if you enlist a number of so-called bird dogs who will hunt down available properties and let you know about them. You pay them only when you finally make a deal on a property they have identified. Therefore, you could have as many of them working for you as you wish and not have any overhead until a bargain is found. Appropriate amounts to pay a bird dog for a referral average between $250 and $500, depending on the size of the deal. Note that in most states it is illegal in the brokerage business to pay a referral fee to an unlicensed party. However, you are an investor and they haven't licensed that activity—yet. You're free to pay for whatever services you wish. Let people know you're willing to pay for leads and you'll find that you'll often have a high-quality lead—one you might not have heard of had it not been for the referring bird dog. Make sure you follow through in paying your bird dog; you don't want to get a bad reputation, or lose a mutually beneficial relationship.

6. *Hand out flyers.* Make up a brochure or a flyer (a less fancy brochure) that you can give out regularly in neighborhoods where you want to do business. An $8^1/_2$-by-11-inch sheet of paper that carries a simple message that you buy houses and may be contacted at such-and-such a number can be handed out by students you hire in shopping centers, malls, fairs—anyplace where people gather. A simple flyer is cheap and will last for years. Thousands can be made and handed out at the right places in a matter of hours.

7. *Go house hunting.* Although previously mentioned, we'll add a bit more as it's an important topic under finding motivated sellers. Just like a prospective home buyer driving through affluent neighborhoods, you need to get out and drive through the neighborhoods in which you wish to do business. Be on the lookout for FSBO signs and, just as important, vacant houses. Vacant houses are proof that motivated sellers are out there. People don't own houses for the pleasure of having them empty. A vacant house often indicates a problem somewhere. You can check with the neighbors to find out who is or was the owner and how to contact that individual. Note that mail sent to a vacant house will often be forwarded. The post office may not give you the forwarding address but will confirm whether there is one. You can also go to the local assessing office, which will have information about the status of the property along with details of the physical structure. It may be the case that the vacant house is no longer controlled by a private owner. Whether it's a bank, or mortgage company, or your municipality (which might have taken the property for nonpayment of back taxes), that entity will most likely be willing to have someone like you with whom to make a favorable deal.

8. *Search assessing records.* You don't always have to drive around neighborhoods or wait for someone to call on your advertising; you can go to one place—your local tax assessor's office. Here you can search through details of property linked to maps showing the outline of each owner's parcel. You will also find valuable information such as names and addresses of owners, property assessments, sizes and relevant details of buildings, land area, or perhaps tax liens or owners who might be beleaguered by high taxes or who have moved out of state. This information source should be used for the investigation of every property that interests you, but it is particularly valuable when tracking down the owner of a vacant house or rented house.

DON'T OVERLOOK OUT-OF-STATE OWNERS

Out-of-state owners are often motivated to sell their real estate. Tenants may have stopped paying the rent or begun damaging the property, or there may not be any more tenants. An empty residence is troublesome to manage and maintain when the owner is far away. It's easy to find out-of-state property owners. Just visit the relevant tax assessor's office and inspect the tax rolls. Write down the names and addresses of the out-of-state owners as well as other known facts about the property. Then write the owners a friendly letter inquiring whether they are interested in selling and indicate that you may be interested in buying. Be sure they know that you're not an agent and would be buying directly, and don't forget to include information so they can call or write back to you.

YOU'RE READY TO MEET THE SELLER AT THE PROPERTY

Once you feel the seller is motivated to make a deal, you can inspect the property. When you meet the seller for a quick visit to the property you probably will not be able to make a thorough inspection. This first meeting is primarily to start a personal relationship with the seller and get a brief tour of the inside. The obvious problems will stand out: interior and exterior painting, foundation, roof, floors. If you decide to go further after this first inspection, you should arrange to show it to tradesmen in order to get prices on repairs. Chapter 5 looks more closely at repairs.

For any problems you can't see on your personal examinations, your sales contract with the seller will have clauses that allow for professional inspections of any termite and wood-boring insect damage, and any foundation or structural defects. Either of these inspections could turn up structural damage.

A distressed property will often be in such bad condition that not only is it at a great price, but you won't have any retail buyers competing with you to purchase it. However, always make sure a house is structurally sound and that repairs are reasonable in cost so that you can ensure a profit for yourself. Properties that have severe damage to the roof or cracked foundation walls should be avoided unless you have an experienced contractor who can fix these problems inexpensively. This is also true for houses with lead paint, asbestos, or radon problems.

You can use the worksheet on this first inspection to gather information.

SEEK HOUSES THROUGH MLS OR THE INTERNET

The Multiple Listing Service, or MLS, is the trade name for a cooperative system of sharing information on property for sale. It is sponsored by the local board of the National Association of Realtors. In some localities, the details of each listing are bound in a printed book or computer and sent out to Realtors who are members of MLS. In many areas, to gain access to the MLS listings you have to have a real estate broker's license, become a Realtor, and join your local MLS (there are yearly dues and monthly fees); once you're a member you can look up listings. In other areas, you don't need to be Realtor, as appraisers and others associated with the real estate industry are allowed to join. In some MLS groups, owners are allowed to post their property for sale.

Perhaps the best part of joining MLS is that you can buy direct; that is, you can buy through the listing agent and often get back one-half or part of the commission. However, many fixer-upper investors work through the right Realtor/sales agent using MLS who is day in and day out searching for the right property, which for you may be a better solution than joining MLS yourself.

You may also be able to use the Internet to seek out property. Many agencies list property for sale on their home pages. Further, the national commercial groups to which many agencies belong also have property listings posted on the agencies' behalf.

WORKSHEET: Initial Property Inspection

Date: _____   Listing/FSBO: _____

Owner's Name: _____   Contact Number: _____

Address: _____

General Location: _____   Neighborhood: _____

Asking Price: _____   Vacant/Occupied: _____

Motivation Level: _____   Seller Financing: _____

Existing Mortgages: _____   Assumable: _____

1st Lender: _____

Balance: _____ Rate: _____ Term: _____ Payment: _____

2nd Lender: _____

Balance: _____ Rate: _____ Term: _____ Payment: _____

Condensed Summary:

Lot Size: _____ House Size: _____ Style: _____

Construction: _____ Foundation: _____ Garage: _____

Landscaping:_____ Driveway: _____ Roof:_____ Exterior: _____

Water: _____ Sewer: _____ Trash: _____

Other Services: _____

Rooms: _____ Bedrooms: _____ Baths: _____ Kitchen: _____

Interior: _____ Floors: _____

Heating/Cooling: _____ Electrical: _____ Plumbing: _____

Hot Water: _____ Appliances:_____

Amenities: _____   Extras: _____

Other: _____

_____

_____

(Continued)

WORKSHEET: Initial Property Inspection *(Continued)*

Specific Problems: _____

_____

_____

Known Structural: _____

_____

_____

Obvious Damage: _____

_____

_____

Probable Unknown Damage: _____

_____

_____

Extent of Repairs: _____

    Standard/Necessary: _____

    Building Code/Health and Safety: _____

    Cosmetic: _____

Description: _____

_____

_____

Comments: _____

_____

_____

_____

_____

_____

GET AGENTS TO BIRD DOG PROPERTY FOR YOU

Call your local real estate offices and spread the word that you are an investor looking to buy a number of properties over the long term. Tell the agents you want the best deals as soon as they come out. Although some agents may ignore you, the good ones will jump. When you find someone who will work with you, don't make him or her run around for nothing. Say what you are looking for, and if you end up buying it, show your appreciation by recommending that agent. That's the way to keep them calling you when something hot comes up after the miserable deal you just gave their seller.

Value these agents and let them know exactly what you want and how you function. Let them call you anytime, day or night, when a good deal comes up. Although you may not buy every house they pitch, the few you do buy will likely be some of your best deals. Note that you can further encourage an agent by agreeing to list the property back with them upon completion of repairs. A word of warning: Don't work with an agent who scoops up the best deals before they reach the market. One who owns only his or her own house is best.

Note, too, that if a real estate agent finds you a property, unless you have the agent's permission, it will be unproductive for you to contact the homeowner directly. The seller will most likely refer you back to the agent. In this case you must ask the seller questions through the agent.

HAVE A CONTACT SYSTEM FOR AGENTS AND PROSPECTS

Until you find the right agent, it may be best to work with several agents. And it's worth finding the few that will work with you regularly. You need a contact system that spurs you to make the necessary telephone calls. First thing in the morning, dedicate an hour to making phone calls. Call the agents you sense are the best ones for coming up with some deals for you. Keep a log of these contact calls. Use three-by-five-inch cards; they'll fit in your coat pocket and, when spread on your desktop, you can see them all at one glance (computers can't do that . . . yet). And sort them as information changes. When an agent gives you a lead, post it on the card, or write a new one.

Keep looking for ways to improve the way you log in information. You'll always be adding and subtracting leads, so keep it simple.

Stay consistent and keep it easy to use—if you make it complex you'll avoid using it. Cards may not be as cutting-edge as the latest electronic gadget, but they're more practical—and cheaper, too. They are what the pros use. Use this system with your potential sellers (and buyers as well).

Note that electronic calendars or personal digital assistants (PDAs) are great for scheduling time because you look at time sequentially. But they fall short as sales contact tools because they don't allow you to see your entire lead base at once, or to easily move leads around. Some investors use three-ring binders. These, too, allow you to move leads around, and a small one can fit in your pocket. Of course, if you're determined to outdo the tax assessor and catalog every property . . . !

WHEN YOU'RE OFFERED A GROUP OF HOUSES

On occasion an opportunity arises to buy a group of houses. For example, a local businesswoman wants to sell 12 houses for a total price of $550,000. Her sales agent says that the price is negotiable if they are bought together as a package. This owner wants 10% down and will finance at 8.5% for 10 years. She will be flexible on financing terms. Rental income on the properties averages $675—roughly $8,100 per month. The agent has told you the seller wants to retire and leave the area. The agent says the seller may be motivated as the property has become worrisome for her.

You start by going to look at the properties. If you are thinking of buying 12 houses as a block, you want to check out the condition of the neighborhood as well as the houses themselves. With 12 units you might have a lot to fix if things fall apart at the same time. Let's say that in this case you find that at least six of them need at least $10,000 in repairs, perhaps more if they are to be fixed up and resold. The others are in good condition. All are presently occupied by tenants. You verify that all the rents are being collected.

You always need to be cautious when a seller is offering what seems like a particularly good deal. You need to verify that he or she is not selling due to hidden problems with the property. Sometimes the current owner is not collecting the rents, or is trying to pass problems to a new buyer. If rent is not coming in, you may have to juggle your money, especially if several tenants don't pay during the same month. So plan ahead on how you would deal with it.

Further, be wary when rents seem cheap. With single-family houses you have a lot of responsibilities. As tenants you want lower-to-middle-income, working people of solid character. At worst, the properties might be plagued with gangs or drug dealers, a possibility you can check by inspecting the houses and neighborhood at different times of day and night. If there are disreputable types hanging around you are likely to see them at odd hours.

Once you have thoroughly checked these properties out and assured yourself the owner is selling for bona fide reasons—divorce, transfer, seller's age, length of holding time—then you can decide whether you want to pursue the deal. After computing repair cost and figuring your profit, you will know what to offer.

IT'S ALL ABOUT PROSPECTING

You should always be prospecting for new properties. In this business you will come across far more property than you will make offers on or even end up controlling. That's why you need to keep on top of lots of resources in order to find the best deal.

You don't need to spend a lot of money; instead it's mainly a contact pursuit. You just have to attack on different fronts, using various methods: telephone, agents, banks, lawyers. You will be surprised at where you will find the best deals. But you won't find any unless you put the word out that you're in play and want property.

In the next chapter we'll talk further about one of the key ways you can find property: negotiating with a lending institution or mortgage company to take over property that has been foreclosed on, repossessed by the lender, or condemned by local government.

4

Finding Foreclosed, Repossessed, or Condemned Property

Before explaining the repairs you should look for and how to price them, we're going to have one more chapter on finding property. In fact, getting a foreclosed or repossessed house is another way to acquire a fixer-upper. Specifically, this chapter looks at the special problems when taking over property that is being foreclosed upon, repossessed by a lender, or condemned by local government. These are all properties that will require repair work. What makes buying them different from the normal acquisition of a fixer-upper is that in order to take control you must negotiate with an institution such as a mortgage lender, or community building inspector.

THE PERILS AND REWARDS OF BUYING AT FORECLOSURE

The three ways you can buy properties in the foreclosure process are: (1) default stage, (2) auction stage, and (3) REO (real estate owned) stage.

1. *Default stage—buying properties in default before foreclosures.* This is the "desperate seller" stage when homeowners who are behind in their bank payments are anxious to make a deal, particularly as these loans may be in or near default. They can be found by searching classified ads for homes for sale by owners, and contacting mortgage banks and companies that are willing to let you know when one of their loan holders is in trouble. Substantial discounts are often available in this preforeclosure stage but you generally have to do a fair amount of rehabilitation work to increase a property's value.

Note that many properties never reach this default stage. An owner who has considerable equity can do a loan workout, a refinance, or a Chapter 13 or Chapter 7 bankruptcy and preserve that equity. In fact, due to favorable bankruptcy laws in many states (e.g., Florida, Texas, California), debtors can emerge from bankruptcy with tens (sometimes hundreds) of thousands of dollars of net worth. Furthermore, almost all communities have not-for-profit debt counseling and restructuring centers. Lenders want workouts—not defaults and foreclosures.

2. *Auction stage—buying at auction.* When you buy a property at auction you have to act quickly. Your competition is a bank or mortgage company holding the mortgage and other investors who smell a bargain. The bidding moves fast. Usually the lender bids in its mortgage amount and then, if the lender is lucky, the price moves up. Occasionally the lender is willing to take a loss and will not bid the mortgage amount. Those are often the best times to get a bargain at auction. As often as not, the lender may be the only bidder. When this happens it usually indicates that the loan balance is more than the market value. In that case the lender acquires the property and is available for negotiation. It is also true that the holder of a second mortgage or a service-related lien may bid at auction.

Remember that when you contemplate buying at auction, you should do adequate research into the property's repairs, if needed, and the current market value. And always decide the limit of your bidding by calculating repair cost, overhead, and profit expectation, and subtracting these amounts from the market value once repaired. Remember, if you lose the bidding battle, you have not lost the war, because someone else may not have done any homework and is going to make less profit than expected. Buying at auction is gambling for a big reward. The possibility of buying at one-half of market value is alluring. But the reality can be daunting when a property goes to foreclosure because its mortgage balance is too high and the property has already been unsuccessfully exposed to the market. Note that behind the delinquent mortgage balance may lurk back taxes or other government service debts that may have to be paid before you can gain clear title. You should not consider proceeding if you are not allowed to inspect the property or if for some reason the title is defective.

3. *Real estate owned (REO) stage—buying a property now owned by the lender.* The most convenient way to buy foreclosed property is to pursue it after the property has actually been taken at auction by the bank or mortgage company. Usually the lender is then willing to make some further cuts in price just to make a deal. Lenders are not in the property business and are usually obliged to move the property quickly. The lender may have been forced to do some of the emergency repairs, such as roofing, if they were badly needed, and may even be willing to negotiate a new mortgage on the property with you. In most cases the lender will have had to ante up additional monies for back property taxes or other municipal obligations. This means that the foreclosed property you buy from the lender is likely to have a clear title but that government liens or other claims may still be active. Note that only nongovernmental liens or claims will be erased by a formal foreclosure. Should there be any IRS liens, back property taxes, water bills, and sewerage claims against the property, they will have to be satisfied before a clear title is issued.

It can be rewarding to buy property that is near foreclosure, or at auction, or that has been taken by the lender. But make sure you examine repair costs as well as market values before you go forward.

FINDING PROPERTIES BEFORE ACTUAL FORECLOSURE

Knowing how to proceed in buying a foreclosed property is one thing, but finding these opportunities is another matter. In some markets, properties near or already foreclosed upon are scarce. However, some ways of finding such properties are easier and more productive than others. The first way is to develop a relationship with staff in the real estate owned (REO) departments of your local lenders. Lenders don't generally want foreclosed property on their books. So, after you buy a few properties from them, they will often tell you about property heading toward foreclosure. It takes time to develop this relationship. However, if these lenders see that you are involved they will likely let you know of properties near foreclosure or in preforeclosure. Preforeclosure is when a lender's mortgage customer is seriously behind in payments and the bank is threatening to step in.

You might find some near-foreclosure or after-foreclosure deals while driving through neighborhoods. These might be houses with trash lying around or the lawn not mowed. Sometimes you can knock on the doors of the houses next door and across the street to find out who owns it and why it is in this condition. Armed with knowledge of how the process works and an observant eye, you will find myriad possibilities. Another source of properties nearing foreclosure is the local tax collector's office, where you can look at public records of tax arrears. Auction houses that specialize in handling property foreclosures can also be a source of upcoming deals.

STEP IN AND NEGOTIATE BEFORE THE FORECLOSURE

In a foreclosure situation you often have the problem that many properties slated for auction never make it to the auction block because deals are made with the owners beforehand. You should do the same. Talk to the owners. Find out how much they owe in back payments and penalties. They probably owe back property taxes, too. Let them know you want to buy the property and save their credit rating. You could offer to purchase it on contract with enough down payment to them to help them catch up on their loan payments and back taxes. You could even negotiate a note for any additional payment they might need. Tell them that they can stay in the house at a reduced rent. (If they don't want to stay as tenants, just work to reinstate the loan so you can produce a quick sale.) Even if there is a due-on-sale clause in the mortgage, you will have time to refinance. Set up an account with an escrow company to make the mortgage payments, which you are obtaining each month from rental income. However, if your new tenants—the former owners—get behind on the rent you will have to evict them. Nevertheless, your conscience will be clear because you gave them a second chance.

SOLVING THE PROBLEMS OF
A HOMEOWNER FACING FORECLOSURE

Remember, as a property investor you must sometimes solve people's problems. This is particularly true in foreclosure cases. Homeowners are often desperate; they do not want foreclosure on their credit record. The homeowner nearing default on a loan, the widower who has recently lost his wife, the couple divorcing—all have real difficulty and uncertainty about their future. It's important that you not discount their needs and fears. Above all you must listen. You must let homeowners in distress tell you what they want. Only then can you figure out a way to help them and still make a good business deal for yourself.

For example, consider the case of a recently widowed homeowner, behind in her property tax payments and remaining mortgage, who is to move to her daughter's home out of state but cannot sell her house due to extensive deferred maintenance. An investor arranges with her to take over the small balance on the existing loan and give her a note for the balance to be paid off after the investor completes the needed repairs and resells the property. The total of the remaining balance on the mortgage note is the purchase price—also fair value considering the present condition of the property. You have to balance your cost with potentially lower price should you buy property through the bank or at auction but without guarantee you will be the buyer.

Someone who can no longer make payments to the bank and has received a notice of foreclosure from the lender deserves compassion. He or she needs someone who can explain the complexities of what is happening and offer a way out at a price that brings both parties fair value. If you're going to do business with people, you've got to help them with their problem. Let them know you'd be happy to assist in any way you can. If appropriate, you can ask if the homeowners have a place to move to. Find them an apartment if you have to, and pay for the movers.

TAKING OVER A QUALIFYING FORECLOSURE

A qualifying foreclosure is a property close to foreclosure with a loan that is not voluntarily assumable but can be taken over upon agreement with the lender that is foreclosing. To take over with the seller's willingness, he or she must get confirmation from the foreclosing lender of the amount needed to bring the loan current. Once established, you record the deed from the seller and send certified funds to the lender. You have completed the sale and will make the monthly payments yourself. If you change the "new address" portion of a payment coupon, new ones will be sent to you.

GETTING STARTED WITH YOUR
FIRST AUCTION FORECLOSURE

So how do you get started with your first foreclosure deal? Let's say you've researched a few properties that went to foreclosure and feel that you would like to try to buy one. You've found one that has been advertised as coming up for auction. You want to know what to do first and how you go about getting inside the property and inspecting it. You also want to know what you do to make sure the property is clear of any liens against it.

Your first step is to see if the present owners are willing to sell directly to you. It is to their benefit to do so as a foreclosure will damage their credit rating. Hopefully, you'll be able to take over by contract and bring the payments up to date, thereby dissuading the lender from following through on the actual foreclosure. However, you will not always be able to prevent an actual foreclosure by auction.

Talk to the foreclosing lender. The lender, too, will be helpful because it is in its interest to have buyers bid at auction high enough to clear the loan balance. Note that the lender will not be able to deal directly with you as it does not technically own the property, although the lender (or other successful bidder) is likely to hold title after the actual foreclosure auction. If the lender gives you some hope that it is not too late to stop the foreclosure, then arrange to do a thorough inspection. It is critical that you know exactly what repairs are necessary and each respective cost.

Next, go to the Registry of Deeds or county courthouse to research any liens against the property. Start with the grantor/grantee index; look up the book and page numbers for the property, and then use this information to check the debts on the property. Ask one of the clerks for help if you need it.

Be thoroughly briefed on all aspects of the property as well as the neighborhood before you proceed. Make sure the neighborhood is primarily owner-occupied, that it has an active sales record, and that prices are rising.

The actual bidding at auction may be intimidating if there is a large crowd. Just focus on the property. You now know it and its potential better than anyone. Have a specific amount (based on your research of final market value minus repair, overhead, and profit figures) that you will not rise above. Remember, you're not at the auction to acquire a property, but a profit. Your entire goal is to get it at the right price. If someone else walks away as the owner, it will be at a price you determined would be too high.

DECIDING WHETHER A DEAL IS GOOD

Let's imagine you're going to your first foreclosure sale at auction. The date is coming up in three weeks. The house has a judgment against it for $127,000 by a local mortgage lender who has allowed you to go in and make an inspection.

You start with some basic research. After thoroughly evaluating the necessary repairs, your estimates total up to $23,000 needed to bring the house up to salable shape. You've been to your local courthouse and found that there is an IRS lien against the property for an additional $4,500. Additional property taxes of $3,700 will have to be paid. Next, and most important, you compare the property in the condition that it will be in when all fixed up with other similar properties that have recently sold in the same marketplace. You determine that on completion of the necessary repairs the renewed property will be worth $195,000.

Now you need to find out if there's enough money to cover your overhead and any contingencies you might meet, your selling costs, and a reasonable profit.

You total up the costs you have researched so far. Since it's a foreclosure auction, you never know exactly what your buy price will be until the bidding takes place. In this example, we'll assume that the bank makes a first bid at its mortgage deficit and is happy for anyone to bid fractionally higher so it can get its money back. In this case your bid will be $1,000 over the bank's cost.

Property:	$128,000
Repairs:	23,000
IRS lien:	4,500
Property taxes:	3,700
Net cost:	$159,200

Now you subtract your net cost that you've totaled up from the property, repairs, lien, and taxes cost from the amount you've determined the property will be worth when refurbished.

Projected selling price: $195,000

Net cost: −159,200

Remaining net: $35,800

Is this a good deal? First, you'd better allow at least 5% of the selling price for selling and legal costs in case you use an agent. This must be calculated from the final amount, not arbitrarily picked from the air unrelated to what the property will sell for. Then you should factor in at least 15%, depending on your profit goal (most investors don't even think about a fixer-upper project unless a 15% profit is available). The question is, do you have enough left over for overhead and contingencies after you subtract selling costs and profit from your net or raw cost?

Remaining net: $35,800

Selling costs: −9,750 (5% of $195,000)

Profit: −29,250

Subtotal: −$3,200

Oops! A negative number! There's not enough money to pay for any overhead or contingencies factor. Warning flag: Do not proceed. So even though the property would be worth more once repaired, and even though there would be enough money to pay for a sales agent's commission, and even though you figure on a tidy profit, there would not be enough to make the deal.

Well, perhaps you can say to yourself, "I'll fudge a little on the repairs, and maybe I can sell it myself, and of course if it's going to be worth $195,000, I could sell it for $210,000." This thinking is disastrous for investors in the fixer-upper market. For example, what will you do if repairs cost you more than you thought and you can't get quite the full $195,000? Or if it takes longer to sell the property than normal? These overruns will come out of your profit. Don't fool yourself. To ensure that you will always get this profit, you need to account for the overhead and contingency amount. Now we hope everything will go along as planned and that you not only will profit but some of the overhead money will come back to you. But to set up the initial deal make sure you have a sufficient overhead set aside (in the range of 10% to 12%).

So, be warned! To ensure your profit in the fixer-upper market, always factor in a figure to safeguard your overhead and contingencies.

SOME REMINDERS ON FORECLOSURES

- Make sure you know what's being foreclosed upon.

- Know the status of all mortgages on the property, not just the one being foreclosed upon.

- Talk directly with the foreclosing party and ask how much it would take to make a deal.

- Discuss the foreclosure with the attorney representing the mortgage holder who is foreclosing.

- Contact someone in the deed recorder's or other appropriate office to show you how to do your own lien search.

- Talk to all creditors who have placed liens on the property.

- Examine the case file at the court to determine as much as possible about the title (i.e., whether it shows any subordinate liens).

- Know that city and/or county property taxes and assessments are usually senior—that is, they take precedence and get paid off first—to mortgages and deeds of trust.

- Beware of liens that get placed just prior to the foreclosure proceedings.

- Make sure the foreclosing is against *all* of the owners of the property.

- Make sure the interest being auctioned off is not a partial interest.

- Make sure that any obligations other than ones you already know about are being wiped away with the foreclosure auction.

- Go to the property and talk to the owners and find out if you can buy it from them.

- Ask the owners if they are interested in purchasing the house back after the sale.

- Hire a competent attorney who knows about foreclosures to guide you.

WHEN THE IRS HAS A LIEN ON
PROPERTY BEING FORECLOSED

Liens by the IRS are not senior to mortgages created before the IRS obligation, and some investors feel you do not need to pay them.

However, the IRS has 120 days from the sale date to take the property (called the right of redemption) at your cost, plus any expense related to securing the property but not for substantial improvements you might have made.

However, when considering buying an IRS-liened house, keep in mind that the IRS seldom tries to get the house back, and is usually willing to negotiate if you don't want to pay off the previous owner's loan.

You do want to satisfy the IRS as much as you can, even to pay the obligation if necessary. Its cost is simply a cost in acquiring the house. If it is too much (in relation to market value), then the IRS may back down on what it receives.

Most conventional lenders will not lend on property within the 120-day redemption period. So you may need a letter from the IRS stating that it would not redeem the property. Or, if the lender does not require an IRS letter, you could wait out the 120 days by renting the house out, just as long as you don't do any major repairs for which you won't be reimbursed.

As an alternative, if all you need to do is make the property presentable by doing inexpensive repairs, you could put it on the market stipulating the IRS contingency, and the planned repairs, and requiring a closing date after the 120 days.

GET ACQUAINTED WITH AUCTION PROCEDURE

As for the auction itself, make sure you have the required deposit in certified funds and that you have arranged for funding to complete the purchase should you prevail in your bidding. Actual bidding procedure is simply raising your hand or a bidding card, thereby gaining the auctioneer's acknowledgment of your bid.

Don't bid at the first solicitation from the auctioneer. Often, auctioneers start by throwing out a figure at which they think the bidding might finally arrive. Those familiar with auctions will remain still until the price drops low enough to attract most bidders. Alternatively, the auctioneer starts at a price requested by the lender, and thereby the lender bids in its loan balance while hoping more bids will follow. If no one else bids after the bank bids in what's owed, and you feel comfortable bidding more, raise your hand or card to the auctioneer.

Note that if the increment asked for by the auctioneer is larger than you wish to bid, wait for him or her to lower it, or, if it is accepted procedure at your auction, acknowledge the auctioneer by moving the flat of your hand horizontally. This means you request only one-half the bid amount instead of the full increment. This may sound complicated, but it's not. If you have any questions on how to proceed, meet with the auctioneer a day or two before the auction. It would be advisable for you to attend a few auctions simply to observe; bidding can proceed rapidly, so it's wise to be prepared before you actually attend an auction in which you plan to bid.

GETTING AN REO FROM THE BANK

Let's move on to property that's already been taken over by a bank. These properties are commonly called "real estate owned," or REO for short. Most of these properties have been foreclosed or simply abandoned by their owners, usually due to high mortgage balances.

Here's a way for you to approach a lender on an REO property. Often, your local banks will have property that they have had to take in for a variety of reasons that usually include foreclosure. As a rule, the banks are anxious to get rid of these REO properties.

You can start by calling the bank that is advertising an REO and ask for the bank officer who is handling the sale. If a property is not advertised but you believe a particular bank is holding a property— perhaps you've checked the property tax rolls—you can start by calling the bank and asking for the name of the particular officer who handles that department so you can send him or her a letter.

Note that the sample letter makes it easy for the bank officer to respond and offers a polite apology in advance for being away from the telephone, which of course you will be as you may have written dozens of these letters at any one time, and are now out on the road scouting other properties. Further, notice the addition of fax number and e-mail address.

When you finally make contact with the appropriate bank officer, you might begin with some questions about the price. You don't need to refer to the "asking" price—that's assumed; besides, you don't want to give the impression that you are going to turn in a low bid—at least not yet. Other questions are: Will they finance? What's the condition of the property? Are there any title problems? Do they know of any other problems? When can you get inside?

Once you are able to talk to the bank officer, either on the tele-

Ms. Mary Smith, Vice President
Real Estate Owned Department
American Savings & Loan
100 Main Street
Escondido, CA 92029

Dear Ms. Smith,

I am interested in buying the single-family house your institution owns located at 27518 Silverpuff Drive, Quartz Hill, California. As I believe you are interested in selling this property, please call me at 813-729-5322. If I am away from my phone, please leave a message and I will get right back to you. Enclosed are my fax number and e-mail address if either is more convenient for you. I look forward to discussing the property with you.

Cordially,

James Lumley
(Address and numbers)

phone or in person, be open and direct. Remember, one of the keys to successful communication is to imagine yourself talking to a good friend across the kitchen table. Bear in mind that this person's expertise is in taking loan applications, probably not in real estate. In the majority of cases you will know more than the bank person does about the property.

Upon this first contact you don't need to say much about yourself. Get the officer to do the talking by asking questions about the property. Listening is the way to learn. The lender doesn't need to know any more than who you are and that you are interested.

USE YOUR REPAIR ESTIMATE TO DRIVE THE PRICE DOWN

In considering an REO property repossessed by a bank, don't dismiss the opportunity just because you feel that what the bank wants is too high. For example, a local mortgage bank has taken over a two-bedroom, one-bath, single-family house in a neighborhood where most houses are rented out. Property appreciation seems to be nil, and

CASE STUDY: Foreclosure

Here's a typical situation: A bank has for sale a property on which it foreclosed. It is asking $74,900 and the value assessed by the tax assessor is $105,000. This difference implies that substantial repairs are needed. You bring in the contractor who normally does work for you and learn that you need to spend only $15,000 to bring this property up to par.

Next, you check out the recent selling prices of comparable properties and find three sales that indicate a value—once the property is fixed up—of $135,000 after repairs. Your calculations show this amount will include buying the property, all repairs and overhead expenses, and profit. You negotiate with the bank. The only hitch you see is that the bank is demanding all cash, and it won't budge. You start by using the insistence on cash to bargain down the price. The bank is persuaded by your inventory of necessary repairs and settles with you for $73,000. But it won't provide the mortgage. You must get the funds from another lender—or come up with all cash.

Asking price by bank:	$74,900
Repairs needed:	15,000
Selling cost (5%):	6,750
Comparable value once fixed:	135,000
Settlement price with bank:	73,000

Note that the assessor's valuation for tax purposes helps confirm value once repairs are completed. The full explanation of establishing the cost of repairs and comparable value once completed will be in the next two chapters.

You put the property under contract with the bank with an inspection and approval clause that asks for 20 days for formal inspections as well as approval by a partner you bring in to raise the necessary amount of cash. Now, since you don't normally use a partner you must endeavor to find one. You might offer a 50–50 split of expected profits with your partner's position secured by a mortgage.

There are several advantages to this deal that are likely to bring in a partner. The first advantage is that often an all-cash

CASE STUDY: Foreclosure *(Continued)*

deal keeps the price somewhat less than otherwise. The second is that the partner's $94,750 (in this case the $73,000 cost, $15,000 for repairs, and $6,750 selling costs) cash investment is secured by a first mortgage. The third is that it's a short-term investment. As soon as the work is done, if not sooner, the property goes on the market and a buyer is found. And if your research on comparables is sound, it should be sold quickly.

Let's say that these incentives enlist a family friend who is more than happy to make one-half of a potential gain of $40,250 (projected selling price of $135,000 minus investment of $94,750, which includes 5% selling cost). The cash is what makes this deal work. Note that you could also resell this property on a lease/purchase agreement with a tenant-buyer. However, because you (actually your partner) have had to put up a substantial amount of cash to make this work, the best strategy to maximize your profits is to get in and out as fast as possible. And once you get your profit, you'll have some cash, and a future comrade, for your next all-cash deal.

---

the property needs at least $12,000 worth of repairs. But the bank wants back its cost, including all sorts of legal and foreclosure fees, of $78,000.

Your investigation shows that even after repairs the most the property would bring would be in the $85,000 to $95,000 range. The bank's asking price can't be met even for a quick wholesale profit. What do you do—walk away or act? You can't give the bank its price.

You employ a commonsense investment strategy and begin to negotiate by laying out the breakdown of repair costs and what the comparables show for value once the repairs are done. Facts can always bring people to reality.

For example, the $12,000 in repairs might break down to:

Roof:	$2,600
Kitchen:	2,400
Floors:	1,200
Plumbing:	1,100

Electrical:	800
Exterior painting:	2,200
Interior painting:	1,300
Trash removal:	400

The comparable sales that you found of similar-sized homes in the same neighborhood, in the same condition, without rehabilitation (you'll see how to make value after repairs over the next few chapters), selling within the last six months, and with no adjustments needed, might be:

Property A:	$44,000
Property B:	$41,000
Property C:	$43,000

Once the bank absorbs the reality that actual selling prices are in the low 40s, that it's going to cost $12,000 to get it into shape, and that all three comparable properties were sold to contractors who put in from $10,000 to $20,000 each, maybe it'll acknowledge that what it has is worth a lot less than it expected. With luck this will make the bank receptive to your offer of something that's a lot closer to the comparable sales prices. In fact, it is close to one-half of what they have been asking. But will they take it?

You'll never know until you ask. If your offer is accepted, the bank would at least recover some of its loss and be able to write off the rest as bad debt. But you know you've offered a fair price from which you can't depart much if you are to make a profit. You have to remember that because this property is in a neighborhood that is stagnant in price, you've got to get an extra bargain in order to move it to a new buyer—who will be either living in the house or wholesaling it to another investor. The worst-case scenario is that you will have to rent it out until the right buyer comes along. This, too, argues against offering a higher price. The point is, don't pass over a property just because the asking price is too high. Document the needed repairs to drive the price down.

FIND CONDEMNED HOUSES
IN RESPECTABLE NEIGHBORHOODS

The last type of institutional buy is the occasional condemned property. A condemned property has been determined by the local health or building authority to be dangerous to the health and safety of any occupant. It is usually a procedure invoked by authorities only when a building is vacant or in seriously decayed condition. Unless a building is in danger of collapse, a condemned property can be a good rehab investment.

Often you can find a list of condemned properties by contacting the local building inspector's office. Larger communities may have a list of 100 or more; smaller, more affluent communities very few, if any. The conditions for buying a condemned property must be optimal. However, if you find one in an otherwise superior neighborhood, and if the property has become neglected through absentee ownership or death of the owner, it may be worth pursuing. While driving around you may even notice such a property because of a red or other-colored tag that identifies it as condemned. If there had been any financing on it at one time, it is now probably owned by the bank or mortgage company.

By way of example, if you spy a red-tagged, empty house in the middle of well-maintained homes that have a good record of recent sales, you will be able to get an idea of what it might bring once fixed up. Your research tells you the fully fixed-up market value of the house is at least $110,000.

First of all, to get the house off the condemned list, you must bring it up to code. Once you find out from the building inspector exactly what defects must be corrected, you can get cost estimates. You want to get all the facts about the property you can. You must also plan on fixing problems that may not be visible, such as plumbing and wiring. Make sure the sewer connection is operable. Sometimes older properties have septic tanks that are no longer functioning or up to code. The power may be off, as it is on many condemned properties, because the electric company will turn off the electricity to any house that sits empty—and often will not turn it back on until the city has inspected the property and it meets code.

The same goes for the title, which may not be able to be transferred until the property meets code. Check with tax collectors to find out what, if any, back taxes are owed. Before going further, make sure you have a clear knowledge of what you must do beyond code violations and their costs. Finally, if it looks like a deal worth pursuing, and not a nightmare making it more trouble than it's worth, you can approach the bank or mortgage company with an offer.

You might check into local government programs for financial help for rehabbing condemned property. There are many dollars available out there for getting property up and viable again, especially as residences for lower-income people.

Condemned houses can be a good choice for rehab property. The keys to buying a condemned property are (1) to find one in a decent neighborhood, and (2) to work out an accurate cost-to-repair list. But a final warning: If the property has any unauthorized tenants, make sure they are out before you take title. You don't want to have to start your ownership and rehabilitation by having to evict somebody. You'll be doing enough for society by upgrading the property to an approved level of safety for the next occupant.

In the next chapter, we'll discuss one of the key procedures in dealing with fixer-uppers: what you need to know about repairs.

5

Repairs That Make
You the Most Money

Now that you've found a potential fixer-upper, you need to know what repairs should be done and what they will cost. As you'll see in the next chapter, knowing the cost of repairs is essential in determining the final retail value of the property, the profit you will gain, and what you should offer.

A key to fixer-uppers is to get firm and accurate estimates. And estimates can vary depending on the type and quality of material chosen. Also, quite often you face the repair-or-replace dilemma. And different contractors will quote widely varying estimates. Sometimes the most profitable repairs require creativity, such as adding a room or the judicious use of skylights. Depending on local practices, contractors may charge for providing an estimate, especially for those with whom they have not done business before and who don't yet own the property. Therefore, lining up estimates can be inconvenient and can require time, yet must proceed rapidly before someone pulls the rug out from under you. But the work will be worth it. And as you gain experience and forge working relationships with repairpeople, the process will become smoother—and take less time.

When you get to the stage when contractors or other competent repairpeople begin work, you may find that a job estimated to be completed in two weeks can turn out to take two months. And although work needs to proceed in a timely manner, precision is not always possible. In this chapter we will deal with tying down all needed repairs and their costs as rapidly as possible.

START BY GETTING ACCURATE ESTIMATES

Before moving forward with determining what you can sell a property for when the time comes, and therefore what you will offer, you need to have a full itemization of what you will do and what it will cost. Repair costs should not be guesstimated. At the same time there's no reason to make pricing repairs an arduous task. A repair estimate form later in this chapter will help make your job easier. You don't need to be a slave to the form, but it will point out many of the repair items that should be addressed. Your job is not to bring the property up to brand-new standards, but simply to fix the obvious problems, such as poor flooring or gutter replacement, structural repairs if needed, and any building code violations such as broken windows. Finally, you may choose to do certain cosmetic repairs that will make your property more salable.

FOUR BROAD AREAS OF REPAIRS

The repairs you will do break down into four major areas:

1. *Normal repairs.* These include replacement of kitchen cabinets, installation of new carpeting, interior and exterior painting, plumbing, electrical work, and floor and roof repairs.

2. *Structural repairs.* Problems such as cracks in the foundation or flooring slab, or termite or wood-boring insect damage are structural.

3. *Building code repairs.* Repairs of a health and safety nature required by law might include violations ranging from broken windows to a lack of a vent fan in a bathroom. If there's any question of what might violate your community's building code requirements, have the building inspector make an inspection. Do this now and you won't get caught later on when a retail buyer has the house inspected.

4. *Cosmetic repairs.* Items done to make the house more pleasing could involve changing the color of the house, sprucing up the front entryway, or planting hardy shrubs, among other possibilities. These are the superficial features that can make a property look better for a modest amount of money.

SIX MAJOR AREAS OF INSPECTION AND REPAIR

Now, within those broad categories let's look at some specific types of rehab problems that fixer-uppers may have.

1. *Foundation.* A common problem is the inadequate drainage of water away from the foundation. This can be spotted by wet conditions in a basement, mildew, water staining, or settling of cracks in the foundation. These uncertainties can usually be solved by improving the landscaping grading around the immediate house so that water drains away, as well as fixing or adding gutters and downspouts.

2. *Roof.* The two key elements in a house are the foundation and the roof. Once you have any foundation problems corrected as may be needed, turn your attention to the roof. Here it's often a matter of shingles damaged by years of weather. The seals, or flashings, around chimneys must be secure to prohibit rain from coming into the house. Although damage to asphalt, tile, or wood shingles may be apparent, if you don't see anything at first, check by inspecting for evidence of water damage such as rotting wood or paint peeling. Inspect the attic and interior ceiling for any indication of water damage.

3. *Wiring.* Another problem is that some older homes have outdated wiring. This is usually referred to as the "knob and tube," which you can recognize because the electricity is carried by two wires held up at junction points by ceramic tubing. This is usually accompanied by a fuse box rather than the modern circuit breakers. Plan on changing the older system, which should also range from 100- to 200-amp service. Unfortunately, another problem you can run into with houses built in the 1960s and early 1970s is aluminum wiring. The actual metal, aluminum, has a chemical reaction when tied into outlets or switches where copper is used. Over time these connections loosen and can create a spark when the electricity jumps across the faulty contact. Again, replace. Further, if there are limited outlets in each room, more should be added so the occupants don't double up on the outlets, like many of us do in the computer age.

4. *HVAC.* The replacement of the heating, ventilating, and/or air-conditioning system is a problem often encountered in fixer-uppers. If a house has a seriously antiquated system, replace it. Even systems installed within the past 20 years can have inefficiencies that make them less desirable today. And even if you have unusually low electric rates in your area, plan on getting rid of that electric heating system. Oil or gas are the heating methods for these modern times. Whatever system you use, make sure the furnace is vented properly. The chimney flue should be lined; that is, the hot exhaust should be encased in high-heat-resistant ceramic tile as it goes up the chimney and leaves the house. With any heating system it's best to check with a heating contractor for efficiency and safety.

5. *Maintenance.* Much of your work on a fixer-upper is often in the area of general maintenance—that is, repairing or rejuvenating the physical wearing away of myriad separate items. These could include fixing cracks and painting walls and ceilings, substituting doors and windows, replacing cabinets, miscellaneous plumbing, outside landscaping, and maintaining walkways and driveways.

6. *Appearance.* Now that you've got the major physical problems corrected, the last hurdle you will encounter will be what can you do to spruce up the property and make it more salable. This is what is usually referred to as cosmetic repair. Don't underestimate the need to give the property some curbside appeal. It's more than just painting, although it is that, too. It is a matter of an attractive appearance so that, when prospective buyers drive up to the front entryway, their first look at the house is a positive one.

FROM PRELIMINARY OUTLINE TO FINALIZED LIST

In Chapter 3, when you met with the seller at the property, you made a preliminary list of repairs. Now you will expand that rough draft to make a full inventory of repair costs, which you will determine with qualified tradespeople on an expanded inspection during a second viewing of the property. Although an experienced rehabber might jump the gun and estimate the repairs found on the preliminary viewing and make an offer to the seller on that basis, this procedure is fraught with danger. No one is an expert at all types of repairs or at pricing those repairs. And nothing is worse than estimating a plumbing job at $600 only to find out when the professional plumber is brought in after the closing that it will cost $1,800.

In addition, you want to make sure you have a clause in your contract with the seller that allows you to escape if you don't like the costs of the forthcoming repair estimates. You won't face a friendly seller if you need to renegotiate. Do it right the first time. That doesn't mean the repair estimate needs to slow you down. Just act as quickly as possible, letting the seller know of your need for an estimate and of your continued interest. Note that most repairs will often center around a main problem, such as flooring, roofing, or painting, allowing you to localize the necessary pricing.

This repair summary worksheet is a way for you to catalog property repairs. Use it as a guide on your initial property viewing as well as during your thorough inspections with repair personnel and contractors. Note that it's a summary and that the details of each price breakdown will be kept on separate paperwork. Although it's comprehensive, it can be modified depending on the type of job you have.

WORKSHEET: Repair Summary

Date: _____

Seller's Name: _____ Telephone: _____

Property Address: _____

_____

_____

Neighborhood: _____

Lead Source: FSBO _____ Agent _____ Bank _____ Other _____

Description: _____

    Bedrooms: ____ Baths: _____ Style: _____

    Age (Years): _____ Condition: _____ Square Feet: _____

    Garage (No. Cars): _____ Outbuildings: _____

    Amenities:_____

    Other: _____

Asking Price:_____

Reason to Sell: _____

(Continued)

WORKSHEET: Repair Summary *(Continued)*

Renovation Summary

Repair Type	*Who Will Do*	*Time Required*	*Cost Estimate*
Basic			
Foundation Cracks	_____	_____	_____
Slab Damage	_____	_____	_____
Structural Repairs	_____	_____	_____
Wood-Boring Insect Damage	_____	_____	_____
Trash/Refuse Removal	_____	_____	_____
Increase Size/Additions	_____	_____	_____
Other	_____	_____	_____
Interior			
Interior Walls/ Painting/Wallpaper	_____	_____	_____
Ceilings/Painting	_____	_____	_____
Plumbing/Drainpipes	_____	_____	_____
Electrical System/ Circuit Box	_____	_____	_____
Hot Water Heater	_____	_____	_____
Heating/ Air-Conditioning	_____	_____	_____
Doors	_____	_____	_____
Windows	_____	_____	_____
Skylights	_____	_____	_____
Flooring/ Hardwood/Carpeting	_____	_____	_____
Kitchen Rehab	_____	_____	_____
Baths Rehab	_____	_____	_____
Bedroom(s)	_____	_____	_____
Other Rooms	_____	_____	_____

WORKSHEET: **Repair Summary** *(Continued)*

Repair Type	Who Will Do?	Time Required	Cost Estimate
Interior			
Light Fixtures	_____	_____	_____
Security System	_____	_____	_____
Appliances	_____	_____	_____
Fireplace(s)	_____	_____	_____
Other	_____	_____	_____
Exterior			
Ext. Surface/Painting	_____	_____	_____
Roof Repair/Replace	_____	_____	_____
Gutters/Drainspouts	_____	_____	_____
Other	_____	_____	_____
Site and Outside			
Site Drainage	_____	_____	_____
Landscaping	_____	_____	_____
Tree Removal	_____	_____	_____
Shrub Replacement	_____	_____	_____
Driveway	_____	_____	_____
Patio/Walkway	_____	_____	_____
Porch/Deck	_____	_____	_____
Garage	_____	_____	_____
Other	_____	_____	_____
Miscellaneous:	_____	_____	_____

Subtotal: _____

Reserve for Undetected Damage: _____

Total Repair Costs: _____

Comments: _____

_____

Don't Underestimate Repairs

A FIRST PRIORITY: ARRANGING
TIME FOR THE REPAIR ESTIMATION

Allow enough time for a proper estimate of repairs. Until you make a detailed cost accounting of all items of repair you cannot establish with the owner the price and terms of sale. As previously mentioned, you will have a clause in your purchase contract that gives you an escape should unseen problems be found later. But the basic repair estimate should be made before the signing of any contract—in fact, even before any initial negotiating.

As you saw in Chapter 3, on your first viewing you should make a simple outline of what work needs to be done. And depending on whether you can secure a deal quickly with the owner, you may also need to make a "best guess" approximating a repair estimate. If a seller will let you go into a property and poke around on your own, that's fine. You may need to arrange two or three more appointments so that you can make certain your inspection is thorough.

If an agent is involved, he or she is normally going to want to be with you. However, since estimating repair cost is time-consuming, most agents are not interested in standing around with you while you do the necessary work. One way to assuage them is to have them open up the building and then let them leave, having arranged a time for them to return when you are done. Or give them an idea of how long it'll take you, and if they hesitate, then request that they contact the owner (or let you do it) so that you can have the owner let you in. You might also point out that if the agent is present when undisclosed problems are found, he or she is obligated to make known all problems to future buyers.

EARLY INSPECTIONS AVOID PROBLEMS LATER

On any fixer-upper you must use a far-ranging inspection process that goes beyond that which the average homeowner would require.

When buying a new property, most home buyers obtain a standard pest control report and a damage or structural report. They review the report and negotiate with the seller about paying for any problems found. Buyers often want to be present at the inspection and ask the inspector questions. The sellers must make sure there are no significant areas that are inaccessible and therefore cannot be inspected, as home inspectors will not drill holes or inspect areas they cannot easily see.

However, even though the property you wish to buy might pass a homeowner's inspection, you need a far more in-depth inspection to determine not only what must be done to satisfy the requirements of your state building code—specifically any health and safety issues, physical deterioration, and obvious damage repair—but also what should be done to improve the salability of the property. You need a list of specific work to be done and what that work costs. This does not mean you are going to remodel completely. But you need to meet required provisions as well as do whatever can be done economically to enhance the property in a buyer's eyes.

TYPICAL REPAIRS YOU MAY ENCOUNTER

One improvement you might make is to paint the exterior. A good paint job is critical to the appearance of a house. You might also upgrade the front yard with hardy shrubs. If the driveway is cracking, you might want to resurface it. Replace missing or damaged storm windows, storm doors, and screens. Sometimes a window itself is so damaged that it's best to replace it completely with a new plastic-coated, modern window that includes storms and screens. These are available at most home centers. If the other houses in the neighborhood have patios or decks you might consider adding one.

On the inside of the house you should replace any bad flooring. This might include wood flooring in the living areas, yard goods in kitchen and baths, or carpeting in a number of locations. You are also likely to find that the interior needs a new paint job. Kitchen cabinets should be refinished or replaced as needed. Fix any plumbing leaks, faucets, and showerheads. Replace any lighting fixtures that may be damaged or not functioning. Often, the refrigerator and stove in a rehabilitation project will not be in good condition. Sometimes it's better to just take them out and keep the space empty, as many potential buyers will have their own appliances.

This roster of repairs is not meant to be exhaustive. Each house in need of repair will have its own particular needs. For more on potential repairs obtain a pamphlet on remodeling at your local home center.

WHAT REPAIRS TO AVOID

Beware of overimproving. You never want to make a property better than the surrounding properties. Even if a house is significantly better in terms of size and quality, buyers will rarely pay $150,000 in a neighborhood where the homes average $120,000.

Similarly, if most of the houses have two-car garages, don't feel you need to spend time and $20,000 on building a garage—especially if it pushes the price of a property beyond the average price. Be aware that if the neighborhood has custom homes with different styles and designs you'll be more flexible in the improvements you can make.

Never change the exterior style of the house to make it different from the neighboring property. For example, you wouldn't change a ranch house into a Cape Cod style, particularly if the neighborhood houses were ranch style and another design would stand out as being too extreme. This doesn't mean that different architectural styles cannot be integrated, but that each must be carefully integrated to match one with the other. If the design of a house isn't complementary to the other styles in the neighborhood, it's possible it could become less salable and even lose value.

The ideal fixer-upper, then, is one that needs only decorating and/or minor remodeling and that doesn't require extensive structural work—you want to make profits, not work.

ALWAYS SOLVE CODE VIOLATIONS

You should look at a distressed property in two ways: what it is going to cost you to make repairs and whether there are any major building code violations. Many rehabbers look only at what they can do to make the property presentable and then get caught short when the property is scrutinized by the new buyer's inspector and code violations appear. And code violations are not something you can escape by ignoring them. You should make a separate list of these violations so that you can ascertain their cost as well as make sure they are dealt with if you decide to follow through and buy the property. The best way to deal with code violations is to have the local building inspector give the property a thorough analysis before you buy so that those requirements are figured into your repair cost. If your seller balks at having the community inspector view the property, a warning flag should go up.

Code violations are the biggest block to being successful with fixer-uppers. In short, you should walk away from a deal when these problems are costly or impractical to repair. Major code violations are nothing you want to deal with if you're just getting started, so at first stick with houses that need only modest repairs. Avoiding the difficulties inherent in major repairs allows you to be more accurate on costs. When you don't feel good about a deal, stay away.

GETTING TO KNOW THE BRICKS AND MORTAR, OR, THE MORE YOU KNOW, THE MORE YOU'LL EARN

Much of what is discussed in this book is on how to buy, how much to pay, how to rent, and how to sell, among other economic considerations. But as important as these financial matters are, you also must learn about the physical aspects of the property. These include the mechanical systems of a building such as heating and cooling system, plumbing and electrical system, and waste disposal and appliances, among others. There are also various structural components, such as foundation, frame, and roof, as well as outside elements such as landscaping, driveways, and walkways.

Some basic knowledge of the workings of these physical aspects of the property will be helpful. After all, most of us are not mechanically inclined. Unfortunately, too many investors jump into a property's ownership without bothering to learn about some of the mechanical or structural systems. They often become unwitting victims of repair contractors who sometimes are confused and chagrined themselves by having to effect the smallest repairs on a building that most professional landlords would have taken care of themselves. In fact, anytime you call a contractor out to do a repair, the cost of labor may very well far exceed the cost of material. For example, filling some cracks in a wall might cost well over $100 with a material cost that is negligible if you have someone come out and do the work.

Now, certainly the average investor can't fix a furnace or repair the internal workings of most appliances, nor should he or she try to, but he or she can replace the washers in a faucet, or patch some wall cracks, or run some caulk around a window frame. It's not carved in stone that to be a real estate investor you should be able to do all these repairs, however minor. What you do need to understand is that with a little education you will save substantially on repairs.

I remember a contractor giving me a price on repairing a damaged spot where a tree branch scraped several shingles off a roof. He quoted me $300, which could rise once he got into the work! And, although at the time I wasn't too familiar with roofs, I got a book out of the library on their repair, and after some study set aside a Saturday morning. So, wearing old clothes, my fishing cap on backward, and with a screwdriver, hammer, and nails in my pockets, I climbed my father's aluminum ladder to the roof's edge while my Mimi stood grousing below me. Fortunately, it was only a one-and-a-half-story house and I could indeed walk up the roof's incline. I pulled away the three broken shingles and replaced them with three of almost the same color I got from the local building supply company. I reinforced them on the underside with some black roof tar. Soon I was off the roof with the tools put away and wondering what I was going to do with the rest of the morning. Needless to say, the $300-plus job had shrunk to $12.50.

Now, I couldn't have done the job on the roof if it entailed more damage. But I was pretty pleased to have been able to do what I did as well as to have saved some money that could go toward other expenses. And something else less tangible but important as well: I gained a bit of confidence in dealing with the property. By this I mean that many of us who approach property from an investing point of view (cash flow, net income, etc.) are often educated for the better when we get a chance to poke around at the bricks and mortar of our properties. It might make you alert to a time when a real roof problem might convince someone to sell before he or she had intended, whereas if you knew a bit about the repair of a roof—or foundation or heating system—you might have more confidence in going ahead with the necessary work.

This is also true regarding a fixer-upper. Some investors want to do all the work themselves, and make a little more money. Others advocate having someone else do all the work. They argue that your own time is better spent finding the next property rather than repairing and refurbishing; the real money is not in doing the repairs, but investing. And after all, you should always estimate the job as if outside repair people were doing the work, so why shouldn't you follow through and use them? If you supervise them properly, and arrange for the sale as you planned, your profit should be enough.

We can leave enough room for both sets of investors. There will always be those who are knowledgeable enough and desire to do the work themselves, as well as those who feel their place is to control it from the outside.

But when you can do the repair yourself and have the time to do it, it can really pay off. So, if you don't know already, it will pay you to learn the basics about inspections and the building code, heating and cooling systems, plumbing and electrical, carpentry and home maintenance.

So, when that contractor throws you an oddball price for a half hour's work you'll have another avenue you can take. And even if you still don't do the actual work yourself, you'll know more about your property and will be able to avoid overpaying.

As I said, the serious money is in investing, not doing repairs. But when you can understand better what repairs, major and minor, are about and what they cost, you will profit more in the end. So don't be alarmed when a few bathroom tiles have come loose. It probably won't take you an hour some Saturday morning to fix the problem.

Where do you go to get information on the ins and outs of your property? I have found that having your own library (perhaps a book or two on each subject—plumbing, electrical, carpentry, roof and window, landscaping, and whatever I left out) will be of great help. Books in these areas are often in a large, inexpensive paperback format. Videos are also available on many of the same subjects. There are also books on home inspection that will help you concentrate on checking out a property. They won't get the job done but they will focus your mind on what needs to be done.

Next, check out the free clinics and the big home centers that have seminars on most if not all the basic construction and maintenance fundamentals you'll need to know.

Also ask your friends who are handy in some aspect of the trades. They are usually happy to be able to expound on some unique way to make a repair that could be valuable to you.

SPECIAL PROBLEM OF DEALING WITH A CRACKED FOUNDATION

Many of the properties you consider for possible purchase are not in the best condition. In fact, they often have formidable problems. That's why they come to your attention. After all, if the property was in perfect shape and ready to sell retail, you might not even hear of it. But before you dismiss a property out of hand, an investigation is warranted. You don't want to approach a property by looking for reasons not to buy it; you want to look at the problems and consider how you might address them. Be objective and positive minded—at least until you're sure a problem cannot be fixed economically.

For example, a fellow investor is considering one property with a crack in the concrete garage foundation and wall that runs from floor to ceiling. In fact, the wall between the garage and the laundry room is buckling and separating from the stucco and metal screen frame to which it is attached.

The problem is major. But there are two ways an investor might approach it.

The first way is technical: Establish a relationship with a qualified construction engineer and a capable foundation contractor. An engineer can tell you why this problem occurred, determine its severity, and clarify what can and needs to be done to remedy it. The contractor can also tell you whether you can repair it yourself and how, and can tell you what it will cost you for a professional to fix it.

The second way is to talk with another investor or homeowner who has experienced the same problem. Again, a contractor may know of someone you can call. Or ask around among your friends. Talking with someone who has solved a supposedly unsolvable problem can give you confidence and remove the fear of looking at distressed property.

If you come across a property with this kind of problem, then follow this general outline:

1. Inspect the property with a qualified engineer.

2. Get a recommendation on whether it's possible to remedy the problem, and if it is how you'd go about it.

3. Get bids from reputable contractors (ask for long-term warranties).

4. Decide whether the costs justify the repair.

5. If they do, buy and repair.

6. Reinspect with the engineer and certify the effectiveness of the repair (in the case of the garage example, the stability and flatness of the foundation).

Note that once you have solved the problem correctly (i.e., you have not covered it up), the property will easily pass any inspection initiated by future buyers. In fact, you may increase the value of the property far more that it cost to make the repair.

However, sometimes you've got to walk away from these deals—especially if the repair estimate is more than the profit you are likely to gain upon sale. You also want to avoid a situation where the estimates have a wide range, like $5,000 to $15,000. You must know your costs before going into any deal.

Furthermore, one of the reasons for the engineer's advice over the contractor's is that the former is the best one to tell you why the foundation cracked in the first place. Perhaps the ground is unstable. Is there any reason to believe that if you repaired the foundation, it would never happen again? Is drainage of the land adequate? Are there any special requirements insisted on by the town building inspector? Ultimately, the cost to fix has to be reasonable, allowing the overall value of the property to rise substantially, and the price to buy has got to be cheap. In fact, you may not be able to get a conventional mortgage until the defect is repaired properly.

Here's how one person solved a foundation problem: One of my associates, relatively new to real estate investing, ran across what seemed to be a superb rehab project. The property had an after-repair appraisal of $149,000, an asking price of $95,000, and a very motivated seller who would take an offer in the high 80s. The hitch was that the house needed over $20,000 of foundation repairs. In fact, to repair the foundation correctly and to guard against future foundation problems, a two-story brick chimney and cement bulkhead would have to be removed.

Fortunately, my associate had contacts in the construction business so that he could obtain several estimates for the foundation repairs. An experienced general contractor did the repair work and warranted it. The job led to more rehab work, though: Additional cracks were found in the foundation and concrete walls, as well as rotted floorboards—necessitating a new floor and a partial movement of a section of plumbing.

It was determined that the possibility of future foundation problems could be minimized by improving drainage around the back of the house. Although this added to the cost, it had to be done and was.

My associate fortunately was able to keep the cost of these extra repairs manageable and still get close to his profit expectation when the property sold.

ANOTHER COMMON REHAB PROBLEM: FIRE DAMAGE

A fire-damaged house makes a complex rehab project, not only because of the difficult work but because of the cost. However, if the original house was of good quality and the damage not too extensive, it may be possible to go forward. Typical fire damage repairs include an extensive roof repair (if not a complete new roof), new drywall, insulation, heat/AC units, and electrical work. Severe smoke damage always requires lots of cleanup. Estimates can range from 10% to 90% of a house's value.

Most of us are not experts in assessing these severe repairs. Fire damage usually requires specialized repair crews. Walls with heavy smoke damage have to be sealed as well as painted with special products. A professional carpet restoration company will be required to clean any salvageable carpets. Duct work in a forced hot air system usually has to be cleaned, too.

Make sure that before you buy a house like this you call the city building inspector to find out what building code repairs are required. Repairs must be completed before the city will issue a certificate of occupancy.

SIX-POINT CHECKLIST FOR FIXING UP

Always remember that your total repair cost is critical in determining value after repairs as well as negotiating price for initial purchase. Here are the basic things you need to know before you buy a fixer-upper: The exact amount of work that's involved in the repairs, how long that work is going to take, how much of the work you're going to hire out, and how much you can do yourself.

1. If you find a bargain, don't procrastinate. Sometimes you need to act on a moment's notice. Do not, however, buy a property just because the price seems cheap, and never sidestep the repair estimate stage.

2. Be wary about what you choose to buy. Don't buy property simply because you have funds or the time or your contractors have no other work.

3. List all needed repairs. Almost every property sold needs some measure of repair or renovation, even if it's just cosmetic.

4. Scrutinize all potential repairs. Start the necessary research on your initial property inspection. Repairs found after closing can eat into profits.

5. If you can't investigate a property, such as the case of a sealed house offered through foreclosure, either take into consideration a tremendous deduction for repairs or stay away from the deal. Totaling up exact repair costs is a crucial element of prudent investing. If anything blocks your determining exactly what repair costs will be, don't buy.

6. Don't feel you need to do the work yourself. Your skills are best utilized in finding potential buys and making proper cost estimates.

The next chapter on how to value fixer-uppers will show you how to take your repair estimate and match the improved property against sales of comparable properties and determine—accounting for selling, overhead costs, and profit—the amount you should not go above in negotiating with the seller.

6

Valuing Properties
Is the Key to Profits

In this chapter you will learn how to determine what your fixer-upper will sell for once repairs are completed. This is done by matching the "after repaired" house with recently sold comparable houses in the same neighborhood. This ensuing value is then used as a base from which you determine your profit after repairs, overhead, and selling costs.

JUDGING THE "AFTER REPAIRS" VALUE

You have already determined what repairs are needed and their costs. You know what the property will be like once you have completed the repairs. Now you use that information to match it against similar properties—same number of rooms, bedrooms, and baths, neighborhood location, style, size and condition—that have sold recently. Note that to determine what you will sell it for you do not merely add together the present property price, the repair cost, and a profit. You need to judge whether your effort is worthwhile; you need to guarantee (as much as possible) that you will make a profit. Specifically, you need to assure yourself what this property will sell for *if* you buy the property, *if* you do the repairs, *if* a profit is available.

REPAIR COSTS LEAD TO FINDING VALUE

Let's look at an example of using repairs to start fixing value. You are talking to a seller of a distressed house for a negotiated price of $95,000. You check out needed repairs and find that in this house they are the bath rehab at $2,000; kitchen floor at $1,600; replacing kitchen cabinets at $4,200; interior and exterior painting at $3,700; replacement of five interior doors at $1,000; replacement of six window sashes at $1,800; miscellaneous plumbing repairs at $2,600; heating and cooling system repairs at $800; repairing a section of roof at $3,500; and general cleaning and trash removal at $1,100. Adding a $2,500 reserve for unrevealed repairs brings the total to $24,800.

After you put $24,800 in materials and labor into the house, what might you plan on for a return? At this point, you start investigating comparable sales—the selling prices of homes similar to the fixed-up condition of your property. Since you know exactly what repair and rehabilitation work will be done to the house, you can easily match the completed house to similar houses. For example, you start by identifying three properties that (1) have an identical floor plan, (2) are in the same neighborhood, and (3) have sold within the last year. This comparison of your repaired property with comparable sold properties reveals several selling prices in the $172,000 to $176,000 range. You therefore figure on a selling price of $174,000.

So far your cost will be $95,000 for the house plus $24,800 for repairs, totaling $119,800. To this amount you add potential selling costs of a 6% agent's commission of $10,440, a 10% overhead of $17,400, and a 15% profit of $26,100—these percentage amounts based on the most probable final selling price of $174,000.

Negotiated price of house:	$95,000
Repairs:	
Bath rehab:	$2,000
Kitchen floor:	1,600
Kitchen cabinets:	4,200

Painting:	3,700
Door replacement:	1,000
Window sashes:	1,800
Plumbing:	2,600
Heating/cooling:	800
Roof repair:	3,500
Cleaning/trash:	1,100
Unrevealed repairs:	2,500
Total repairs:	$24,800
Net cost of house and repairs:	$119,800
Average selling price of comparable house:	$174,000
Net balance prior to selling, overhead, and profit:	$54,200
Selling costs (6%):	$10,440
Overhead (10%):	17,400
Profit (15%):	26,100
Total costs based on final selling price:	$53,940

Now you ask yourself whether there is enough leeway between what you're going to sell it for ($174,000) and your net cost of house and repairs ($119,800) to take care of your selling and overhead cost and give you a fair profit. And, yes, there is, as the net balance of $54,200 is sufficient to pay back these costs and provide a 15% profit.

The key here is that you, as a savvy investor, have thoroughly checked repair costs and comparable sales for the house, that is, what it is likely to be worth after you complete repairs, before you buy it. Don't do it by the seat of your pants. Once you have gone through the process a few times you will be more efficient at it. We'll see this in more detail in the next chapter.

Now let's take a closer look at how you go about finding comparable property.

GETTING STARTED IN VALUING HOUSES

Value in real estate has much to do with a property's location. This is in part the neighborhood setting and the property's distance to schools, parks, and shopping, or for commuting to and from work. Another consideration is whether the other properties in the neighborhood are similar. If a property is next to a commercial building or apartment complex, this may influence your opinion about what would otherwise be construed as an environment of the same composition. One definition of value is what people are willing to pay, based primarily on the home's location, surroundings, and condition.

The way you find value is with a mini-appraisal. Although the basics are similar, a mini-appraisal is different from a full-blown value analysis done by a professional appraiser. It requires only minimal paperwork, not a formal report. You're doing it to assure only yourself, not a tax assessor, of the property's value. You do some simple math, and keep track of figures.

Like most real estate businesspeople, your ability to keep track of values and match them appropriately in the marketplace is a part of the key to success. For this purpose, you need to have access to your local assessor's office or other town government offices that hold information on recent selling prices as well as the details on specific properties. Another source for selling prices is the Multiple Listing Service sponsored by the local board of Realtors. Note that in ascertaining value you are not looking for advertisements for property or MLS asking prices to see what property is offered at, but rather what property has actually sold for. Real estate agents and professional appraisers can also be helpful, particularly agents, as they are interested in your business. You must—and this cannot be stressed enough—you must find properties that have already *sold*, for only by those actual selling prices can you determine what your property is worth now and what it will be worth after it is fixed up.

YOU START BY FINDING COMPARABLE PROPERTIES WITH RECENT SALES

Comparable properties or comps should be comparisons of your potential property with actual sales of similar properties (ranch with a ranch, two-story with a two-story, two-bedroom with a two-bedroom), from the same neighborhood or from one close by. Therefore, it is necessary to consider all of the recent sales in the immediate area near the subject property.

Cultivate a relationship with a Realtor or sales agent who will allow you to review these records. Most agents and brokers are likely to be willing to let you view the records because information on sold property is usually part of the public record and does not infringe on their current selling efforts. Agents are also familiar with the idea of seeking out homes with similar attributes. That is, they are experienced in finding qualities that new buyers look for, and are very aware of how the location, style, and size determine the price of a home.

You can also go to the Registry of Deeds, land planning offices, or county assessment offices to research and verify selling prices. Just ask for the recent sales reports. Much information on actual sales is found in local newspapers and easily obtained public records. Some newspapers keep a weekly log of property sale transfers. Banks, too, will have records of sales, as it is their business to lend money in mortgages.

DOING A MINI-APPRAISAL

An appraisal is an estimate of value. The three basic techniques to arrive at a value judgment are the sales comparison approach, the cost approach, and the income approach. The sales comparison approach is the one you will be primarily interested in for determining value. It is based on the selling prices of similar properties. The cost approach estimates how much it would cost to build the house today, subtracts depreciation, and finally adds back the value of the land. The income approach is primarily geared toward a rental property, where a stream of income after operating expenses is evaluated using capitalization rates and rent multipliers. We'll see more on the income approach as it pertains to investment property in Chapters 14 through 17 on multiunit buy-and-hold techniques.

To find value for a fixer-upper you use the sales comparison approach to match a property's intended attributes as imagined after repairs—location, rooms, baths, size, age, style, condition—to properties that have sold recently. In that way your matches give an indication of what your subject property will sell for.

Your task, then, is to find at least three properties similar to your subject property—the one you want to appraise—that have sold recently.

WHAT TO CONSIDER IN DETERMINING VALUE

Let's take a closer look at each of the factors you'll consider in choosing a similar property. Again, those factors are location, rooms, size, amenities, age, style, and condition:

1. *Location.* In seeking property, location is the primary factor in real estate value, so you want to look only for comparables within the immediate area to your subject property. With luck, the houses you find will be in the same neighborhood. Obviously, the best location for a comparable house would be one just down the street from you, or at least in your immediate neighborhood. Those are the first houses you should search out. But this does not mean that you might not find a comparable house in another neighborhood. Specifically, if there is a general similarity of surroundings, style, and size, as well as price level, in a neighborhood other than yours, then these houses might be potential comparables for yours. But first look in your neighborhood.

2. *Rooms.* A comparable house should have the same number of rooms, particularly the same number of bedrooms and baths. Everything should match as closely as possible—the existence or lack of a basement, the state (finished or unfinished) of that basement, the number of car spaces, and even the existence of a swimming pool. If something does not match up in an otherwise suitable comparable, an adjustment will have to be made. (See next section on valuation.)

3. *Size and amenities.* The number of square feet of living space should be very close to that of your potential property for it to be a comparable house. Small adjustments can be made for size if other attributes are close. Extra space like garages or outbuildings ideally should be similar or you will have to make adjustments there as well. Lot size also is a factor. If the lots are similar in size—yours is an acre or so, for example, and other lots in your neighborhood are also an acre—they are obviously comparable.

4. *Age.* Age, like size, should be similar because adjustments, if possible, should not be made for age. Age is always an important factor. Generally, if a house is a little older, built perhaps 40 or 60 years ago, the style of the house is likely to be different from the designs built today. The American bungalow style that was popular in the 1920s and 1930s can often predominate in some older neighborhoods. Although in recent years these homes have remained popular

as preowned structures, this style is not built anymore. So, if you have a style like that, you'll want to keep that in mind.

5. *Style.* As you've just seen, style often relates to age. Further considerations of style are: Is it a one-story, a split-level, a two-story garrison, or a Cape Cod cottage? Is it a contemporary? Generally homes of the same style will be similar in market value, particularly if they share the attribute of size. This determination is usually done by measuring the outside dimensions of your house. It does not count a basement or attic. If you have a 1,500-square-foot one-level house, and others in your neighborhood are of similar size and style, they are likely to be comparable.

6. *Condition.* Perhaps the most important attribute for evaluating a distressed property or a fixer-upper is condition, especially since you are going to be looking at two sets of comparables: one as is and the other imagining repairs as completed.

It won't be easy to find comparables for every property you would like to evaluate. You have to deal with the activity that occurred in the marketplace and the information you can get from it. Sometimes there just aren't sales of homes exactly comparable to yours. You may need to compromise a little and make adjustments.

This worksheet shows the type and amount of information you should gather to compare properties. Use it to log in the specific attributes of your subject property. You can also use it to gather information on similar properties that you may be able to use as comparables.

MAKING ADJUSTMENTS TO EQUALIZE VALUE

In searching for comparable properties you will rarely find an exact match. You will often need to make adjustments for those factors that make one property slightly different from another and balance the major attributes, doing both as closely as possible, making small positive and negative adjustments for what are relatively minor things. For example, if another house that sold within the past year is comparable to your subject but has two and a half bathrooms where your house has two, you would subtract an amount from that property's selling price to adjust it to the value of yours.

Making adjustments does not mean that you manipulate the value of the comparables to conform to a preconceived notion of

WORKSHEET: Property Information Mini-Appraisal

Subject Property: _____

(or) Comparable: _____

Name: _____

Address: _____

Neighborhood: _____

Shopping: _____ Type: _____ Distance: _____

Property Description: _____

Building Size: _____

Style:

   Split-level ___ Garrison Colonial ___ Colonial ___ Cape Cod ___

   Ranch ___ Bungalow ___ Contemporary ___ Condominium ___

   No. Stories ___ Wood ___ Brick ___ Stone ___ Stucco ___

   Other _____

Rooms: _____ Bedrooms: _____ Baths: _____

Age: _____

Condition:

   Poor __ Fair __ Average __ Good __ Very Good __ Excellent __

   Other _____

Outbuildings:

   Garage _____

   Barn _____

   Other _____

Land Size: _____

Major Amenities:

   Swimming Pool _____

   Special Landscaping _____

   Other _____

(Continued)

WORKSHEET: Property Information Mini-Appraisal
(Continued)

Construction:

Exterior ____ Interior ____ Basement ____ Roof ____ Heating ____

Cooling ____ Plumbing ____ Electrical ____ Kitchen ____

Appliances ____ Cabinets ____ Condition ____

Land Area: _____ Describe: _____

_____

Special Features: _____

_____

_____

Comments:_____

_____

_____

_____

_____

what you feel they should be worth. In making adjustments you are only making up for the obvious lack or existence of a particular feature of a property that would be in most other ways similar. Typical features that might be adjusted would be the lack or addition of a half bath, a one- or two-car garage, and a difference of 10% or less in the amount of square footage.

For example, let's say you find a comparable that sold six months ago. It is in the same neighborhood and like the subject property is a one-level ranch-style single-family house. It also has almost the same amount of square footage as your subject property. However, it needs to be adjusted by subtracting for a one-car garage, which your subject property does not have. It also lacks a half bath, which your subject property does have. You find out from other sold property in your marketplace that the relative resale value difference for a one-car garage in current condition is $2,700 and for a half bath it is

$1,200. As the other features are roughly similar, you subtract from the selling price of the comparable the $2,700 for the garage and add $1,200 for the half bath.

Note that these cost additions and subtractions are not what it would cost a contractor to install the given feature but what that specific feature would sell for in the marketplace. You do this by comparing the sales of houses with and without the feature you are trying to value. In other words, the dollar adjustments are not determined by the actual contractor's cost, but by the market—what a particular feature will be valued when sold as part of a similar property. For example, a contractor may charge $4,500 for the installation of a half bath, but it may be valued at only $3,200 when sold within the entirety of a house. Note that the cost of adjustments may vary in a different market as well as in a different neighborhood.

FEATURES TO ADJUST IN THE MINI-APPRAISAL

How many features do you adjust for? Only those that bring into conformity minor differences in an otherwise similar property. You find the best matching properties to your subject property, then adjust those similar properties for their small differences in an attempt to bring the comparables into a more precise match. The following features are often adjusted if different between subject and comparable property:

1. Date of sale.
2. Location.
3. Age of property.
4. Condition of property, construction quality.
5. Size of living area.
6. Number of rooms, extra bedrooms, baths.
7. Outbuildings, extra garage.
8. Porch/patio.
9. Amenities, swimming pool, landscaping.

This chart/worksheet shows you how to compare homes and make adjustments for minor differences. Note that selling price and square feet of living space are listed first as they are of prime

EXAMPLE: Comparable Sales Analysis

Information Sheet

Property Owner: S. Smithson   Telephone: 354-555-8484
Address: 23 Pleasant St., Anytown

Feature	Subject Property	Comparable #1	Comparable #2	Comparable #3
Address:	3 Winston Lane	23 Portia Place	10 Janna Road	332 Milhous Ave.
Selling Price:		$136,000	$128,000	$121,000
Living Area Sq. Ft.	1,625	1,780	1,650	1,550
Description		Description Adjust +/–	Description Adjust +/–	Description Adjust +/–
Date of Sale:		($1,500)	—0—	—0—
Location:	Palmdale	Same —0—	Same —0—	Same —0—
Land:	120 × 180	150 × 200 ($2,000)	130 × 175 —0—	140 × 150 —0—
Living Area:	1,625	1,780 ($3,000)	1,625 —0—	1,560 $2,000
No./Rooms:	7	8 ($2,500)	7 —0—	7 —0—
Quality:	Good	Good —0—	Good —0—	Good —0—
Condition:	Good	Exc. ($3,500)	Very Good ($1,500)	Good —0—
Age:	15 years	8 years ($1,500)	14 years —0—	17 years —0—
Basement/ Garage:	1 car	1 car —0—	2 car ($2,500)	1 car —0—
Porch/Patio:	No	No —0—	No —0—	No —0—
Other:				
Net Adjustment:		+/– ($12,500)	+/– ($4,000)	+/– $2,000
Indicated Value:		$123,500	$124,000	$123,000

Final Adjusted Value by Market Analysis Approach: $123,500
                                             (or) per Square Foot: $76 per Sq. Ft.

Remarks: All comparables are in same neighborhood. #1 is slightly larger and in better condition. #1 also has more adjustments but others corroborate similar value. #2 is four houses away and in similar style. #3 is on the other side of the development but similar.

importance. As you can see by the example, the gross values for each of the three properties are totaled and averaged to determine a final estimate of value.

PRICING ADJUSTMENTS ACCURATELY IMPROVES WITH EXPERIENCE

In this example, certain adjustments have been made for number of rooms, number of garage spaces, age, and condition. In other words, you are not going to throw out a house that meets the overall degree of comparability just because it does not have a new roof. You solve this by asking an experienced real estate agent or a property appraiser what the value of a new roof is in the marketplace—that is, how much a new roof adds to the selling price of a house that needs the repair. As discussed earlier, this amount is likely to be less than what a roofing contractor would charge. However, in some markets, the full cost of such an important repair as a roof may come back on resale.

The same goes for other things you need a price on, say for a swimming pool or other amenities. Real estate agents can be very helpful in this area, as they might tell you that a particular size swimming pool is worth only six thousand dollars reselling in the market even though it cost fifteen thousand to build. Well, herein lies the problem: Certain items are discounted heavily in the marketplace. That is why it's always good to talk to a real estate agent. Something that is very utilitarian, like a garage, will have a value very close to its construction cost, but if something is more of an amenity, like a swimming pool, it's more particular to that owner and does not automatically appeal to all owners, even if you're in an area where every other house has a swimming pool. As your experience grows, your accuracy at pricing adjustments will improve.

MAKE SURE COMPARABLE SALES ARE ARM'S-LENGTH TRANSACTIONS

As you gather comparable sales, note the prices at which they sold. Ideally they would all be similar, and if this is so, it will give you a good indication of your property's value. However, if you find a comparable sales price that is markedly different from the others, you need to check it out further. Drive by the property and look at it. If it sold for a low price, you may find that it was a foreclosure, or that it was a private sale within a family. If it sold for a markedly higher price, see how it was sold and the number of days it was on the market. Sometimes people pay a premium for a home because they do not want to lose it by having other potential buyers see it.

If a broker was involved in the sale, call and ask what information the agent can give you about why it sold for the price it did. You may find in your investigation that it sold quickly due to circumstances beyond anyone's control. If the price is higher, perhaps there are improvements that are not indicated in the other information you have from the assessment data. If you encounter a sales price that seems unusually high or low, you probably should not consider that sale in your analysis, particularly if you have other comparables you can use.

NEIGHBORHOOD PRICES TEND TO CLUSTER

The selling prices of homes in a given neighborhood tend to cluster within 10% above or below an average price. Rarely does a house sell for more than 15% above this average price no matter how much one improves the property. This rule is more evident in neighborhoods where houses are of similar size and style and less true in neighborhoods where the houses have been custom-built for their owners and are separated on large lots. For example, other three-bedroom, two-bath ranches in the same neighborhood are likely to be of the same value, only varying due to condition or amenities such as a swimming pool.

In ascertaining value you should always be guided by the average selling price of houses in the particular neighborhood where the house is located.

In the next chapter we'll use the pricing information we've gained here to negotiate an offer with the seller.

7

Negotiate to Get
Your Offers Accepted

In the previous chapter your goal was to determine what the property would sell for once the work was completed. You did this by judging what your newly repaired and spruced up house would be worth when measured against houses in a similar and comparable state. In this chapter we'll take this final value and decide, after deducting for repair expenses, selling costs, overhead, and profit, what we will offer the seller. We'll also discuss how to negotiate that offer.

HOW MUCH PROFIT DO YOU TAKE?

Perhaps you are planning your first investment purchase and are wondering what return you should expect. The answer will depend on several factors. The first is the size of the deal. It would not be unusual if selling a repaired property brought you $15,000 to $25,000, particularly if its final selling price was upwards of $90,000. That's a good markup. Some have made over $30,000 in the same price range, while others have barely squeaked by with little profit. It also depends on whether you are the one doing the fixing up or you are wholesaling the property to another fixer-upper investor. Certainly, in the latter case your profit is less, but so is your risk.

Whether you do the fixing up yourself or pass it on, what is crucial to understand is that you should compute your profit before you go into the deal. You deduct your profit (as well as other costs including repairs) from a final selling price to determine what you will offer the seller.

The minimum you should expect is a 15% profit margin. Any less and you are not getting enough for the time and risk you take. As you can see, you calculate backward so you know how much money you can pay for a property before you buy it. For example, suppose that by using the appraising method comparing comparable sales outlined in the previous chapter, you've confirmed that a house is worth $135,000 after substantial repairs are done. Your researched repairs are $18,000, profit at 15% equals $20,250, overhead and holding costs (unforeseen expenses and operating costs) at 10% equal $13,500, and selling costs of 6% are $8,100, thereby limiting your property acquisition to a maximum of $75,000. This is the amount of your highest offer. When you can buy the property for under $75,000 it could add to your profit.

Estimated value after repairs:	$135,000
Repairs needed:	−18,000
Overhead and holding costs:	−13,500 (10%)
Selling costs:	−8,100 (6%)
Anticipated profit:	−20,250 (15%)
Net balance:	$ 75,150

Note that this $75,000 is the maximum amount you can offer the seller in which to secure your anticipated profit of $20,250.

In other words, to make a 15% profit on a house in this price range, one that requires $18,000 in repairs, you should pay at the most $75,000. If you wish, you can allow more money for repairs and holding costs than you think it will take.

A further note: Don't get confused by trying to relate the price at which you buy to the price you sell at. You are not necessarily buying the property at a discount from an entirely different selling price. Because of the extensive repairs needed, the "as completed" value will have radically changed.

What you make in profit has more to do with a proper accounting of needed repairs and an accurate comparison of the rehabilitated house to comparable sales than it does with whether you bought a bargain. Sometimes you can find a distressed house in a neighborhood of fine homes where you stand to make a huge profit. But always figure a minimum profit of 15%, in addition to a modest overhead and selling cost, and hope with sound management you will make more. Once you get the numbers written down (use the investment potential worksheet) you have a guideline to follow.

Now let's see how assuring your profit translates into making an offer.

HOW TO DETERMINE MAXIMUM OFFER PRICE

So now you have your final selling price with subtracted profit, overhead (holding and contingency costs), selling costs, and, of course, repair costs, and you have arrived at a price that you must not go above in making the seller an offer. Remember that in your costs calculations you should always allow for unexpected expenses and a reasonable holding period before the property sells. For the purpose of our examples, we will set aside at least 15% off the top for profit. Let's look at the other expenses you must consider.

Overhead is the amount you want to set aside to cover the normal cost of business operations. Some investors have an office, while some work out of their home. Overhead pays for telephone, travel, and miscellaneous expenses that shouldn't eat into your profit. Overhead also includes holding costs, the amounts you must pay in interest expense, utilities, property tax payments, and insurance for the period it takes to complete the repairs and find a buyer to close. A nominal 5% to 10% is typically used for overhead.

Overhead also includes contingencies, or the planning for problems you were not able to anticipate. This might include an inaccurate cost for repairs, or a hidden repair item that was found after you purchased the property. These could mean extra repair expenses, extra fees for inspection, or even something as awful as a new septic system mandated by your community. Plan on 5% to 10% for contingencies.

Selling costs are those fees paid to sales agents as a percentage to find a buyer, as well as legal fees charged by your attorney or title company. Although you may sell the property yourself, it's judicious to set aside an amount to pay for an agent in case you need

WORKSHEET: Investment Potential

Date: _____

Property Address: _____

Neighborhood: _____

Lead Source: _____ FSBO _____ Agent _____ Bank _____ Other_____

Description: _____

   Bedrooms: _____ Baths: _____ Style: _____ Age (Years): _____

   Condition: _____ Square Feet: _____

   Garage (No. Cars): _____ Amenities: _____

   Other: _____

Asking Price: _____

From Repair Summary Worksheet: Repair Cost Estimate: _____

                              Reserve for Undetected Damage: _____

                                     Total Repair Cost: _____

Estimated Comparable Sales "Repairs Completed" Value: _____

Most Probable Resale Price (Final Selling Price): _____

   Profit: _____ ___ %

   Overhead/Holding Costs: _____ ___ %

   Selling Costs: _____ ___ %

   Fixed Repair Costs: _____

   Other: _____

Subtotal: _____

Maximum Offer Price: _____

Best Possible Purchase Price: _____

Most Probable Purchase Price: _____

Final Profit Reconciliation: _____

Comments: _____

_____

_____

to use their services; 5% to 8% should cover agents' and attorneys' fees.

As we've detailed in a previous chapter, repair costs are the material and labor expense to get the property ready to sell at top dollar. This is never a percentage but an exact amount found from an accurate estimate of each specific cost and then deducted from the final selling price.

The guideline, then, for determining the highest offering price for the property is the figure you get when you take the final selling price found through comparable sales, and you subtract profit, overhead and contingency costs, selling costs, and repair costs. For example:

Final selling price:	100%
Subtract:	
Profit:	15% to 20%
Overhead/holding costs:	10%
Selling expenses:	5% to 8%
Total repair cost:	From cost estimate

This means in the previous example that you will buy the property for $75,000 or less, put in repairs of $18,000, have an overhead cost of $13,500, a selling expense of $8,100, and sell the property at $135,000 to net yourself a profit of over $20,000!

NOW THAT YOU KNOW YOUR LIMIT, WHERE DO YOU START?

In the previous example it may seem like an extreme difference between what you will sell the property for and what you will pay for it. However, you have to remember that the property is worth $135,000 *only after* you have made extensive repairs to fix it up.

In negotiating the actual price at which you will buy, the seller's motivation helps. If in the example the seller is asking $85,000, he or she may not realize the extent of the repairs that are needed. And if you start with an offer 10% lower than the maximum $75,000 you will offer, or $67,500, you're a considerable distance apart. But if the seller realizes the extent of the repairs that are needed, it may not be hard for him or her to counter with a figure that's closer to your top

CASE STUDY: What Do You Offer?

Let's say that you find a 45-year-old single-family home that needs minor repairs but is generally in good shape. Subject to an inspector's judgment, you will make an offer. The seller was initially asking $150,000, dropped to $135,000, and is now asking $125,000. Your estimate of rehab work is $26,000 for a detailed list of exterior and interior work. You've checked the prices of comparable property—as if your repairs were done—and after much comparison work as explained in Chapter 6 the future fair market value seems to indicate a price of over $175,000. From this final selling price you can calculate the profit you want at $25,000.

You want to structure an offer to give to the seller. You subtract $17,500 for overhead, contingency, and holding costs. You further anticipate a selling cost of at least 5% or $8,750 in case you use an agent to sell. You also subtract your repairs of $26,000.

Remember, in finding comparable value you don't compare property in its present condition but with ones that reflect the improved condition. Note that this method is a standard way used by lenders that make improvement loans—they confirm the new value of the improved property with comparable selling prices. With your friendly MLS agent you come up with three recent similar house sales. In this example, the selling prices are close together in price: $175,500, $174,500, and $176,500, averaging a bit over $175,000. Knowing this you are already encouraged because you can see that the money you will be spending on repairs and overhead will be gained back in selling price—as long as you can buy the property within reasonable parameters as outlined here.

Next, you calculate what you can offer the seller, based on your projected repairs, overhead, selling expenses, and profit. Your total is $26,000 (repairs), plus $17,500 (overhead), plus $8,750 (selling costs), which equals $52,250. Adding in your profit (treating it as a cost) of $25,000 to this amount gives you $77,250, which you deduct from your final estimate of value—$175,000 minus $77,250 equals $97,750.

CASE STUDY: What Do You Offer? *(Continued)*

Initial asking price:	$150,000 (unrepaired)
First drop in price:	135,000
Current asking price:	125,000
Estimated repair cost:	26,000
Overhead:	17,500
Selling cost:	8,750
Profit:	25,000
Subtotal:	$77,250

Probable selling price after repairs:	$175,000
Repairs, overhead, selling costs, profit:	–77,250
Maximum amount to be paid for property:	$97,750

Now you're armed with facts and figures, and you can feel your confidence growing. But wait a minute—the seller is asking $125,000, $27,000 more than you feel you can pay. You are not close on price and it's unlikely to expect that he will accept an offer in the $90,000 range. You know you can go up more, at least to $98,000. Beyond that and you're in the danger zone. And, you don't want to start fudging your figuring. You're buying this for the $25,000 profit, and nothing less should satisfy you.

Probably the seller will not take your first offer. That's all right. In fact, it's better to have your first offer turned down—if the seller accepted it, you'd end up wondering if you should have offered less. Let him reject $90,000 and counter with something less than his latest asking price. After several counteroffers, your buying price might end up close to your original target of $98,000. One gambit might be to increase your offer slightly (perhaps 5%) and ask the seller to help finance (see Chapters 9 and 10). In that way you might make a good deal better.

price of $75,000. Remember, the price of distressed homes is subjective. An extensive rehabilitation is required for the house to reach its potential value.

USE REPAIR COSTS TO CONVINCE THE SELLER

In each prospective purchase be aware of what you can tell the seller that will increase his or her realization that what you propose is fair. Let's look at a typical deal: You come across a former neighbor's house that, after having originally been her home, has been a rental for 12 years. The owner has moved out of state. The house is 35 years old and needs at least $30,000 in repairs to bring it up to respectable selling condition. You do a comparable market analysis and determine that after repairs it would bring $175,000. It is assessed at $120,000.

The current tenant is two months behind in rent and has given notice that he wishes to leave by the end of next month. The nonpayment of rent has upset the owner who has had to retain a local attorney to file a claim for back rent. You suspect that this current rent loss is in part what is making the owner consider selling.

The owner thinks she can come back to supervise a few thousand dollars' worth of repairs and some minor cleanup and then list the property with an agent for $165,000. You know the owner is unrealistic. She has not seen the property in three years and does not know that a wide range of repairs are needed. You believe the best way to bring her to reality is to write down some details of just what she would have to do to bring her house up to top dollar. You intend to show her that she might make almost as much money in the long run with your offer.

You start with a list of what's needed:

Cost of repairs:
Roof:	$6,580
Exterior painting:	3,248
Interior painting:	1,235
Plumbing repairs:	1,160
Electrical panel problem:	937
Furnace replacement:	4,350

AC repair:	1,175
Interior door, replace:	975
Windows, thermopane:	1,435
Kitchen cabinets:	2,750
Kitchen floor:	1,350
Interior floor, refinish:	2,275
Bath, redo:	2,450
Cellar leak, repair:	3,675
Plantings, replace:	825
Cleanup:	545
Repairs subtotal:	$34,965
Sales agent (7%):	$11,550 (est.)
Attorney's fee:	2,300 (est.)
Travel back and forth:	$1,700 (est.)
Rental loss:	$7,300 (est.)
Tax and operating loss:	$4,800 (est.)

You put in your list everything that will be a legitimate cost to the owner or whoever sells the property at full value. You've inspected the property thoroughly with a contractor and come up with fair prices. You haven't overlooked anything that can be done to bring the house up to current building standards. You want to convince her that it will be difficult to do the upgrade herself and that she'd be better off with your offer. Estimate how long the place would sit empty before it is sold. You can also estimate how much she will lose in rent by having it on the market. You've added the cost of property taxes, insurance, and utilities while it is vacant. The key with your seller is to show all the costs that will stack up if she decides to fix it up and sell it herself. You do not, however, want to show the seller what you will sell the house for when the repairs are completed, or your anticipated profit.

Seller's Cost

Best possible selling price:	$165,000
Repairs:	−34,965
Agent's cost (7%):	−11,550
Legal charges:	−2,300

Travel from out of state:	−1,700
Loss of rent:	−7,300
Tax and operating loss:	−4,800
Net balance	$102,385

Now, applying your own method for purchase you subtract from the best possible selling price of $165,000 a preplanned profit of 20% or $33,000. Further, you take off an additional 10% or $16,500 for your overhead, selling, and legal expenses. Deduct for repairs of $34,965. You have reached a figure of about $80,000 as your purchase, or offer, price.

Investor's Cost

Best possible selling price:	$165,000
Repairs:	−34,965
Profit (20%):	−33,000
Overhead (10%):	−16,500
Net balance:	$80,535

The seller, then, would have the potential of making a bit over $20,000 more if she came from her present home and supervised the work needed rather than accepting your offer. In reality, she is likely to do a lick-and-a-promise of fix-up and get substantially less than the highest possible selling price. And these figures will help her to understand this. Remember, most decisions are emotional. When the seller becomes upset over the late rent payments, this may influence her decision making. She may get to the point that she decides she just does not want to hassle with it.

The paperwork you provide is likely to have just enough severe truth to make her throw up her hands and realize that she is better off with your deal. You can even offer a bonus—like offering her the missing rent payments and indicating that you will deal with the tenant. It will help her save face and feel better about your terms. You want her to see your offer as one that saves her a lot of trouble.

And here's a tip: Make sure all this information is typed up neatly and sent to her at once. Its power is in the details. Use overnight mail or Federal Express. The more you do to make it assume importance in the seller's eyes, the more important it will become.

How quickly can you shift gears? If the seller does not accept your offer, is there an alternative to walking away? If she decides to do it herself, she will still be burdened by the long distance. Offer her a compromise where she enters a partnership with you—you front and supervise the repairs, and after your costs for repairs are covered, you split the profits. Since you've proven your expertise in the repair costs, she just might agree. Always think of the alternative while pursuing the most winning possibility.

BE READY TO WALK AWAY IF NO SOLUTION

You just looked at a property that has been listed by an agent at $135,000. After 90 days it remains unsold and now the seller will sell it to you directly for $100,000 as is. The problem is that it has been rented out for 10 years and is in terrible condition. You estimate it needs at least $23,000 in rehab costs. Can you make this deal work?

Unless there is something more to this deal, you're going to have a hard time making money here. A $135,000 listed price does not mean that it will sell for that figure, even if it is fixed up. And, selling expenses can be 5% to 7% if you sell through an agent. You must have your net profit figured into the deal before committing.

Possible solution: Start by obtaining a realistic price of what the property will sell for when fixed up. If your research with comparable properties and the recommendations of capable agents lead you to a price of $135,000 to $140,000, you still need to subtract the cost to improve ($23,000), overhead and contingency expenses ($14,000), selling costs ($10,000), and profit ($20,000), which would mean you have to buy under $70,000. If your seller doesn't agree, you must walk away from the deal. Once you negotiate the right deal, you could also assign the option to someone who will follow through and do the work, allowing you a minimal profit.

MAKE OFFERS ON A REGULAR BASIS

Don't send offers out in bulk. Be judicious. It takes time to arrive at an accurate repair estimate, as well as an estimate of final value. However, if you stay in touch with your local market you will soon become familiar with values and what it costs to make repairs. Study property being offered for sale. Once you find a motivated seller, make a repair estimate, ascertain value, and make an offer. You can easily do this once a month; if you are really active, once a week. Work out a systematic plan to make offers on a regular basis.

Remember that you want to find out as much as possible about a property before making an offer. Although you should do this beforehand, if you have not been able to make a thorough inspection, or price out all repairs, make sure that in any contract you sign you leave an escape clause that allows you to cancel the deal if you find that repair estimates go over a certain sum. A cancellation clause could also spell out a time period, such as any time during 20 days after signing a sales agreement in which you could cancel if repairs go over a certain sum.

It is not advisable to make offers on property you have not seen, let alone inspected, properly valued, or priced for repairs. Continual offers mean you are throwing out hurried, unresearched prices that have little chance of being accepted or garnering a profit for you. And, perhaps most detrimental to you, you are likely to upset both owners and agents, whose goodwill you need to operate effectively in your market. Over a period of time you may scare some nervous seller into accepting a low offer, only to find that the property's currently priced at twice what it's worth and has some horrendous defect that will bury you in extra costs. In order to gain business, you've got to work in a local market and earn the trust and confidence of numerous people. Be trustworthy and professional!

SEVEN-POINT STRATEGY TO GET YOUR OFFERS APPROVED

The following are some guidelines to help you get your offers accepted. These guidelines by no means include all ways of negotiating with sellers, but they do provide the basics, to which you can add as your experience grows.

1. *Always treat the seller with respect.* You and the seller will often have opposing points of view about a property's value. But that does not mean you should treat the seller as an adversary. Very often you will meet this person again and need his or her help in your community. He or she may also own more property that you may be able to buy on advantageous terms. Never allow a relationship to take a nasty personal turn. If something does go wrong, it means you can't make the deal; it does not mean you make an enemy. If something in the negotiations makes the seller tense, you can usually improve the situation by informing the seller that you respect his or her position but circumstances make it unfortunate that you cannot meet his or her requirements.

Courteous persistence in sticking by your own dollar limits is the right path. If the seller likes you more than he or she does your offer, that will go a long way to getting the latter accepted. So, in conclusion, always treat the seller with respect and dignity. Trust is an important part of negotiations. If the seller believes you have violated that trust, it simply provides a reason not to accept your offer.

2. *He who leads with price, loses.* An old axiom in negotiating is that he who speaks first, loses (said before, but we can't say it enough). Here, it means specifically that if you make an offer first, you're likely to end up losing more than you first offered. Start by establishing a level of trust and confidence with the seller before you deal with hard numbers. After all, you want the seller to accept an amount for the property that is probably less than he or she wants. To do that you first need to establish a relationship of fairness. Start settling the easy items first. Perhaps the closing date is important to the seller and not so for you. Or perhaps it is a question of how to handle the utilities. And of course there are the details of the property itself. What does the seller think must be done to the property, and what it will cost? Although you need an independent judgment of any of these components, the seller does help in a general way to key you in on what's going on with the property and how he or she feels about it. It also gives you a chance to spend time together in a positive way while saving for later the big items of price and financing. Allow the seller to mention price first. Negotiate all other details—inspections, property description, closing date, financing terms—before price. In that way you may establish enough rapport with the seller for agreement on a price that is less than might have been initially acceptable. So, in conclusion, save your best price for last. When you discuss price, don't throw out the top dollar you will pay, even if you know the seller wants still more. Expect some wrangling over price. Most deals usually have several counteroffers going back and forth before one is accepted.

3. *If possible, get the seller to take financing.* You may want to get the seller to give back financing on the sale. That is, you should get the seller to give you the first mortgage on the property. Or, failing that, try to take over the existing mortgage. If you don't have to go to the bank or mortgage company to make the deal work, you have one more good reason to go ahead with the deal. The key in getting the seller to do this is to give assurance that the mortgage is safe because you are going to put a substantial amount of cash into the building in order to make improvements and the seller's mortgage will be paid back shortly—when you resell the property; the mortgage will not continue with the new buyer. These two points can often relieve a seller's resistance to giving financing. Even if you offer a point more interest than you would have to pay to the bank, it's worth it because it's not a long-term loan from a bank and so you won't have to pay points (usually added on by a bank)! And once you know whether the seller will finance the deal, you know what you can offer for price. Allow a better price if the seller will finance. If the seller will carry back some or all of the mortgage, you won't need to price the house at rock bottom. The seller may agree in a fixer-upper deal as he or she won't have to carry the mortgage for more than a short period of time. Anytime you can get a seller to finance it's worth it to you in terms of interest rate as well as applications and points.

4. *Know when to offer cash.* An all-cash deal is a strong motivator in any real estate deal. Sellers never like to finance; they often must do so because of the reasons stated in item 3. However, the advantage for you in offering cash is to drive down the purchase price. If you can get the property at a low price only by making a cash deal, and you don't have the cash, then consider a private mortgage source or bringing in a partner. If it's a good deal, don't lose it. Only in the details of a particular deal can you determine if it's best for you to get substantial financing help for the lowest possible price. But generally avoid asking for financing help, if possible.

If your offer is low and you know the seller is not in a financial position to help, you are likely to need some other form of mortgage financing. And although your agreement may be conditional on financing, to the seller this means he or she will receive all cash—as soon as the property closes the seller has all his or her money. If the seller will not agree to your low offer, you may be able to pose a negotiation strategy—for example, that since difficulties are likely to arise in financing the repairs, perhaps the seller will finance that much. A lender will often balk on lending until the repairs are made, and the seller will not likely prefer this trade-off, so your suggestion may save your low offer.

5. *Let the seller know of extensive repairs.* Let the seller know the extensive list and cost of repairs that you will do. This is to show the seller that in order to take on these major expenses they can't be added to an overpriced house. In fact, the seller has to consider the fact that a bank isn't likely to make a loan on a building that needs repairs. This is particularly true if health and safety violations of the building code are present. This can be a powerful motivation to get the seller to give financing.

6. *Make your offer work.* Now that you have a relationship with the seller, get ready to make your offer. By now you have determined if the seller will take back financing—either the entire first mortgage or a second mortgage for the down payment—or if the seller insists on cash. These parameters will allow you to determine the price you will offer. Note that whatever offer you make is likely to be countered with another price. Allow for that in making the first offer. Another alternative is to give the seller a choice of two offers. Rather than one all-or-none proposal, submit a choice of two acceptable alternatives. These could be with or without seller financing and an appropriate price difference. One could be for all cash with the seller's price discounted, and the other could include seller financing but at a better price.

7. *Never close negotiations.* And finally, when you think the seller has held firm and rejected your final offer, don't close the negotiations. Sometimes a seller needs to think your offer over, or perhaps just needs to reject it with some time to give it a second thought. Arrange to meet again, perhaps the next day when the seller realizes that your offer is the best one he or she will get. Time can make someone under pressure come around. Always leave room for another counteroffer and have your offer ready to be written out in a formal agreement. This agreement doesn't need to be complicated. It could be a simple form that outlines the details of the sale, which will be elaborated by the respective attorneys. It shows your professionalism and gains the commitment of the seller.

ALWAYS USE "CONTINGENT ON FINANCING" CLAUSE

If you are not obtaining financing from the seller and are dependent on seeking a loan from conventional sources, you should make sure you have a clause in your offer-to-purchase contract that says the deal is contingent on financing. Normally you would be expected to apply for a loan within a certain time frame, such as 20 days of the date of the signed contract. You have to apply at several mortgage sources before you can tell the seller that you are not going to get the loan. Another clause that would get you out of a sale would be one that states that "purchase is contingent upon partner's approval."

This latter clause allows you to cancel the sale should your partner, or other investor, perhaps even a buyer, for any reason decide against the deal.

Now that you have found a property, priced out its needed repairs, matched its fixed-up state with comparable sales, and negotiated a favorable price with the seller, you can choose whether you do the deal yourself or, as we'll discuss in the next chapter, wholesale it to a fellow investor for a fee.

8

Wholesale Property
for Steady Gains

Before going on to financing and selling the fixer-upper, there is another decision to make: Specifically, do you go ahead and buy the property and do the fixing up, or do you wholesale your deal to another investor? This chapter explores the advantages of using the wholesaling, or "flipping," strategy.

WHAT ARE THE BASICS OF
WHOLESALING, OR FLIPPING, A PROPERTY?

Wholesaling, or flipping, a property happens when you assign a contract for a modest profit to a buyer soon after you sign it, in most cases not closing at all. In this case you would pass the property on as is, without making repairs.

If the deal is structured so that you actually take title, you would likely have two separate but simultaneous closings to pass title. This means that you buy and sell a property in the same sitting and walk away from the closing with your profit.

The idea behind wholesaling a property is to avoid the steps of taking title on the property, doing the necessary amount of fixing up, and then waiting for a retail buyer to come along. Instead you skip right to looking for a buyer; in essence you are performing the job of a real estate agent, except that you control the property through a sales contract. And for little risk you are willing to take a modest profit rather than a large gain. However, these transactions are easy to do and take little time. They can often be arranged and ready to go quickly, perhaps in a week's time.

However, wholesaling does not mean you don't invest effort and cost out repairs and research the final selling price. In fact, this work is essentially what the new investor is buying, and your appraisal of expenses and final judgment of value will often be the clincher to make the deal. Furthermore, time is of the essence. If you are not going to do the rehabilitation work yourself, you need to turn the property over as soon as possible because it's not customary for a seller to agree to wait an extended time to close.

GETTING STARTED WITH WHOLESALING

Sometimes you are not always able to follow through with fixing a property and reselling it yourself. It may be time for someone else to make the profit. But since you've found the property there must be a way for you to profit, too. In the wholesaling business your profit will be modest, by which I mean you will not get as much money as you would have if you had taken control of the property yourself on the repairs and resold for top dollar. You can expect a modest amount, perhaps 3% or 4% of the purchase price. This would be a decent profit for property you did not have to take control of and didn't have to take title to.

Some investors wholesale property to the exclusion of all other techniques. They call it flipping. I feel that its original name, wholesaling, gives a better explanation of the actual process. Flipping, however, is the accepted term in the business. But for most situations, when you need to refer to the strategy you are likely to say that you wholesaled the property.

In some ways wholesaling is similar to the rent-to-own or lease/purchase strategy (which you will read about in Chapters 11 and 12), in that you don't actually take title to the property. In most cases you will be assigning the contract you negotiate with the seller to the new investor-buyer.

Usually properties that are wholesaled are those that require some amount of repair. This isn't always true, but most of the properties that are in this category either have been on the market and for one reason or another have not sold, or have had such repair problems facing them that the owners have not put them on the market, and are undecided about what to do. Like many owners trying to sell, they are in a must-sell situation because they're being transferred or divorced, or are moving away from the area for retirement purposes.

Note that just like in practicing the fixer-upper strategy, in wholesaling property you must be very careful about the price at which you are buying. Certainly all the criteria you would use for buying a fixer-upper must be followed. As a general rule, the buy price of these properties is a fair distance away from the market price after the repairs are made. For example, you buy a property for $85,000 that requires $25,000 of work. You determine its after-repaired value as described in the fixer-upper chapters of this book. Your comparable sales analysis tells you that you can sell it for at least $135,000 after repairs are made. Note that in this sales analysis you have measured your subject house against comparable property and found that it is equal to properties selling for $135,000. Even though in the example I'm describing you are not going to actually follow through—taking title, doing the work, and finally selling— you still need to know what the final profit margin will be in order to present the property to another investor.

Your main job in wholesaling is going to be to find a motivated seller with a property that you can buy at a bargain price because of its worsening condition. As noted, you need to get a general idea of how much the repairs will cost and what the property will be worth after one makes the repairs. As with many real estate transactions, your job is to negotiate a contract with the seller that can be by and large a straightforward real estate contract. It should, however, allow you plenty of time to find a party to whom you will sell. You must also make sure that there's nothing in the agreement that would prohibit your assigning this contract to another party. Further, you must have a clause that allows you to get out of the contract if you should for some unforeseen circumstance be unable to find a buyer and not be able to proceed. Wording of this nature could be: "This contract is subject to the approval and inspection of the property by buyer's partners and/or colleagues."

For the seller, this latter condition of partner's approval can raise a question. But if you explain to the seller that it's reasonable for you to need extra time to investigate the repairs and their respective costs, the seller should agree, knowing that it's going to take a fair amount of work to bring the property into salable shape. After all, the seller has probably already offered the property for sale and is currently quite anxious about making a deal.

Also make sure that any item, major or minor, that might create some disagreement upon taking title is dealt with in the contract itself. You don't want any disagreement with sellers who may conveniently forget what they said they would do, particularly since a new buyer is now standing in your place.

Note that like when buying a fixer-upper, much of the hard work of investigating repairs and prices should be done before a price is negotiated on the contract. The key here is to get a reasonable buy price so that once the repairs are made and overhead and selling costs accounted for, the repaired property sells at a new market value ensuring your profit. It's relatively easy to determine the market value once you know what repairs are to be made and can match the property in its repaired condition, because there will likely be comparables available with which to match your subject property. In contrast, it's often hard to match a distressed property, as there may be few other similar properties. This is a problem that appraisers often have. In fact, appraisers often reach a determination of a distressed property's value by matching its potentially upgraded condition to comparable sales. Mortgage lenders also project a value for property on which they lend funds for repairs. And, as you will read in Chapters 9 and 10 on financing, the federal government, in its Federal Housing Administration (FHA) 203(k), Fannie Mae "HomeStyle" loan, and FHA/HUD/Title I lending programs, also projects as-repaired value.

The key in wholesaling, also true for most real estate transactions, is the seller's motivation. If the seller is not reasonably motivated, he or she is not likely to agree to your price and conditions. So be warned: You may need to talk to a number of sellers, investigating the relative worth of their properties, before you find a property that will work.

The other side of the equation is, to whom do you sell? Investors who wholesale frequently have prospects lists, buyers they can contact as soon as they have secured a deal with a seller. Those on their prospects list may come from newspaper ads; may be local contractors, investment mentors, fellow investors, or members of local real estate investment clubs; or simply may respond to an ad you might place in the newspaper. Most potential buyers using the wholesaling strategy will be people like yourself, those who can participate and who have the capability of financing and following through with the necessary repairs, as well as selling the property. Typically this would be the investor-contractor working in the fixer-upper market.

That's the basic outline of the wholesaling, or flipping, procedure. And as mentioned, some investors specialize in wholesaling and rarely take title of a property on their own. In my experience, as well as from communication of the activities of other investors, wholesaling works well as an adjunct to buying, fixing up, and reselling single-family houses. As always, let your marketplace be your guide. If most of the property in your marketplace is already in pristine condition, you may decide to commit to wholesaling only when an unusual opportunity arises. Under these conditions you certainly want to make sure that your buy price is an exceptionally good one before you make the deal. However, if in your marketplace or one nearby there are a number of properties being renovated and resold, then perhaps the wholesaling and the fixer-upper strategies will both work well for you. To find out more about which neighborhoods within your general area are active in renovation, inquire at your local assessor's office.

ADVICE FOR A NEWBIE!

Let's imagine you're getting started in real estate investing. You don't have much money, but you do have some you can use to get started, and you also have a couple of friends who will participate with you if you find the right deal. You might even have a favorite aunt who could help a little with some extra financing. You've read a few books, taken some courses, even paid money for a personal mentor. All this just made you even more motivated to get busy so you could pay off those expenses.

You don't know if you should start by finding some property that would be suitable to wholesale, or roll up your sleeves and find a place to fix up and resell, or be the lease/option holder between a seller and a tenant-buyer (Chapters 11 and 12), or—if some secondary financing were available—buy with the thought of holding a duplex, or even a three- or four-family building. The choices are many. Certainly your first thought—finding a property to wholesale to someone else—would give you some ready cash that would help pay expenses as well as build a reserve fund for future deals. You know that some investors wholesale property during their entire investment career, but you've also heard stories that many start out that way, make a little money, and then expand into other areas, buying some small apartment or commercial buildings, or some properties to fix up. In fact, your mentor told you many of those who did other techniques return at the end of their career to finding and securing property to fix up and wholesale to others. But how to decide? You're not sure where to focus, where to start, and where you should concentrate your efforts.

Wholesaling gives you an excellent opportunity to put together a buyer's list of investors you can market properties to, before you ever place one under contract. You can separate this list into categories that fit these buyers' needs. You can even search out properties that fit a particular buyer's needs. If your buyer seems interested on hearing basic information (without the address), it's likely that other buyers will be, too, so place the property under contract.

One of the basics of conservative wholesaling is that if you are not sure you will be able to flip a particular property to an investor, you should not place the property under contract unless you would be willing to close on it yourself. The potential buyers list is important then. If you have a list of financially well-established buyers who have sufficient cash and don't need owner financing, you shouldn't have to put down more than $100 to $500 earnest money.

Making the sale should be straightforward, as all you need to do is to assign the contract to your prospect and collect your fee.

SEARCHING FOR A PROPERTY TO FLIP

The reason this chapter on wholesaling has been put here is that many of your potential properties to flip come from your search for fixer-uppers. And in order to prepare yourself for these opportunities, you need a list of those other investors and contractors who, like you, buy and fix up distressed property. You can start by making contact with these prospects and asking what kinds of property they look for and in what price range.

Put properties that meet these objectives on a list of properties you will evaluate. Then keep in mind these objectives when you evaluate the properties in question.

Many who wholesale concentrate on lower-income neighborhoods; but this is not necessary, as sellers in affluent, white-collar areas have the same determined reasons to sell (i.e., transfer, divorce, estate purposes, etc.), as previously discussed.

Note that in finding properties to flip you must still study comparable sales. You must also still estimate repairs and determine what the final selling price is likely to be. Even though you are not going to be taking title, doing the needed repairs, or finding the final retail buyer or homeowner, in order to get a commitment you need the facts of repair and value to convince another fixer-upper investor that you have negotiated a good deal.

TO WHOM DO YOU WHOLESALE?

The advantage of wholesaling is that if your funds are tied up, or you've already got too many deals going, you don't need to walk away. You can still be involved, just not for as much profit. Now, the question comes up, if you're not going to buy it, who is? First, in preparation for this inevitability, make a list of potential short-term operators who could jump in and take over.

One of the other investors who buys fixer-uppers in your community might be interested. Another possibility is contractors who want to keep their crews busy on a project during a slow period—they can resell it themselves after the job is done. In this case, the contractors may be more interested in keeping their workers busy than the big profit at the end, so they may be willing to go into the deal giving you more money than you anticipated. As a general rule they are not in direct or continual competition with you for property of this nature. This type of buyer is not likely to have a financing problem because they should already have credit lines established with commercial and mortgage banks.

Offer the property for 3% to 8% more than your agreed-upon price with the original seller. If your new buyers want the deal, get a deposit from them and assign the contract over to them, letting your attorney and title company complete the transaction. You get your money at the closing. Note that if you can't find anyone at all who wants the property, you tell the seller (or agent if you are dealing with one) that your associates—in this case, your potential buyers—did not approve the purchase and you're out of the deal.

RUN AN AD TO ATTRACT INVESTOR-BUYERS

Does wholesaling sound easy? It's not difficult. But you do need to keep in mind the specific highlights talked about in this chapter and understand that these deals may not come along every day. In fact, if you're working in a fairly narrow market that doesn't have many fixer-uppers and there are already a few investors to jump on them when they become available, the opportunity to wholesale may be minimal.

Therefore, to increase your chances of success in wholesaling, reach out to potential investor-buyers. If you've got several wholesale possibilities, put an ad that would attract other investors in the classified section of your local newspaper. It could say something like this:

"Do-it-yourself special. Need to sell. Discount for cash!" Add your telephone number.

You want to pull in buyers of investments, those willing to rehab, or a potential homeowner who is willing to put some sweat equity into a home. When you do get calls, make sure you record their name, address, and telephone number, as well as what they are looking for. Use telephone record forms that you can examine and use to recontact those who appear to be looking for the kind of property you've got. Arrange to meet with these future buyers, first to investigate their needs more thoroughly, and then to show them the property if it seems right for them.

MAKE SURE YOUR WHOLESALE
BUYERS HAVE CASH OR CREDIT LINE

If you are wholesaling potential fixer-uppers to other investors, you need to be sure that they are capable of closing within a relatively short time. Many sellers with whom you will be making deals will want a quick closing in order for them to agree to the best or lowest price. Therefore, in negotiating with a seller get as much time as possible before the closing. There's nothing more aggravating than someone who takes a fair amount of time before getting back to you but at the same time wants a quick closing. In this case you can say that you just bought a few properties in the prior week and in order to buy theirs you are going to need more time, such as 45 to 60 days. The negotiation often gives you the extra time you need.

Unfortunately a lot of those who advertise "I buy houses for cash" can't really perform as implied. Many of those who advertise that way think that although the seller gets all cash, it doesn't mean the advertising investor has that money in the bank. Usually he or she still needs to go out and get financing.

So, if you're looking for property to wholesale and in your negotiations with a seller need to know that the buyers to whom you will wholesale are ready to act, be warned that they may need to get financing from a lender. Therefore, because of this need to finance on the part of these buyers, you may have a tough time working out the deal in a short time. Not all can close within the 30-day limit your seller may demand. In fact, financing a fixer-upper (reassuring the lender on your repair list) can often create a time lag.

The trick is to get to know your buyers and weed out those who can't perform quickly. That way you can assure yourself that you have real cash buyers. Many investors who have a track record for taking over fixer-uppers already have a credit line, formally or informally, that will provide them with the necessary funds.

So, before you assign a contract with anyone, make sure he or she either has the cash or is prequalified with a financing source. And make your own verification. If possible, have the buyer approved for the loan before you assign the contract.

FINDING CASH BUYERS FOR WHOLESALE PROPERTY

Other than advertising in your local newspaper, there are some excellent ways to find cash buyers to whom you can sell property wholesale. You can start by searching the public records at the county recorder's or registrar of deeds' office for houses that have been rehabbed in the past. Often a property sold by a bank or other mortgage lender, or the Department of Housing and Urban Development (HUD), Veterans Administration (VA), or Federal National Mortgage Association (FNMA), has been bought by a rehabber. It's likely that this individual or company bought the property to flip it or rehab it as an investment. The deed should give the address of the new buyer. You could send such buyers a letter and tell them you have properties for sale or that you will be getting some soon. Or give them a phone call if they are in the book.

Unfortunately, most of the companies won't have a listing in the phone book, so you could check with your local assessor's office or even the Secretary of State or the Board of Corporations in your state, find out who the officers of these companies are, look them up in the phone book, and call them at home. This is a bit of research but it will pay off in the end.

Another way to get the information you need is to network, either in person or on the Internet. Let sales agents, real estate attorneys, and title companies know you are an investor and may have some properties to sell. Further, stop at single-family construction sites and talk to contractors.

IT'S ALL ABOUT ESTABLISHING RELATIONSHIPS

In order to wholesale you need connections with other investors who fix up houses and resell them. At first glance it may seem that they are your competitors, and to a degree they are, but it's not like losing out to someone on buying an apartment building that might be held for an extended time. In the fixer-up and wholesale field there are many possibilities. You are often in and out of a deal within a year, and plenty of properties exist in which you and other investors can participate.

So, establish relationships with others to whom you might wholesale, and establish yourself as someone who will take in a property wholesaled to you. In other words, get deals back from them, and use each other's talents at prospecting. And then turn the deals over to others, making a small profit for yourself. Or if someone has told you about one and you've made the direct buy, give one back to that person.

Just don't get greedy with those from whom you want to buy. They won't begrudge you a small profit if they make a bigger one. In fact, that will only encourage them to come back to you. Where else can you create profits of 3% to 8% or more, depending on the size of the deal, in less than a week or so? It's a no-money-down or very-little-money-down deal. The key is prospecting for sellers. One of the biggest reasons to wholesale is that you yourself can't take in all the properties that need fixing up in order to resell them. Wholesaling gives you a chance to pass them on and a way to benefit from the extra property you investigate and secure.

WHY A 3% TO 8% PROFIT IN WHOLESALING FIXER-UPPERS?

How much profit do you take in wholesaling? If you received 15% to 20% or more (on completed value) when you took in the property and made the repairs, then when you merely turn it over to someone else you would expect more modest profits, perhaps in the 3% to 8% range on the unrepaired value. This seems a lot less, but you will not have to take title or carry out the repair work. Remember, if you were looking for 15% on final value by doing the work, another fixer-upper investor would be, too. The new investor can never exceed the after-repair value set by the marketplace. Therefore, your margin has to be modest.

Note that properties in higher price ranges don't work as well as those in an average range for the purpose of either buying and fixing up or wholesaling. This is partly because of their higher cost and partly because, being newer, these properties don't usually require as much repair, and therefore do not have as much profit margin available. Although no universal statements apply, many investors who wholesale feel that property in the low to middle price range in each market offers the best profits. Generally, homes in lower price ranges are in neighborhoods of the same composition; the majority of homes will be alike in age, perhaps 20 to 50 years old, and are beginning to require considerable maintenance that owners don't always keep up with.

CONTRACT PROVISIONS FOR WHOLESALING

In wholesaling you do need to limit your financial and legal exposure. First, put down as little deposit money as possible, and, as in your fixer-upper contract, include a provision that allows you to cancel should you not be able to obtain partner's or colleague's approval or should the property fail to pass the building inspection code without error.

If you know the person to whom you are wholesaling the property, you don't need a large deposit to be put into escrow. But if his or her credit is not established with you or the community, it is advantageous to ask for a sizable deposit to protect your deal from falling apart should your buyer default.

Additionally, make sure you allow enough time in your contract with the seller to find a new buyer to take over. Two weeks

SAMPLE FORM: Assignment of Contract

Assignment of Contract of Sale

By assignment of contract, and in consideration of an earnest money deposit of $_____, and other good and valuable consideration, and the mutual benefits to be derived by all parties to this assignment, the undersigned, _____ (original buyer), does hereby exercise his or her unqualified right to assign unto _____ (new buyer) all his or her rights, obligations, and responsibilities in the above-noted contract dated _____ (contract date) with _____ (owner) concerning such property known as _____ (address) and further described as Lot _____, Block _____, Book _____, Page _____ in the City/Town of _____, County of _____ in the State of _____. The new buyer of this property hereby agrees to fulfill all of the same conditions and terms of the above-referenced contract, including but not limited to all settlement requirements as originally stated. This assignment does not transfer any earnest monies the assignor may have on deposit with the owner.

The total consideration for this assignment is $_____ to be paid _____ .

Executed this _____ day of _____ (month), _____ (year).

_____
(Original Buyer)

This assignment of contract of sale accepted this _____ day of _____ (month), _____ (year).

_____
(New Buyer)

_____
(Phone)

_____
(Address)

only allows you to go through your current list. You'll need more time if you have to reach more possible buyers.

As mentioned before, make sure your position in the contract with the seller can be assigned to another buyer. In this way and using the same contract you could assign your rights to someone else for a minimal finder's fee. (See sample form.) However, as you don't necessarily want your buyer to know the specific details or price of your deal with the seller, you may wish to use two contracts. (As with all contracts, have them thoroughly examined and adapted as needed by your own legal counsel.)

USING TWO CONTRACTS TO SEPARATE SELLER AND BUYER

Let's say you have a seller of a fixer-upper who has agreed to your purchase price and you have a wholesale buyer who has agreed to buy from you without your doing the repairs. Sounds great. Now how do you sell a property when you do not have title to the property? You want to make the deal without having the buyer find out your buying price or taking title yourself. How should you proceed with this transaction?

You start by making sure your contracts are in order. Your first contract essentially works like an option where your liability is limited. You make this first contract subject to your (and your associates', if appropriate) inspection and approval within a specific time period, such as 10 to 20 days. This contract allows you to show the property to repairpeople, carpenters, or contractors; private and public building inspectors; agents and appraisers; and potential tenants or buyers. It should even obtain for you the right to place a sign on the front lawn. Most important, your position in the contract is assignable to another buyer.

Then use a second contract to sell to the buyer. This second contract will have minimal contingencies for the new buyer. This buyer states that he or she is aware of the needed repairs and is capable of doing the work. For example, you find a single-family home that needs repair work and for which the seller is asking $125,000. With the local building inspector and a maintenance contractor you thoroughly check out what repairs must be done and their cost and determine they could be done for less than $18,000. You conclude that comparable values for the property as repaired are in the range of $175,000 to $178,000. You negotiate a price of $122,000 with the seller. Your contract with the seller allows you 60 days before you have to close. It also contains a clause that allows you to assign your position to another buyer should you wish it. You immediately check with other investors working in the fixer-upper market who buy from you on occasion. On the strength of your research into repair costs and final value, in two days you find three skilled tradespeople willing to close as soon as possible and do the necessary repairs. In a second contract you assign your rights in the contract to one of these new buyers for a $5,500 profit.

To close, use an attorney with whom you have worked before and who is experienced in simultaneous closings. Make sure this attorney can be trusted at the closing to keep private the details of your original agreement, particularly in terms of price. If you have to use an attorney who is not well known to you, or another party's attorney will be handling the closing, communicate with him or her and express your concern for privacy regarding details on your side of the transaction. Use your own attorney to make this contact if you feel it will help.

So, if you wish to keep private the amount you are gaining for profit, make sure you use separate agreements and have the attorneys at the closing keep this information confidential.

PROBLEMS AND SOLUTIONS IN WHOLESALING

Let's take a look at some of the real-world problems, as well as the solutions, you may encounter in wholesaling property.

Problem: *Often there can appear to be a fair amount of competition. For example, in your Sunday newspaper you see 12 "I buy homes" advertisements. What can you do?*

Solution: Lots of advertisements may indicate that these investors have plenty of property on which to bid. Get out there and capture your share.

Problem: *Often when a great number of investors are dealing in the wholesale market, many will recklessly make bids on properties, causing prices to rise beyond the possibility of making a fair profit.*

Solution: Turn these investors into buyers for the property you do secure. And, to keep your own wholesale prices fair, don't do any work on the houses.

Problem: *Numerous real estate agents in your area have gotten into the investing business and because of their access to MLS are quick to make offers.*

Solution: Be more aggressive and try to get the lowdown on properties before the agents do. Send out inquiries via letters, postcards, flyers, and so on to owners of vacant or distressed properties.

Problem: *Properties in lower price ranges are gobbled up faster than you can bid on them.*

Solution: Move to a higher price level. This will allow you to get into a sector with less competition.

Problem: *You weren't able to wholesale or assign a property you contracted.*

Solution: Rehabilitate those houses you decide to keep (or couldn't wholesale) for the retail market, or, in some situations, to hold.

Problem: *You've got the money to close on the house but none is left over to do the repairs.*

Solution: Bring another investor into the deal for the rehab money.

Problem: *There are plenty of properties to buy but not a large enough pool of potential homeowners.*

Solution: Put more effort into acquisition when the sales market is slow. Show up at every foreclosure auction, visit mortgage lenders for leads, and contact owners of distressed property and out-of-town owners.

Problem: *You have a lot of potential homeowners but find it hard to find properties to wholesale or fix up.*

Solution: You won't have to repair every last detail with your rehabs or spend as much effort on the selling side.

Problem: *Most of those who attempt to wholesale property for resale move slowly and have a reputation of tying property up.*

Solution: Be professional by moving quickly and decisively. If you perform on your contracts and are reliable, you will develop a reputation as the one to call when someone needs to sell.

Problem: *You haven't found a property lately and you're becoming discouraged.*

Solution: A number of would-be investors get frustrated and quit. Above all, don't be one of the ones who give up trying. Success will come your way in due time.

Problem: *Sellers are constantly telling you that others are looking or making offers on their property.*

Solution: Tell them to call you when the other parties' offers fall through. This keeps them less than eager when dealing with current offers and still interested in the potential price you might offer.

The next chapter returns to the assumption that you'll opt to take title, complete the rehabilitation, and resell the property, and will therefore need to explore ways of financing.

9

Financing I: Working through Conventional Lenders

Let's start this chapter with a primer on basic financing and discuss the differences as well as the similarities of home and investment loans. We'll also cover fixed and adjustable rate loans, blanket loans to help cover the down payment, home equity credit lines, and specialty loans to finance repairs. We'll finish with a special section on the FHA 203(k) loan program for homeowners, followed by a discussion of the Fannie Mae HomeStyle loan that allows investors as well as homeowners to buy and rehabilitate property.

THE DIFFERENCES BETWEEN
HOME AND INVESTMENT MORTGAGES

If you are considering your first investment, even buying your first home such as a duplex in which you will live in one half, you may have some basic questions about the home financing process. There are differences between financing a home in which you will live and an investment property. These differences are primarily in qualifying for the loan and the interest rate. Specifically, if you already own your own home, it may be easier for you to qualify for an investment loan due to the importance placed on the value of the property over your own income.

The interest rate for an investment loan, however, can range from one point to two or more points above the average rate for a home in which you will live. Otherwise, many of the other qualifications for financing the small investments are similar. As a general rule you usually can qualify for a home mortgage loan of two to two and one-half times your household's income (and this is true if you are buying that duplex and going to live in one half). For example, if you have an income of $30,000 a year, you can qualify for a mortgage of $60,000 to $75,000. But with the investment loan, the loan will be weighted toward the value of the property and the percent amount of the loan in relation to value (called loan-to-value, or LTV) which is usually less than what is available for a home loan. The investment property lender will also consider your regular income and credit history, including your current income and how you repaid past loans, but will look more closely at rental income and operating expenses.

DOWN PAYMENT AND CLOSING COSTS

How much money will you need for a down payment and closing costs? When you bought your primary residence (and this might include a small investment property in which you were going to live) you probably made a down payment of between 10% and 20% of the house's price and paid closing costs of 3% to 6% of the loan amount. If you made a down payment of less than 20%, the lender probably required you to pay for private mortgage insurance (requirements for VA or FHA loans may differ). By contrast, a lender of investment property funds usually will require up to 30% of value of the property be put down either in cash or from secondary sources.

SHOP FOR MORTGAGE LOANS

Mortgages can be quite different from one lender to another. Always investigate the various choices to find the one best for you. For example, check the real estate section in your local newspaper for the names of lenders, mortgage interest rates, and advantageous mortgage packages. The Yellow Pages will also have a list of mortgage lenders in your area. Call various lenders for information on rates and terms for the type of investment property you are considering. One lender may charge a rate for a fixer-upper close to its regular home rate, while another will want its full investment rate of 1% to 1.5% more than the regular home rate.

Compare the mortgages offered by several lenders before you apply for a loan. Whether you are applying for a home or an investment loan, most lenders require a fee when you file your loan application. The amount of this fee varies, but it can be $100 to $300. Some lenders refund this fee if you are not approved for the loan, or if you decide not to accept the loan terms offered. Ask the lenders before you apply whether they charge an application fee, how much it is, and under what circumstances and to what extent it is refundable.

WHAT TYPES OF MORTGAGES ARE AVAILABLE?

For either homes or investments there are two major types of mortgage loans—those with fixed interest rates and monthly payments, and those with changing rates and payments, or adjustable rate mortgages (ARMs). Many variations of the ARM loans are available, and you should shop carefully for the mortgage that best suits your needs. The traditional fixed rate mortgages include 30-year, 20-year, and 15-year mortgages with the 30-year generally offering the lowest monthly payments. The 15-year fixed rate mortgage enables you to pay less interest overall, thereby paying off the property loan at less than one-half the interest costs of a 30-year loan but at higher monthly payments. In addition, with shorter-term loans, you have smaller mortgage interest deductions on your income tax.

Note that because the financing of a fixer-upper is usually short-term in nature, it is often, but not always, a fixed rate loan. These shorter-term loans can often appeal to a lender as they usually bring a higher rate than a regular home loan (unless you'll live there), and it's a quick-in and -out transaction that puts the lender in the best position to obtain the long-term commitment from the homeowner when the property is sold.

Many forms of adjustable rate mortgage (ARM) loans are available. The most common generally offer interest rates and monthly payments that are initially lower than fixed rate mortgages. However, these rates, and thereby payments, can vary according to changes in a predetermined index—commonly the rate of return on U.S. government Treasury bills, on which the ARM bases its adjustment.

Some ARM loans allow you to convert at some future time to a fixed rate loan. For this a small fee may be charged. Another type of mortgage loan carries a fixed interest rate for a number of years, frequently five to seven, before adjusting to a new interest rate for the remaining balance of the loan. A "buydown" or "discounted mortgage" is another type of loan with an initially reduced interest rate that increases to a higher fixed rate or to an adjustable rate, usually within one to three years. For example, in a lender buydown, the lender offers lower monthly payments during the first few years of the loan.

COMPARING DIFFERENT MORTGAGES

The first factor to consider in shopping for a mortgage, whether it is for a home or an investment, is the annual percentage rate, or APR. This APR includes the cost of credit, such as interest, "points" (fees often charged when a mortgage is closed), and mortgage insurance (when part of the loan package). Lenders must disclose the APR under the Truth in Lending Act. The lower the APR, the lower the cost of your loan. Note that when you see in an advertisement mention of a "simple" interest rate, it does not include other costs such as points or loan insurance.

In looking for ARMs compare the following:

- The initial interest rate.
- How often this interest rate can change.
- The cap—or how much the interest rate can increase/decrease over the life of the loan, and how much the rate can change at the end of each adjustment period.
- Similarly, how much and how often the monthly payments and term of the loan can change.
- What index is used to determine the rate changes.
- What margin is used—or how much a lender can add to the adjusted interest rate.
- The limits, if any, on "negative amortization"—the loss of equity when low monthly payments do not fully cover the interest rate charges agreed on in the mortgage contract.

■ Any balloon payment—a large payment before the end of your loan term, often after a series of low monthly payments.

TWO WAYS TO QUALIFY FOR FIXED RATE LOANS

The traditional way to buy any property is to borrow from a conventional mortgage lender. There are two conventional financing choices: conforming and portfolio.

Conforming financing generally requires 30% down on a nonowner-occupied property, whereas portfolio financing typically requires 20% down. Conforming financing may get you lower loan fees and a lower rate. It also uses your income to qualify you. This should not be a problem if you already qualified for one loan (such as your home) with your current income as it doesn't usually matter that you have an existing mortgage.

Portfolio financing is not as concerned with your income. The lender judges the worth of the property based on rental income and operating expenses. Portfolio financing occasionally has a prepayment penalty, but conforming financing may not have a prepayment penalty. You can obtain conforming financing from almost any mortgage bank or broker. As a general rule, however, you can obtain portfolio financing only from banks. As a strategy, you should constantly be looking for lenders that will compete against each other and offer portfolio-type loans.

SECOND MORTGAGE FINANCING
FROM A CONVENTIONAL LENDER

As many investors know, there are other ways to borrow money from lenders. For example, you may want to explore second mortgage loans. Although this loan places an additional mortgage on the property, second mortgage money is usually loaned in a lump sum made available by writing checks on an account, rather than in a series of advances common with other loans. Also, second mortgages usually have fixed interest rates and fixed payment amounts.

You also may want to explore borrowing from home equity

funding, as well as credit lines that do not use your home as collateral, such as those available with your credit cards or with unsecured credit lines that let you write checks as you need the money.

In addition, you may want to ask lenders about loans for specific items, such as cars or tuition, that will free up your existing funds for investment.

Here we'll review some basics of what second mortgages are and discuss how to get one from your local lender.

If you are like most homeowners, you probably have a first mortgage loan on your home. Typically, such loans are for 25 to 30 years, with the monthly payments adjusted so that the loan is paid in full at the end of the term.

As you make monthly mortgage payments and the value of the home increases, your interest in the property (called equity) grows. After a while, some homeowners may wish to borrow against the equity in their home to get cash, to make home improvements, to educate their children, or to consolidate personal debts. Because such loans are in addition to the first mortgage on the home, they are commonly called second mortgage loans.

Second mortgage loans are different from first mortgages in several ways. They often carry a higher interest rate, and they usually are for a shorter time, 15 years or less. In addition, they may require a large single payment at the end of the term, commonly known as a balloon payment.

Traditionally, second mortgage loans are offered with a fixed loan amount and a predetermined repayment schedule. Some lenders now offer lines of credit that allow you to obtain cash advances with a credit card or to write checks up to a certain credit limit. These often are called home equity lines of credit because the equity in your home is collateral for the amount of credit you request. As you pay off the outstanding balance, you can reuse the line of credit during the loan period.

Now let's look at some answers to common questions people ask when they begin shopping for a first or second mortgage or home equity loan. Topics discussed include choosing a lender, the meaning of some mortgage terms, costs, disclosure documents, and contacts for resolving problems.

How do I choose a lender?
When you are looking for a lender, shop around and make comparisons. Interest rates, repayment terms, and origination fees may vary substantially. Ask your local banks, savings and loans, credit unions, or

finance companies about their loan terms. Although you will want to select the lender that offers you terms most suited to your needs, be sure to ask and compare the annual percentage rates (APR), because they will give you the total cost of the loan, including financing charges.

If you have not done business with the lender before, or if the lender is unfamiliar to you, you may wish to ask your local Better Business Bureau or consumer protection office if they have any complaints against the lender.

How long will I have to repay the loan?
Some second mortgage loans may extend for as long as 15 or 20 years; others may require repayment in one year. You will need to discuss the repayment terms with the lenders and select the most appropriate one. For example, if you need to borrow $20,000 to make repairs, you may not want a loan that requires you to repay the entire amount in one or two years because the monthly payments may be too high.

Will my interest rate change?
If you have a fixed-rate loan, the interest rate is set for the life of the loan. However, many lenders offer variable rate mortgages, also known as adjustable rate mortgages or ARMs. These provide for periodic interest rate adjustments. If your loan contract allows the lender to adjust or change the interest rate, be sure you understand when the lender has the right to do so, whether there are any limits on how much the interest or payments can change, and how often the lender can change the rate. You also should know what basis the lender will use to determine a new rate of interest.

How much will my monthly payments be, and will they pay off the loan?
Be sure you understand how much your monthly payments will be and what they cover. Your lender should be able to give you this information in advance. With some loans, you will be required to make monthly payments on the principal and interest. With other loans, you may be required to pay interest only on the borrowed amount; in these loans, your monthly payments will not reduce the principal amount of the loan. With such a loan, you will be required to pay back the entire borrowed amount at the end of the loan period. These loans are popularly known as balloon loans.

If your loan has a balloon payment, you should consider how you will arrange to repay the entire amount when it becomes due.

On home equity lines, the lender does not have to give you the exact amount of the monthly payment, but must explain how it is figured. This is because the borrowed amount will vary and your outstanding balance will change if you use the line of credit. However, if your monthly payment term is 5% of the outstanding balance and your outstanding balance is $5,000, your minimum monthly payments would be $250.

Will I have to pay any fees to get this loan?
Many companies will charge a fee for lending you money. The fee is usually a percentage of the loan and is sometimes referred to as "points." One point is equal to 1% of the amount you borrow. For example, if you were to borrow $10,000 with a fee of eight points, one point would be $100 and you would pay $800 in points. The number of points lenders charge varies, so it may be worthwhile to shop around. If the fee seems too high, you may be able to bargain for or find a lower fee. Be sure to get the amount of the fee in writing before you take the loan. Many states limit the amount a lender may charge in fees on a second mortgage loan. You may want to check with your state's consumer protection office or banking commissioner to determine whether there is a limit in your state.

What should I get in writing?
If your loan is primarily for personal, family, or household purposes, the lender is required to give you a federal Truth in Lending Act disclosure form before you sign the customary loan documents, such as a note or deed of trust. This Truth in Lending form will tell you the actual cost of the loan. It includes the annual percentage rate, the finance charge, and the fees included in the loan. For home equity lines, your lender must send you a periodic statement, usually monthly. The lender also is required to give you a notice of your right of rescission. The right of rescission gives you three business days after signing for the loan and receiving the Truth in Lending Act disclosures to reconsider whether you want to take the loan.

CASH FROM A HOME EQUITY CREDIT LINE

To raise needed cash on a short-term basis for a down payment on a fixer-upper or for repair funds, many investors use a credit line to borrow against the equity in their home. Lenders offer these home equity credit lines with variable interest rates or fixed rates. These variable rates may offer lower monthly payments at first, but during the rest of the repayment period the payments may change and be higher. Fixed interest rates, if available, may be slightly higher initially than variable rates, but fixed rates offer stable monthly payments over the life of the credit line.

The home equity loan may also be accompanied by one-time up-front fees, closing costs, and even annual fees similar to what you had when you financed your original mortgage. These include items such as an application fee, title search, appraisal, attorneys' fees, and points (a percentage of the amount you borrow). These expenses can add substantially to the cost of your loan, especially if you ultimately borrow little from your credit line. You may want to negotiate with lenders to see if they will waive or pay for some of these expenses.

Lenders may structure home equity loans with balloon payments at the end of a period, or with no balloons but with higher monthly payments.

No one loan is right for you all the time. What loan you choose will depend on many variables, such as the length of time you plan on holding the property and whether you plan to use the loan for a down payment or repairs. For example, you might be in and out of a fixer-upper in 60 to 90 days. Or it might be a more extensive job and take 120 days or more. You need to contact different lenders, compare what they offer, and select the home equity credit line to best fit your time schedule.

A home equity loan can provide you with a large amount of cash at relatively low interest rates. At the same time, you should be careful of these because home equity lines of credit require you to use your home as collateral for the loan. This may put your home at risk if you are late or cannot make payments, so it should be used only when you want the money for a deal like a fixer-upper where you'll be in and out in a relatively short time. Plus, as the money will be used for the purchase and/or repair of another piece of real estate, and not a boat or other depreciating asset, a substantial asset is being used to help secure the loan's repayments.

A further advantage of a home equity loan is that once you pay one off by reselling your fixer-upper, you will again be quite welcome at the lender's office for borrowing when the next deal comes along.

What Is the Interest Rate on a Home Equity Loan?

Interest rates for home equity loans can vary from lender to lender. Always check for the latest prices. Further, you want to compare the annual percentage rate (APR), which indicates the cost on a yearly basis. And be aware that the APR for a home equity loan is based on interest alone and you must add in points and closing costs for a true comparison. Note that when you compare a home equity credit line with a traditional installment (or second) mortgage, the APR for the latter usually includes the total costs for the loan.

If you are considering a variable rate, check and compare the terms with a fixed rate. Check the periodic cap, or the limit on interest rate changes at one time. Also, check the lifetime cap, which is the limit on interest rate changes throughout the loan term.

Further, ask the lender which index (such as the prime rate) is used to determine how much to raise or lower interest rates, and how much and how often it can change. And check the margin, which is an amount added to the index that determines the interest you are charged. Margins may vary considerably between lenders. In addition, inquire whether you can convert your variable rate loan to a fixed rate at some future time.

Sometimes lenders offer a temporarily discounted interest rate—a rate that is unusually low and lasts for only an introductory period, such as six months. After the introductory period ends, however, your rate (and payments) will increase to the true market level (the index plus the margin). So ask if the rate you are offered is discounted, and, if so, find out how the rate will be determined at the end of the discount period and how much larger your payments could be at that time.

How Much Money Can You Borrow on a Home Equity Credit Line?

Depending on your income, credit rating, and the amount of your current debt, home equity lenders may let you borrow up to 85% of the appraised value of your home minus the amount you still owe on your first mortgage.

If you are using the home equity funds for rehabbing and need to pay your obligations with repairpeople on time, it's important to ask your lender about whether there are minimum or maximum withdrawal requirements after your account is opened. And make sure you know about how you gain access to your credit line—with either lender drafts or checks.

You also want to know if your home equity plan sets a fixed time—a draw period—when you can make withdrawals from your account. Should you need funds you have not drawn upon, you don't want to be stopped from receiving funds once the period expires.

BE PRUDENT IN RISKING THE EQUITY IN YOUR HOME

It's tempting to use the equity in your own home, through either a second mortgage or a home equity loan, as a down payment on another property. However, there are several pitfalls, such as getting your home payments too high, raising your interest rate, and lowering the home equity you might need in a true emergency. If you don't disturb this equity, you'll have greater peace of mind.

So, try to keep your own home as free as possible of debt. You don't want to put your home in jeopardy. Remember, debt is what causes bankruptcies. Contrary to the advice of "fast money" gurus, for example, you should never buy a property and receive money at the closing. That usually means you are borrowing more than you should for the property—a recipe for financial disaster.

Furthermore, borrowed money is not tax-free. You have to pay this money back with after-tax dollars. Besides, if the worst happened, the IRS considers any foreclosure a sale where there is any mortgage over the current tax basis; this additional sum is treated as profit, giving you a large tax liability. Having received this warning, if you need a small amount from a home equity loan, and you are absolutely sure about the property (it will sell quickly for top dollar once repaired) and its price (you're buying at rock bottom), go ahead—cautiously.

USING A BLANKET MORTGAGE
TO COVER THE DOWN PAYMENT

Another way to finance with a conventional lender is to use a blanket mortgage that covers a number of properties. It is an excellent way to use your current equity in several properties to finance the purchase of more property or your down payment. It works like a line of credit. There will usually be a loan commitment fee of 1% of the total loan amount paid up front. You will also have appraisal costs. The lender holding the blanket mortgage will probably want you to provide to the lender an updated financial statement each year. However, as you plan on being an active investor, this is a good financing device to use.

Note that in qualifying for a conventional loan for the first time, a borrower with good credit normally should not have over 38% in total debt in order to qualify for the lowest interest rate. However, this is only a guideline and the percentage can be higher. Once you have several properties, the accumulated loan amounts throw this formula out the window. A borrower whose credit is not perfect can be moved into a higher-interest loan or a lower loan-to-value (LTV) mortgage. Lending is an art, not a science, and it changes depending on the marketplace.

CONSIDER A CONSTRUCTION LOAN TO FINANCE REPAIRS

You will often use the seller's equity to finance a distressed property. This is in part because conventional mortgage lenders are, on occasion, apprehensive about funding damaged property. They are used to lending their money to the homeowner, the person who is going to reside in the ready-to-live-in property. However, if the lender feels that the projected repairs are well thought out and add value to a property, you may be able to borrow funds through a construction loan.

A construction loan is normally given to contractors who build a house from scratch. These loans are offered on a short-term basis until the work is completed, at which time the lender normally provides a long-term loan to a new buyer who will reside at the property. Sometimes construction-type loans are not available from a traditional mortgage lender. A commercial bank that lends short-term for business, car, and personal loans usually makes available construction and repair loans.

When you can show a bank a detailed list of improvements to be completed by professionals and your research that shows the property will be worth considerably more once these repairs are done, you should be able to assuage any of the bank's fears about making the loan.

CREDIT WITH A COMMERCIAL
BANK IS BETTER THAN GOLD

Being able to act quickly with cash may be important in the foreclosure market. Let's say you've located a property that is going to hit the auction block in two weeks. The owners have defaulted on their mortgage payments. You verified today's value with comparable sales to be 30% more after a small amount in repairs. You've checked the title and it appears there are no other liens on the property. How do you go about getting the money for the purchase at the auction? You qualify for a conventional loan but the loan officer has said she cannot get the approval before the time of the auction. What do you do to gather the money prior to the auction?

Consider a commercial bank for a short-term business loan. As long as you have good credit and the assurance that your mortgage lender merely needs more time to complete the transaction, the commercial bank is likely to make the loan. Commercial banks are often the best source for quick, ready cash to get deals started. Such a loan also continues a track record of your good credit. Since you never know if you'll be going through with the actual purchase at an auction until the bidding is completed, you need an arrangement where you can get cash within a day or two of the sale.

REHABBING THROUGH THE FHA 203(k) LOAN

In an effort to restore properties in need of substantial repair, the Federal Housing Administration (FHA) has developed a rehabilitation mortgage insurance program called the FHA 203(k). This program enables home buyers and current homeowners wanting to rehabilitate to finance both the purchase or refinancing of a single- or multifamily property and the cost of its rehabilitation through a single mortgage.

The purpose of the program is to encourage lenders to make mortgage credit available to borrowers who might not otherwise qualify for conventional loans on affordable terms and to residents of disadvantaged neighborhoods where mortgages may be hard to get.

The program is designed to allow homeowners to buy properties to fix up with a loan that pays for repairs. Its goal is to give more purchasing power to buyers and to help improve neighborhoods. Some of its features include a minimal down payment of 3% to 7%, which can be money from a gift; low fixed or adjustable interest rates; and the financing of all repairs including appliances, carpeting, painting, and outside landscaping.

Whether purchasing or refinancing, the 203(k) program allows homeowners to make improvements to their home while financing the cost of repairs into a permanent fixed rate mortgage. No construction financing is necessary and the loan is fully dispersed in one closing before the repairs are made. A portion of the loan proceeds is used to pay the seller, or, if refinancing, to pay off the existing mortgage, while the remaining funds are placed in an escrow account and released as rehabilitation is done. The mortgage amount for these loans is based on the projected value of the property with the work completed.

For example, let's suppose a typical property that you might encounter for $60,000 needs $20,000 worth of repairs and is valued at $100,000 when finished. Because you have an FHA 203(k) loan, you could put down only 15%—a little over $12,000—and borrow the $60,000 for the property and the $20,000 for the repairs as well as a substantial part of the closing costs. But that's not all. If you are going to occupy the property with a 203(k) loan you could borrow 97% or $97,000 of the prospective selling price of $100,000, which if you are a first-time home buyer can be no money down, as this down payment can be waived, gifted, or made as a second mortgage. If it's not the first home for the home buyer, a 5% down payment can be arranged. And, of course, your closing costs are minimal because the loan is assumed.

To summarize, the FHA 203(k) loan allows almost full financing as well as pre-approval on a loan at new market value for the new home buyer. The program allows you to finance 97% of the purchase price of the home plus all the repairs plus part of the closing costs! No other mortgage program on the market allows you to do this in one mortgage and one closing.

Highlights of FHA 203(k) are:

- Both owner-occupants and new home buyers are eligible.
- Funds are available after closing for property and repairs.
- Prearranged mortgage funding is available for new owner-occupant.
- Owner-occupant puts only 3% down.

- Minimum repair amount is $5,000.
- Planning meeting prior to contract costs $200.

Which kinds of properties are eligible? One- to four-family residential homes that have been completed for at least one year; homes that have been demolished or razed as part of the rehabilitation process are eligible as long as the existing foundation system is not affected and remains intact; any property the buyer wishes to convert, such as a single-family unit into a two- to four-family unit, or a two- to four-family unit into a single-family unit.

The total value of the property must fall within the FHA mortgage limit for the area. The value of the property is determined by whichever is less of either (1) the value of the property before rehabilitation plus the cost of rehabilitation, or (2) 110% of the appraised value of the property after rehabilitation. Note that the maximum mortgage amounts may vary within each state.

Since FHA maximum mortgage limits are updated constantly by local HUD office staff, please contact the single family housing director in your local Department of Housing and Urban Development (HUD) office for current information.

Here are some guidelines that will help you ensure a hassle-free transaction through the 203(k) loan program:

- Work with a lender who is familiar with the 203(k) process.

- Make sure repairs are necessary; cosmetic or amenity repairs like swimming pools are generally not allowed.

- Loan amount may be limited to the borrower's ability to qualify for enough mortgage to fund HUD-required repairs.

- Rehab money is provided *after* completion of part or all of the work on a reimbursement basis. Not all contractors will agree to front all of the material and labor costs without the owner's assistance.

- As the inspection program is rigorous, licensed contractors provide the best insurance of a timely and quality completion.

- HUD requires a thorough termite inspection report, which should be completed as early as possible.

The extent of the rehabilitation covered by Section 203(k) insurance may range from relatively minor to virtual reconstruction provided that the existing foundation system remains in place. Section 203(k)-insured loans can finance the rehabilitation of the residential portion of a property that also has nonresidential uses; they can also cover the conversion of a property of any size to a one- to four-unit structure. Remembering that $5,000 is the required minimum of eligible improvements, the types of improvements that borrowers may make include:

- Repair or replacement of structural damage.

- Structural alterations and reconstruction, including chimney repair.

- Improved function and modernization, such as remodeled kitchens and baths, including permanently installed fixtures and appliances.

- Replacement or installation of flooring, tiling, and carpeting.

- Energy conservation, such as new double-pane windows, insulated exterior doors, solar domestic hot water systems, insulation, and caulking and weather-stripping including replacement of leaky jambs and sills.

- Finishing of attics and basements.

- Repair of termite damage and treatment against termites and other infestation.

- Elimination of health and safety hazards, such as resolution of lead-based paint or asbestos hazards.

- Reconditioning or replacement of HVAC (heating, ventilating, and air-conditioning) systems and electrical systems including connections to public systems.

- Installation of wells and septic systems.

- Landscaping and site improvement such as patios, decks, and terraces that improve the value, or that preserve the property from erosion, including grading and drainage improvements.

- Improved accessibility for the handicapped, such as providing space for wheelchair access, lowering kitchen and bathroom cabinets and fixtures, widening doors, and providing ramps.

Luxury items and improvements that do not become a permanent part of the property are not eligible uses.

Note that lenders may charge some additional fees, such as a supplemental origination fee, fees to cover the preparation of architectural documents and review of the rehabilitation plan, and a higher appraisal fee. However, unlike other FHA mortgages, Section 203(k) borrowers do not pay an up-front mortgage premium.

FANNIE MAE HOMESTYLE LOAN

An alternative to the FHA 203(k) is the Fannie Mae HomeStyle loan available to investors, which allows you to borrow the money, at low first-mortgage rates using one loan, for the purchase and improvement of a home. It is available for one- to four-unit principal residences, single-family second homes, and one-unit investment properties. The HomeStyle loan may be an appropriate choice if you are over the FHA mortgage limits for your area or are not an owner-occupant. Down payments can be as low as 5% for one-unit homes. Refinance options are available. A HomeStyle remodeler loan is also available as a second loan for remodeling jobs under $50,000, or up to $15,000 for a condominium. Further, a HomeStyle energy loan is available for energy improvements that typically include replacing central heating and cooling systems, water heating systems, windows, and doors. A HomeStyle community mortgage is a low-down-payment option to help low- and moderate-income buyers purchase and renovate a home or refinance a mortgage on an existing home to fund improvements.

Note that the Fannie Mae HomeStyle loan is similar to the FHA 203(k) loan program but allows investors to participate. You can get up to 100% of the rehabilitation amount. For example, a lender may give you a loan of up to 90% of the "after improved value" on an investment property up to four units. That means that if you find a property for $100,000 with a construction amount of $100,000 that has an "as improved value" of $300,000 based on an appraisal, you could get 100% of the purchase and rehab and up to $10,000 of your closing costs financed. In practical terms you've put nothing down!

In the next chapter, we'll explore seller financing, mortgage assumption, contractual takeovers, credit cards, and another FHA/HUD loan program, Title I.

10

Financing II:
Help from the Seller

This chapter explores various ways—seller financing, mortgage assumption, contractual takeovers, credit card borrowing, and Title I, the second major FHA/HUD loan program—to finance or control a property. In the previous chapter you read about second mortgages from a conventional lender. Here, let's start looking at arranging secondary financing from the seller.

SECONDARY FINANCING FROM THE SELLER

From an investor's point of view the most popular way to finance a property is certainly to have the seller provide the financing. And, as you will read in Chapter 17 on multiple dwelling units, this is one of the major ways to finance. In fixer-uppers you are not always able to obtain seller financing, though. Since most of the property you are looking at in the fixer-upper area is distressed to varying degrees, many sellers may be in a difficult situation themselves, and perhaps heavy with existing financing as well.

Plan on other alternatives. Getting a lower price may be more important than seller financing. That does not mean, however, that you do not ask. As part of any offer, unless you know otherwise—either by the agent telling you or your personal contact—ask for the seller to provide some financing help. This could be in the form of a first mortgage, although that is not likely. More common is some form of secondary financing—perhaps even a delayed portion of the down payment. As the seller knows you are buying the property to fix it up and resell it, you can make it clear that this loan will be for only a short time until the property is resold. A seller who has the equity and is not unduly pressured may accept. Let's take a closer look at secondary financing.

SELLER FINANCING WITH SECOND MORTGAGE

Say you buy a property for $76,000 that needs $24,000 in repairs. With the help of a cooperative sales agent you have verified three houses in the same neighborhood that are closely comparable and have sold during the past six months at an average selling price of $145,000. The mortgage lender from whom you borrowed the money to buy your own residence is happy to lend you the money to buy the fixer-upper. Since the new purchase is not a house in which you will reside, the lender will charge you a percentage point and one-half more than is currently charged for homes, and will not lend more than 70% of the purchase price and repairs. This means you have to fund 30%, plus closing costs. You have approximately $18,000.

Purchase price:	$ 76,000
Repairs:	$ 24,000
Subtotal:	$100,000
Mortgage available (70%):	$ 70,000
Difference needed:	$ 30,000
You have:	$ 18,000
You need:	$ 12,000

You go back to the seller and request that he or she fund one-half of the repairs until the work is completed and the house is resold. This is not an unreasonable request. As you have both the sales agent and the bank endorsing the deal, it should give confidence to the seller that his or her loan will be only for a short time. And, since secondary financing usually brings a higher interest rate, you could offer another point or two more than the bank charges to make it more attractive for the seller.

Other alternatives are available if the seller cannot participate, but often the seller will. In this case the seller agrees to a loan of $12,000 until the property resells, at an interest rate 2 percentage points above what the bank is charging you for the investment mortgage.

Note that on occasion you can base the financing on the projected selling price. That is, in this example you would be able to finance 70% of the final selling price of $145,000, or $101,500, allowing the seller to be paid off at the closing and essentially funding the repairs.

WHEN SELLER FINANCING IS ALL THAT'S AVAILABLE

Now let's look at a more complicated but not uncommon example of getting a mortgage note on the sale of a fixer-upper while at the same time selling the note to get cash. In this example financing is not available from conventional sources and the seller finances both a first and a second mortgage.

Here's how the terms of the deal work out:

A fixer-upper is bought for $58,500; it requires $19,000 of repairs—for a total investment of $77,500—to come up to building code and be resold. All financing is with the seller and includes a first mortgage of $54,250 (70% of $77,500) at 8.25%. It is agreed that if the property is not resold and the loan not paid within one year payments will be based on a 20-year term with monthly payments of $462.25. The seller also gives a second mortgage of $14,000 at 9.5% with a five-year term or until the property is resold.

The mortgage broker arranging these notes sells the first note at a 10% discount for a cash payoff of $48,825, increasing its yield to 9.72% ($48,825 principal paid monthly at $462.25 for 20 years yields a return of 9.72%).

The selling of this first mortgage gives cash to the seller and allows him to keep the higher-yielding second note until the property is resold.

WHAT "NO MONEY DOWN" REALLY MEANS

For you, a "no money down" deal is where none of your own money goes to the seller. The seller of course gets money. His or her money comes from the mortgage loan, commercial loan, equity line of credit on your personal home, family personal loan, partners you bring in, even credit card debt. But you don't take cash out of your pocket to finance the deal. Assuredly, you are liable for the debt you incur; yet, if you buy the right property for the right terms or price, then carrying a debt should work out satisfactorily. This type of deal happens all the time.

What is more common is to buy with a little money down. That is, you have some capital of your own in the deal. It may not be a lot, perhaps a small percentage of the price.

Here's how a no-money-down deal might work. You have $50,000 of equity in your home. You arrange with your bank for an equity line of credit. You buy a single-family fixer-upper for $85,000 by obtaining a 70% first mortgage of $60,000 and tapping into your equity line of credit for the remaining amount (to the seller) of $25,000, and $20,000 to renovate. Three months later you sell it for $120,000, clearing $15,000.

That's what is meant by no money down. It's not that you don't put up some cash; it's just that you do it through your existing equity. In other words, your cash—for purchase and renovations—is borrowed.

Note that in this example you could have gotten a first mortgage of 70% on the value as fixed up. In this case let's say the final value after repairs will be $130,000 (an extra $10,000 for overhead and legal expense is plugged in), permitting the mortgage lender to lend you $91,000, thereby covering the full cost of purchase and a bit of the renovations, too. With the balance being made up with your equity line of credit, it's still a "no money down" deal—you don't use a dime out of your own pocket. You use your credit based on the equity in your current asset to fund the deal.

BUYING "SUBJECT TO" AND "ASSUMING" AN EXISTING MORTGAGE

No discussion of seller financing would be complete without touching on taking over existing loans. It must be mentioned that with today's relatively low interest rates and availability of funds, taking over "subject to" or by "assuming" an existing mortgage is not as popular as it has been in the past. Not many sellers today will agree to having their loans taken over unless they pocket a large down payment and are able to protect their credit by using a payment in escrow with the right to reclaim the property if the investor defaults. They are not likely to allow someone else to take over their existing loan while at the same time they remain liable on the note. A seller would have to be frantic to agree. It will be difficult to buy the property at as much of a discount as possible and also find a seller who would agree to such burdensome terms. The discussion is included here so that you will be able to follow through should the unlikely but occasional possible opportunity occur.

In fact, one of the first considerations in buying property is assuming an existing loan. This means that the lender allows you to assume lawful responsibility for the seller's loan, relieving the seller from further obligation. The only problem is that most mortgages written over the past 20 years contain a "due on sale" clause in them that prohibits them from being assumed by another party. Lenders do this because they can make more money writing new loans. This "due on sale" clause means that if the property is transferred to a new owner by a change in official records, such as a deed, the mortgage must be paid off. In an attempt to get around this, you buy "subject to" the mortgage and continue making payments on the existing mortgage. By strict definition you are not "assuming" but taking "subject to."

Buying "subject to" means you take title acknowledging the existence of the prior mortgage. This has the practical effect of limiting your liability to whatever cash you may have in the property. For example, if you had $6,000 as a down payment "subject to" a $60,000 first mortgage, you have limited your liability to your $6,000. You may service the loan by making payments, but you can always walk away and lose only your equity. Note, however, if the original loan agreement contained a "due on sale" clause the lender may, but not always, call the loan.

"Assuming" a loan, rather than taking "subject to," is not as simple as just taking over the payments. If an owner wants out and is offering to let you take over his or her loan, the questions you need to ask are: Will the bank make it difficult, and will the bank require you to go through an application process as if you were starting from scratch? Note that nearly all loans can be assumed upon bank approval. However, that process is virtually the same as qualifying for a new loan.

Taking over a loan, either "subject to" or "assuming," is not just a matter of not having to borrow that amount in a new loan. It also keeps the seller's favorable interest rate intact for you, and it should help you avoid spreading your credit too thinly. However, while taking title "subject to" (seller still responsible) is often good for you, it can be a drawback for the seller. A seller acquainted with the pitfalls—continuing liability and a credit claim—may shy away from this option. However, the seller is more likely to agree if you carefully explain the benefits for both of you—ease of transfer, quickness of sale, favorable interest rate, and that it will be only temporary (if that is your wish) until you make repairs and find a buyer.

Generally, you would prefer to buy a property subject to the existing loan, as it doesn't tie you formally to the liability on the loan, whereas assuming the loan usually does. And although in "assuming," the seller usually remains primarily responsible for the loan, many sellers request a release from liability. Note that such a release usually involves an application and approval of the lender. In taking "subject to," you avoid dealing with the lender; this is also true if the property is put into a land trust. However, if a third or more equity is in the property, or you aim to sell soon, you should not worry about liability in assuming a loan.

A solution where you don't actually assume the loan but you get control is when the seller deeds the property into a land trust with you as the trustee. Additionally, the seller assigns his or her interest in the property to you. The purpose of the land trust or similar arrangement is to avoid triggering the bank's nonassumption clause. This deal can be made attractive to the seller by giving him or her a substantial deposit or some amount of equity. Use your attorney to structure the paperwork.

PROBLEMS OF BUYING "SUBJECT TO"

If you take a property subject to a mortgage (with little or no money in it), your risk is minimal. Knowledge, however, will help you avoid some potential problems. For example, if you are trying to resell the property to a current tenant, you could get stranded in a situation where your tenant cannot qualify for a loan and so cannot buy it. Make sure you don't misjudge the marketability of the property—or the financial situation of the tenant. As long as your tenant can qualify for financing, a new loan will pay off the old "due on sale" loan. If for some unforeseen reason you can't rent the property, either because you misjudged the real estate market or this market took a sudden nosedive, the liability falls to the original signer on the loan.

Note that in most cases when you take a property "subject to," the seller is months behind on mortgage payments, if not in default. If you deeded the property back to the seller, he or she would be in no worse a position than at the start (in the interim, you helped his or her credit by making payments on time).

An additional problem in buying "subject to" might be the case where you are unable to get the bank or mortgage company to transfer the name and mailing address on the account to yours. Therefore, the payment notices continue to get sent to the former owner at a forwarded address. One way to solve this problem is to set up a post office box and have your seller send a letter to the lender changing the address to the box number. The same is true for property tax bills and year-end interest statements. These are likely to have the previous owner's name and Social Security number on them. However, the ultimate test for deductibility according to the IRS is who pays the bills. So if you pay them, claiming the property tax and interest deductions on your tax returns should not be a problem. If the IRS questions it, you will have your records and can easily prove that you bought the property "subject to."

Property insurance can be handled another way. As is sometimes the case, the previous owner may be paying for insurance along with the mortgage or tax payment. This is not by itself a problem except that some policies are not assignable and will continue to have the former owner named as the insured. You can solve this at your closing by having the seller endorse you in his or her policy as an additional insured with a statement that you are managing the property. (See also the next section, on a management-purchase takeover.)

Sometimes a mortgage company will become difficult and insist that you file the forms verifying the assumption. This is like qualifying for a new loan. If you fail to do this, the company could foreclose. While personal liability might be a problem only for the former owner, if assumption is denied and you can't refinance, you could lose whatever you have put into the property. A way to avoid this problem is to make all payments with unsigned money orders, noting, of course, the proper account numbers for what is being paid. If this isn't successful, at worst, in court a judge might well throw out the foreclosure action if you can show you've been trying to pay but the mortgage company refused to accept the funds. If all else fails, you must hustle and refinance.

Do not be put off by the problems that go with buying a property subject to the existing mortgage. In fact, you should always make some effort to do so, particularly if the interest rate is favorable and you have a willing seller who will give you a second mortgage for near or close to the balance. Just be aware of the potential problems so you can be ready to solve them.

TAKEOVER WITH MANAGEMENT AGREEMENT AND ESCROWED DEED

Another variation in acquiring a loan is to have the owner sign over the deed, which you then hold in escrow, unrecorded, at your attorney's office. The seller further hires you by contract to manage the property, thereby giving you the direct authority to make the owner's mortgage payments. You have an option to take over formally at an agreed-upon price at some time in the future.

In this arrangement you are basically constructing an artificial sale: You will not be sending the seller any rent, but you are giving him or her monies up front to satisfy equity needs, if any, and making the mortgage payments as you unofficially take over the loan. To protect your equity under this arrangement, the seller gives you a so-called paper-only second mortgage for an approximation of your equity (deposit if any, repair cost, equity buildup, loan reduction, etc.) that becomes valid only in the extremely improbable circumstance of a sheriff's sale. That way, if some unknown judgment fell out of the sky on the seller (whose deed was not technically transferred), your equity would be protected.

Note that the sheriff's sale, in most states, is the worst-case scenario seizure of assets. In the case of the loan itself, you don't need to protect against a bank foreclosure as you are the one making the payments. Although these cautionary protections seem more complicated than a straight lease/option, they must be done when there is a longer-term arrangement where current and future equity must be protected, or when the capital cost of repairs needs to be protected.

USING A LAND TRUST

A trust is a property interest held by one person for the benefit of another. For the purpose of our discussion here, a land trust is an agreement between an originator, or grantor, of a trust, and a trustee, where there is a deed from the originator to the trustee. The deed held by the trust does not breach the "due on sale" clause of the mortgage. It is, therefore, a way of assuming a loan that is normally nonassumable. You do need to check in your state for the proper procedure to establish a land trust.

Taking title in a land trust (in most states) allows the trustee to obligate the trust to "assume and agree to pay," avoiding personal liability beyond current equity. It's great if you have a seller who will get a new mortgage and let you assume the loan. The legalities of land trusts vary from state to state, but basically you get the current owner to place the property into a trust (you may do the paperwork), whereupon at closing the owner transfers the trust over to you as the buyer. The property is yours and you start making payments. The bank is unaware of the change of ownership since the deed doesn't get recorded a second time as it stays in the same name as the trust. You do need to check the laws in your state, as each is different.

USING CREDIT CARDS TO HELP WITH DOWN PAYMENT

Some real estate investment gurus suggest using credit cards to pay for short-term real estate purchases. Is this a good idea? Should you do it? Most credit cards have $3,500 to $5,000 limits. If you need to raise a large sum, you will need several credit cards. But be careful that if you use credit cards to make a down payment, you use them only on a temporary basis.

As long as your income and credit card limits are sufficiently related, you should not be disadvantaged by extra cards. You can't regret having more than enough credit available, except when you apply for a conventional mortgage; then you do not want a pocket full of credit cards. Conventional lenders look at credit cards as potential (or actual) debts and consider them in calculating your debt-to-income ratio. Even a card with a zero balance will add about $20 per month to your debt payments as calculated by the lender. The lenders know you can use the card at any time and dramatically increase your debt.

While it's true that many lenders look askance at borrowers who have a dozen or more credit cards, neither the Federal Home Loan Mortgage Corporation (FHLMC, or Freddie Mac), FNMA (Fannie Mae), FHA, nor VA loan underwriting guidelines have any such provision for negatively affecting a borrower's debt-to-income ratio calculation. Someone with numerous credit cards and $50,000 available but zero balances on these cards should have no such problem qualifying for a mortgage.

WORD OF WARNING

Credit card balances do affect your credit and therefore the opportunity to qualify for a loan. If you must use credit cards, use them wisely. Credit card debt is the biggest cause of personal bankruptcies in the United States.

It's better to get cash from equity you have in property, either by increasing a mortgage or bringing about a credit line on your home equity. Often these are safe deals because at some time after closing, the same bank will offer a standard mortgage on the property that you just purchased for the amount you pulled out of your home equity line of credit. Once you fix up the property you will sell it and pay off these debts.

Alternatively, if you use credit cards for a down payment, you could pay down some of your credit card debt by having a bank take a mortgage on the property, then fix up the property to develop additional equity and pay off the whole amount of your credit cards and mortgage when you resell. Be careful, though, because doing a deal like this taps out your entire credit limit, and you should allow yourself some room just in case you need it.

TITLE I LOAN GUARANTEE

For housing rehabilitation, in addition to last chapter's FHA 203(k), borrowers may also consider HUD's Title I home improvement loan program.

This program works by HUD insuring local lenders against most losses on home improvement loans. The Federal Housing Administration (FHA) makes it easier for consumers to obtain affordable home improvement loans by insuring loans made by private lenders to improve properties that meet certain requirements. This is one of HUD's most frequently used loan insurance products.

The Title I program insures loans to finance the light or moderate rehabilitation of properties, as well as the construction of nonresidential buildings on the property. This program may be used to insure such loans for up to 20 years on either single- or multifamily properties. The maximum loan amount is $25,000 for improving a single-family home or for improving or building a nonresidential structure.

For improving a multifamily structure, the maximum loan amount is $12,000 per family unit, not to exceed a total of $60,000 for the structure. These are fixed rate loans for which lenders charge interest at market rates. The interest rates are not subsidized by HUD, although some communities participate in local housing rehabilitation programs that provide reduced-rate property improvement loans through Title I lenders.

The FHA insures private lenders against the risk of default for up to 90% of any single loan, with maximum insurance coverage limited to 10% of the total amount lent. The annual premium for this insurance is 50 cents per $100 of the amount advanced; although this fee may be charged to the borrower separately, it is usually covered by an additional 0.5% interest charge.

Only lenders approved by HUD specifically for this program can make loans covered by Title I insurance. While most lenders and contractors use this program responsibly, HUD urges consumers to be cautious in choosing and supervising home repair contractors conducting Title I repair/renovation work. HUD has uncovered some instances of unscrupulous contractors and shoddy work; therefore, HUD encourages homeowners to work directly with their lender in selecting a home repair contractor in order to prevent inflated estimates.

Eligible borrowers include the owner of the property to be improved, the person leasing the property (provided that the lease will extend at least six months beyond the date when the loan must be repaid), or someone purchasing the property under a land installment contract.

Title I loans may be used to finance permanent property improvements that protect or improve the basic livability or utility of the property, including manufactured homes, single-family and multifamily homes, and nonresidential structures.

Contact your local lender and FHA's home improvement insurance branch for information about how to obtain Title I funding.

QUESTIONS AND ANSWERS ON FINANCING

The following information refers to both conventional and seller financing.

Where do you find nonconforming lenders who don't require top credit?
Start looking in the Yellow Pages under Lenders and/or Finance
Companies. Call other investors and knowledgeable agents to see
who offers the right program. Also check with your state's banking
division and see if it will send you a list of all mortgage lenders
statewide.

What is nonrecourse financing?
Nonrecourse financing means the lender cannot come after you for
any loss in the loan amount. Its only redress is against the property.
This would come into play on a loan you took subject to an existing
mortgage.

What part of a transaction is actually the mortgage?
Two documents make up a real estate mortgage: One is the proof of
debt called the promissory note, which comprises the details of the
agreement such as the terms of repayment and the default conditions; the other, depending on your state, is the mortgage or deed of
trust recorded at the county courthouse or Registry of Deeds, which
binds the debt to the property. This mortgage specifies the formal
boundaries of the land.

What does assuming a mortgage mean?
The lender allows you to assume legal responsibility for the seller's
loan, relieving the seller from further obligation.

What is buying "subject to"?
The seller deeds you the property "subject to the existing mortgage."
You now own a property with a mortgage that has someone else's
name against it.

*What happens if you take over a property via a "subject to" deed that has a
mortgage with a "due on sale" clause in it?*
A "due on sale" clause means that the loan is officially nonassumable. If you take over and the lender calls in the loan, you may have
to refinance or sell the property in a relatively short amount of time.
This is particularly true if the lender is a private individual. Usually a
conventional lender does not monitor deed transfers and therefore
does not know when one is transferred. The lender is not likely to
catch up with the problem before you've got the work done and, we
hope, found a buyer. Although you put the existing mortgage in

jeopardy of being called in since ownership of the mortgaged property has transferred, even a lender who does find out may not call in the note if it's being paid on time and the interest rate is high enough.

How else might you avoid the lender calling in the loan because of a "due on sale" clause?
If you could hold the deed in escrow, unrecorded, while continuing to make the seller's payments, the lender is not likely to know or call in the loan. If you go to the lender and explain the circumstances, the lender is likely to consent to the takeover due to its short-term nature and the fact that the property is being upgraded.

What about insurance?
If you have not told the lender about taking over the existing mortgage and the lender gets a notice of insurance being in someone's name other than that of the person who originally got the financing, it could cause a "due on sale" problem. If you keep up the insurance payments, the lender is not likely to receive such notice.

A FINAL NOTE

This chapter has explored various ways—seller financing, mortgage assumption, contractual takeovers, credit cards, Title I—to finance or control a property. Perhaps the first choice in financing any investment purchase, certainly in the case of fixer-uppers as well as investment property, is to have the seller finance the purchase.

"Assuming" or taking over the property "subject to" the existing financing were considered. Even though the current lender may have a "due on sale" clause in the seller's mortgage contract, the lender is likely to let you proceed, primarily because of the short-term nature of the agreement. Perhaps the biggest obstacle to taking over financing is that there must be some financing to take over.

Another alternative is to arrange to take over the property on a temporary basis—at least until the work is completed—through a management agreement or some form of contract that gives you legal control. In this way, you direct the fixing-up work and final ownership settlement of the property without having to take title; a lease/option could also be used to accomplish this task.

Land trusts were explained. Also examined were the use of credit cards to fund the down payment or rehabilitation work on a property and the inherent dangers in doing so. Finally, basic information on the FHA/HUD Title I property rehabilitation program was offered.

The next chapter discusses lease/options, also called rent-to-own.

11

Lease/Options I: Arranging Rent-to-Own with Tenant-Buyers

There is one more popular short-term strategy to explain before we leave the buy-and-sell techniques and go on to buy-and-hold techniques.

In this chapter we'll show you how to take control of a property with little or no cash by leasing with an option to buy. It's called the lease/option, or "rent-to-own," and it's a way to produce positive cash flow while waiting for an additional amount at closing. You can do the lease/option without having to become a real estate expert or look at hundreds of houses.

A lease/option allows you to lease a property on which you have an option and sublease and/or sell it to a tenant-buyer. It is a process where you have a rental agreement or lease with a seller that includes an option contract allowing a purchase on or before a future date at a prenegotiated price. You, in turn, find a tenant who occupies the property for a monthly rental and agrees to make the actual purchase at some coming time to which you both agree. The tenant/buyer may have a percentage of the rent credited to the down payment or taken off the purchase price.

The lease part of the lease/option means that under the arrangement you will rent the property monthly while rerenting or subleasing it to another person who will actually live in it with part of the rent going toward the purchase price. The option part of the lease/option is a right to purchase or assign that right to another. In most cases this will be the tenant-buyer with whom you have negotiated a lease/purchase agreement that will close prior to the expiration of your option. This book uses the convention of the term "lease/option" when referring to the deal you make with the seller, and "lease/purchase" for your arrangement with the tenant-buyer.

The lease/option has everything you need to make prudent and profitable investments in real estate. Often, with very small down payments (1% to 2%), you can control properties that normally require a substantial down payment, and you don't even have to visit a lender and get a mortgage. The lease/option permits you to control a property and obtain strong cash flow and high profits with minimal risk. Lease/option can be the best way to create quick cash flow for either beginning or experienced investors.

In a lease/option you search for property you can lease under favorable terms, which in turn allows you to sublease the premises for a higher price. In effect, you become sandwiched between the current owner and a tenant-buyer. You can do this with minimal management or maintenance problems. A lease/option involves negotiating a long-term commitment for a low monthly rental amount that allows you to sublease to another and obtains for you or your tenant the right to purchase at any time. Generally, the longer the term of the underlying lease, the more valuable your position.

The main benefit of this method is an immediate cash flow from rents while you wait for a substantial gain at the time of sale. It is essentially a low-cost financing tool for controlling property without actual ownership—without the headaches associated with maintenance, management, or expenses. You control a sort of de facto ownership while waiting for your profit to develop—all with limited risk.

Through a lease/option you could control six or a dozen properties with the same amount of money you would need for a down payment on one. Now, that's leverage. You can even help finance the new buyer, thus generating more profit. It's also an area where there is little competition even though it's considered by some to be one of the best ways for both the beginner and the seasoned investor to be involved in real estate. Lease/option is a protected way to do real estate business. You don't need mortgage financing; you don't pay operating costs such as taxes, utilities, or maintenance. You have almost the same authority as does the owner. You can sublease, sell, or assign the arrangement, all without transferring ownership. A lease/option, then, allows you to profit in several ways: the difference between what you pay the owner and what you receive from the tenant-buyer; the difference between the agreed-upon price stated in your option and the price at which you are selling it to the tenant-buyer; the amount by which you might profit by assigning the agreement to another; and the profit in interest if you give financing help to the new buyer. Generating high profits with minimal risk is a win–win concept for all the parties involved.

BE A MATCHMAKER

When you use the rent-to-own strategy you match a motivated seller whose goal is to get rid of a piece of property and a tenant-buyer who sincerely wants to own his or her own home but for varied reasons can't qualify to buy a home the conventional way. And in making this match, you will profit.

It's a little like acting as a real estate broker, and there's less competition. And you don't need a license as long as you do it the way outlined in this chapter. In fact, you're often dealing with properties that have already been offered for sale through traditional channels and failed to bring about a sale. Now all the sales agents look at the house as a dog. There can be a similar bias against the potential tenant-buyer. He or she may have suffered through bankruptcy, after which it takes up to seven years to clear one's credit. But often these are people with good jobs who can pay a fair rent and within a few years qualify for a new loan.

Let's look again at our seller. Tommy Typical, like many home sellers, must move. His job has transferred him to a new city, so he has to sell, and the sooner the better. Our motivated seller has already tried to sell his house through local sales agents, who failed. Unfortunately, he's got to start work 1,500 miles away in two weeks. He could give his house away at a substantially discounted price, but he's not quite willing to do that. He could rent out the property, but he knows it's hard being a landlord for a single-family house at a great distance. He would have to hire a property manager, who would incur extra fees.

Here's where you come in. You agree to lease Tommy's house for five years while further agreeing to buy the house at a set price at any time during those five years. Tommy's payments on the house are $1,250 a month including principal, interest, taxes, and insurance. You will pay Tommy this amount on a monthly basis until such time as you arrange for its purchase.

After negotiating with Tommy on the price, you and he settle for $130,000. Although this is somewhat less than he was asking, it is more than he would get in a distressed sale. Using the rent-to-own strategy allows you to pay fair value for a property and still make a profit. Certainly, any amount less than current value will bring you greater profits.

Now what else does it take to gain the seller's approval? Often, but not always, there is no option consideration put down. The logic of this is that since you are taking out a long-term lease on the property, the option is a secondary provision, and because of the lease a compelling need for money down doesn't exist. Certainly, in your negotiations with the owner you don't discuss any amount down, unless it's mentioned by the seller first. Then, if needed, you can use the rationale that you have already made a major commitment yourself by entering into a long-term lease and feel constrained to avoid an additional financial commitment.

However, sometimes in order to make the deal you may need to put a modest amount down. And, it's true that you may be more successful at negotiating a lower price on the property as well as the monthly rental if you put some money up front with the seller. Perhaps Tommy Typical (or his attorney) insists on at least some money down. Let's say you both agree to $2,500 down—$1,000 now and the other $1,500 when the actual occupancy or lease starts, usually within 30 to 60 days. Note that as in most real estate deals some money is put down, but most of that amount doesn't need to come from your own pocket!

You probably can guess the next step. You go out and hustle up a tenant-buyer. This might be someone you already have a lead on in your prospect folder or someone who might come to you through a classified advertisement. It's this tenant-buyer who is going to rent as well as have an option on the house from you. He or she will be the one who puts up the down payment. In this case, you would ask for the $2,500 (or more if possible) as a deposit on the tenant-buyer's deal with you.

To summarize what's going on here: You have agreed to lease the house from Tommy Typical for five years with an option to buy at any time for a set amount of $130,000. You bind this agreement with a deposit of $2,500 that will be applied to the purchase price. Note that your lease with Tommy must stipulate that you personally will not necessarily be the actual tenant but that you will be responsible for the rent. You in turn rerent the house to an actual tenant who will take residence and agree to buy the property for a set amount at some time during the owner's agreement with you. This tenant-buyer puts down a deposit that is equal to or more than that which you had to put down with the owner. For a rent-to-own it is always a good idea to get a deposit equal to several months' rent or 3% to 5% of the projected selling price to help ensure the tenant's purchase.

Now, where do you profit? First, it should be understood that you are optioning a house at some advantageous discount to market value due to your making a special deal to relieve the seller of much of his responsibility for a difficult-to-sell house. Plus, since your actual sale with the tenant-buyer may not take place for several years, your price to him or her does not need to be discounted. A similar rationale goes for monthly rent. Since you are making a long-term commitment, you should logically get a better deal on monthly rent than one would if renting for only a year. Your rental price to the tenant-buyer, however, although favorable, reflects the market rental price more closely. Your tenant-buyer, then, will pay you more each month in rent than the amount you've agreed to pay in rent to the seller.

Let's look at how these figures might work out:

Current owner receives from you:
Monthly rental: $ 1,250
Buy price on option: $130,000

You receive from tenant-buyer:
Monthly rental: $ 1,450
Buy price on option: $145,000

Your profit on rents is $200 per month, or $2,400 per year.
Your profit on future sale is $15,000.

If your tenant-buyer exercises his or her option at the end of the third year, you would have earned three times $2,400, or $7,200 on rental income, and the difference between selling prices—the $145,000 you receive from the tenant-buyer minus the $130,000 you pay the seller—$15,000.

In other words, for no investment you gain an extraordinary $22,200 in three years' time!

But this story is not just about you. The seller, Tommy Typical, improved his position by your arranging a much fairer price for his property than he would have gotten in a forced sale. He also received a continuing stream of payments that matched his obligations on the property. The tenant-buyer also gained by securing a fair rent and guaranteed price on a property that he or she controlled and could take over at a definite time in the future after saving up the necessary amount of down payment and/or repairing his or her credit.

Note that no mention of a rent credit for the tenant-buyer was used in this example. However, it could be included if negotiated.

Also note that tenants who plan on becoming owners tend to take much better care of property than regular month-to-month renters. Your maintenance job is notably reduced.

OWNER'S REASONS TO PARTICIPATE IN LEASE/OPTION ARE VARIED

You might ask yourself why a seller would agree to a lease/option with you when he or she could do essentially the same deal directly with a tenant. The intermediary isn't always necessary. It depends on your local market as well as the ability of sellers to manage a tenant, which isn't easy if the owner is leaving the area—you're there and he or she may not be.

Sellers' reasons for participating in a lease/option are varied: Perhaps he or she wants to delay any sale for tax reasons, wants to avoid a sales commission or avoid needed repairs, doesn't need to discount the price in lease/option as much as if selling as fixer-upper, has offered the property for sale but it remains unsold, asked too much money initially, or needs to move but wants to lease to one responsible person rather than a succession of tenants. These are just some of the reasons someone might have to agree to a lease/option.

MAKE THE LEASE/OPTION APPEAL TO THE SELLER

Let's say you are negotiating with a seller on several single-family houses she has rented out for a number of years but is now considering selling. She will consider a lease/option with the first and last month's rent plus a security deposit. As this is almost what you will be getting from a prospective buyer, what can you do to get the seller to take less? The seller is used to renting and those are her normal terms. One way to make this more appealing is to offer several extra months in rent. This may satisfy the seller's need for cash and allow you to reimburse yourself when your tenant-buyer starts paying rent. Note that your lease/option agreement should be contingent on your finding a subtenant. And when you do, the subtenant will be paying the first month's rent and security deposit along with an option consideration or down payment on the agreement.

Sometimes sellers balk at having someone sublease their property. They are afraid that someone they don't know will cause damage. Even though you are responsible, it appears to them that they just have less control of who lives there. One way to approach their concern is to explain to them that you will screen any potential tenants carefully, and that these tenants are going to be buying as soon as they can. If the owner cannot accept this, it may be a warning sign to you that the owner is not motivated enough to go through with the deal.

MAKING A LEASE/OPTION OFFER

Here are two letters to make an offer on a lease/option deal. The letter to the seller even throws in a gratuity of paying maintenance to help grease the deal. That's being creative.

You do have some latitude in negotiations to be more favorable to the tenant in such areas as price and rent. Certainly your object is to have this tenant buy eventually, but if he does not exercise the option, he loses the $4,000 option consideration and all rent credits. At the beginning of year two, you can start over by either renewing with the same tenant or getting a new tenant while charging an additional $4,000 in option consideration.

Your profit: Your tenant pays you the $4,000, $1,500 of which you give to the owner as prepaid rent and option consideration. You collect and keep the first two months' rent ($900 each month) and keep the difference in rent paid by your tenant to you and rent you pay to the owner of $300 per month on the next 10 months' rent ($3,000). You've made a total profit of $7,300 in the first 12 months. If your tenant exercises the option, he pays $115,000 minus the $4,000 option money and $1,800 in rent credits ($115,000 – $5,800 = $109,200). You pay the owner his $90,000 and you keep $19,200.

Dear Mr. Owner,

My name is Sam Suchandsuch and I live in the town of Whereisit. I am interested in the property at 123 Main Street and would like to ask you to consider accepting a four-year lease and option with the right to assign and renew for four more years. I would then pay you $600 per month with no rent credit. The purchase price would be set at $90,000. You would retain all tax and depreciation benefits. Furthermore, I would be responsible for the first $100 per month on general repairs and maintenance. Any required replacement or failure of systems other than normal wear and tear would remain your responsibility until final closing. I would give you $1,500 down as follows: the first two months of prepaid rent and $300 as option consideration. I'll give you the $300 option consideration and sign a contract immediately. You'll receive the balance within 30 days before I take possession.

Sincerely yours,

Sam Suchandsuch

Dear Mr. Tenant-Buyer,

In regard to the 123 Main Street property, if you will take a 12-month lease with option to buy with $4,000 down as option consideration, then I will rent it to you for $900 per month with $150 monthly rent credit toward the purchase price of $115,000. You would also be responsible for the first $200 in monthly maintenance and repairs. When you close at the end of the year you will have in property equity $4,000 plus $1,800 ($150 × 12), which equals $5,800.

Sincerely yours,

Sam Suchandsuch

You've made $7,300 plus $19,200, which equals $26,500 in total profit. If none of your tenants exercise their options, you could then renew a new four-year lease with the owner, or you could buy the property yourself and keep renting and optioning out. Note that closing costs are not completed in this example. They should be minimal as no agent was used in the transaction.

DOING THE TYPICAL LEASE/OPTION DEAL

Here's how a typical lease/option deal works: You begin your search through the local classified ads and answer some of those that advertise single-family homes for sale. You find an owner who has had her property for sale for over a year and would consider renting with an option to buy. Her house is a single-family, three-bedroom, one-and-a-half-bath in a neighborhood where most of the properties are owner-occupied. The property had had a rental tenant at $650 per month for six months and is now vacant. The owner is motivated but not despairing—she simply wants to get her money out as soon as possible.

You check on the property's value as compared to other, similar properties and note what they have sold for. You find that the average comparable selling price is approximately $80,000 and that your seller initially overpriced her property at $110,000 and lost prospects who were turned away by the high price. What she is willing to take now is the much more reasonable $85,000.

You start by offering her a monthly rent of $525 a month with a rent credit per month of $150 and a four-year option at $70,000. She counters with $78,000, agrees to the monthly rent with a rent credit of $100, but insists the option last only two years. If she will accept $75,000, you will agree to the shorter time period. You do not mention offering any consideration for the option, and she does not ask for one. You both agree to the following:

Term:	Two years
Price:	$75,000
Rent:	$525 per month
Security deposit:	$525
Rent credit:	$100 per month
Option consideration:	None

The original asking price was $110,000, but was dropped to $85,000 with a negotiated price at $75,000. The property is in reasonably good condition and nothing major needs to be done for a renter. However, some cleanup and cosmetic sprucing up costs $500.

You agree to take over at the beginning of the next month, which is in three weeks. You immediately contact several of the rent-to-own prospects you have found from running your classified ads. A young couple who are just starting out and building up their down payment for a future home but who have minor credit problems decide they want the house if they can work out a deal where they could eventually own it. They both have jobs and figure they would, with some help from their families, have enough for a down payment by the end of next year.

Now, you say to yourself, isn't that just what lease/option is all about? You make the deal with them for the full two years of time. They put down $2,500 they have saved as a deposit to be credited to their purchase price of $83,000. You agree to a monthly rent of $675 with a credit of $200 per month toward the $83,000.

Your profit on the deal is as follows:

Option consideration from the buyer-tenant:	$2,500
Your option consideration to current owner:	–$0
Spruce-up costs:	–$500
Immediate profit:	$2,000
Rent difference ($675 – $525 = $150 × 24 months):	$3,600
Price difference ($83,000 – $75,000):	$8,000
Rent credit difference ($200 – $100 = $100 × 24 months):	–$2,400
Gross profit over two years:	$11,200

One of your breaks on this deal is that you did not have to put up any consideration for the option with the owner. This is often avoided as the owner is so relieved—read "motivated"—that you are taking over responsibility for the property that he or she doesn't think or care to ask.

This is a win–win deal for both you and the ultimate buyer. The tenant-buyer gets to commit on a house at a fair price in today's market—but doesn't have to pay for it until two years from now. Hence, the buyer gains price appreciation over that time, and also gets a buildup of rent credit over the two-year period of $4,800 that is added to the deposit. You've made a small investment of sprucing-up costs and taken a minimal risk for an ample gain. You've controlled a property without taking title; at the same time you used leverage by making a small amount of money go a long way. Imagine doing a dozen of these deals a year. No wonder investors like to lease/option!

CASE STUDY #1: Using Prepaid Rent as Option Consideration

First example: The investor negotiates with the owner a four-year lease with an option to purchase a midsize, four-bedroom, single-family home with two full baths. The rent is $800 per month and the agreed-upon price for the property is $105,000. The owner will keep up the maintenance on the property and pay the taxes and insurance.

A difficulty is that the owner wants $2,500 cash up front for the option. This along with the first month's rent and an equivalent security deposit come to the healthy sum of $4,100. A resolution is reached by the investor and the seller to change the amount of the initial payment of the option to $1,600 plus prepayment of three months' rent (3 × $800 = $2,400). The investor will recoup $450 of his option over the next three months by keeping the rent ($950 per month) to be paid by the tenant, as the investor will not owe additional rent to the seller until the fourth month.

Within two weeks the investor has a tenant-buyer move in with a nonrefundable $2,800 down and a firm agreement to rent until purchase. The tenant-buyer pays $950 per month with $200 each month going toward the purchase price of $115,000.

To summarize:

Option amount:	$1,600
Positive monthly cash flow:	$150
Annual cash flow:	$1,800
Nonrefundable deposit from tenant-buyer:	$2,800
First-year gross proceeds:	$4,600

If the sale is completed by the tenant-buyer at the end of the first year, the investor will receive an additional $4,800, which is the difference between the two purchase prices or $10,000 ($115,000 − $105,000 = $10,000), $2,800 of which has already been paid minus a rent credit of $2,400 ($200 × 12). Should the tenant-buyer back out of the deal, he or she will forfeit the $2,800 and the investor can rent out the property to another party under the same conditions.

CASE STUDY #2: Up-Front Repair Expenses

Second example: An owner would consider a five-year lease and option on a three-bedroom, one-and-a-half-bath, single-family house in a favored neighborhood. The owner is not asking for money for the option or a security deposit. The rent will be $550 per month.

The only problem is that the inside needs some cosmetic fixing up that will cost about $2,500. The seller realizes she should spend this money if she expects to sell for retail value, and if she does not, she must take less. She and the investor settle for $87,000, with which the investor is quite comfortable. Once the minor repairs are done, the house is quickly leased out to a tenant-buyer for $800 per month and an agreement to close within two years at $95,000.

The investor's financial picture the first year is the initial expenditure of $2,500 for repairs, which is balanced by the extra $250 per month in profit, or $3,000—a $500 gross profit the first year. The second year brings in the full $3,000 difference in rents. Unfortunately—or fortunately, depending on how you might want to look at it—at the end of the second year the tenant-buyer is unable to close because his job takes him to another area. The investor then leases with an option again for another $100 per month in rent and another $3,000 added onto the purchase price—a bit of extra profit.

YOUR FIRST LEASE/OPTION DEAL

You're thinking of using a lease/option but still have a few questions. You understand that you negotiate the price on the house at a discount from market value and that you seek a time period of not less than three years. You know that you do this with as little money down, as low a rent as possible, and with as much of this rent being credited to the purchase as possible.

Now let's say you've found a single-family house in a good neighborhood with three bedrooms and two baths, and you have found by investigating recent comparable sales that it should sell for $105,000. The seller's asking price is $115,000. The seller has agreed to rent the property with an option to buy for $1,000 (for the option) and $750 per month rent with anything over that credited to the purchase price. Current rents for similar houses run at approximately $800 to $850 per month.

You're concerned about the risks. You wonder if you will lose your deposit and rent credit if you choose not to purchase. Can the owner-seller come after you for additional money?

If you have a willing seller, tie up the property with $100 and an agreement to pay an additional amount when you place a tenant-buyer in the property. Perhaps the seller is willing to take less in rent. If $115,000 is the asking price and you've determined the fair market value is $105,000, perhaps you can get a discount from the seller's price.

The key is the seller's motivation—transfer, divorce, and so on. If the house must be sold, then you have a chance. A discounted price may be your margin of profit when you retail the property to a tenant-buyer. Be up-front with the seller about the need for the future buyer to go in at a fair price. After all, the seller has had the property on the market for a while and it did not sell. It needs time and a better price.

These are ideas; find out what motivates your seller and what his or her needs are. Give the seller a way to save face when having to take a lower price—most sellers will come down when reminded they don't have to pay an agent, for example. If you can't get the seller to come down as much as you would like, extend the time on the option. Gain six or eight years so you can bring the house into a new and probably higher price range.

MAKING SURE YOU'VE GOT A GREAT DEAL

One morning, before you've had your first cup of coffee, you find a seller advertising in the newspaper who will let you take over with a lease/option. His three-bedroom, two-bath single-family house is appraised at $115,000 and is in a predominantly owner-occupied neighborhood. He will rent at market value for $800 per month. He will lease/option for $3,000 down and $1,000 per month for a year while crediting the whole amount to the purchase price. You're excited. Within a year you could own the property while having $15,000 credited to the price. You think it's too good to be true. You think you've got a great deal cooking. In spite of your excitement, here are some rules to consider:

- Don't pay retail. You're not in this business to pay a retail price on any property. Any definition of property value includes a real estate commission, which adds 6% to 7% (or more) to the price. Always think wholesale, which would take an additional 10% to 20% off the commissionless fair value as an initial offer, assuming no repairs are needed. Furthermore, your wholesale margin will allow you to deal with another investor if you choose. For you to secure eager tenant-buyers you've got to be able to offer the house to them at fair value or less.

- Always carry out a market analysis to establish fair value. Just as with any other technique in real estate, lease/options also require you to know your local values well.

- Offer rent credits to your tenant-buyer unless he or she is already buying at a reduced price. Generally, rent credits are a marketing device to make properties look more attractive to retail buyers. They becomes pointless when based on an inflated asking price. You've got to be fair with your prospective tenant-buyer, whose rent credit has value only if he or she is not overpaying.

- With the seller, negotiate a discount from market rent. For a lease/option deal the market rent should be discounted 25% or more—a $1,000 monthly should become no more than $750 to the lease/option investor. As with price, you've got to be able to offer your tenant-buyer a good deal on rent price.

- You should avoid paying any rental deposit more than the first month's rent to get the deal going.

- Only pay a fee for the option itself if the seller insists. Attempt to limit that fee to no more than a month's rent. Negotiate that any option consideration you agree to put up will be in the form of prepaid rents; $100 for each year makes sense. Furthermore, make sure that what fee you do pay is credited toward the purchase price when you, or your assignees, do close. As an investor you shouldn't have to take money out of your pocket to bring about a lease/option. The down payment, or option consideration to the owner, should come from the new tenant-buyer's payment.

- Make sure your contract with the seller allows you to sublease to another without having to ask for the seller's approval.

- Word the contract with the seller so as not to consummate the deal until you have found a suitable tenant.

- Forget about deals where you can't negotiate for an agreement that will extend beyond one year. An exception to this would be if you had a tenant ready to occupy and buy within the year. He or she would have to sign a purchase-and-sales agreement committing the tenant-buyer firmly to the purchase. Normally you want more time to take advantage of price appreciation on the property as well as the rent. Plus, you may need more time to find the right buyer. This is particularly true for properties that have been for sale before and not sold, or for those that need some repairs. Four to six years on a lease/option gives you time to maneuver for best profit. In negotiating with the owner, perhaps you could ask for eight years and get four.

- Arrange for the right to renew the time period of the option. This will allow you to extend the time to find a buyer before you need to exercise the option. Additional monetary consideration could be given for this right.

- Avoid lease/options on a property that needs repairs unless the owner will move forward to fix what's needed. Have a professional property inspection.

- As a general rule, lease/option only single-family houses. Multifamily units ordinarily require too much regular maintenance and it's extremely complex to get them moved on to a new buyer unless you are the owner. If sellers are motivated, they will finance your purchase now. If they are not motivated, you have no reason to deal with them until they are. Avoid condos, too, because their group association and maintenance obligations, as well as financing constraints, make for problematic lease/option deals.

- Always have a clause in your lease/option contract with the owner-seller that allows you the right to assign your position. This lets you make a profit by selling the deal to another investor or use it for your tenant-buyer to close.

- Check that there are no liens or other judgments against the property. Make sure that the contract with the seller guarantees that the mortgage payment will be paid and that there is a provision for you to make payment, credited from the seller's lease money if you so choose, directly to the bank.

- Have separate agreements with the seller-owner and the tenant-buyer. Depending on your attorney's advice, you may want two agreements with your tenant: one to rent, and the other to option.

So now that you've had a chance to size up how to make a profit in this business, how does the deal in question look? Maybe if you paid only $90,000 instead of $115,000, $600 for the rent instead of $1,000, and two months' prepaid rent as option consideration instead of $3,000 down, and had four years on the deal instead of one—the key in this example is to start thinking wholesale, the way an investor thinks, not retail. And, yes, what the seller wants here is too good to be true.

FIVE WAYS TO FIND TENANT-BUYERS

Most people want to become homeowners. The lease/purchase allows more people to have an opportunity to buy—to stop renting and own a home of their own. As an investor you are an intermediary between an owner you have convinced to lease out and sell, and the final homeowner who is looking to be part of the American Dream.

Here are five ways to find tenants for the rent-to-own properties under your control:

1. *Use classified advertising in the local newspaper.* Run either an ad on a specific property or a general ad on letting potential tenant-buyers know that you offer lease/purchase arrangements. Your ad can have details on rent and location, size and style, bedrooms and baths.

2. *Send out brochures or preprinted letters.* Use a brochure or a letter stating your intentions and describing how renting in a rent-to-own program might benefit a potential homeowner who may not have saved up enough down payment or needs some extra time to build up credit. You can distribute the brochure and letter to anyone you wish to let know of your service. Distributing them to local apartment buildings is a good place to start.

3. *Work with mortgage bankers and brokers.* Let those in your financial community—like mortgage officers at both banks and mortgage companies—know that you offer rent-to-own

homes. These people will often refer prospects to you, as the lease/purchase you offer is a way for them to give temporary aid to those who may not be ready to meet the full qualifications of purchasing and only need time until they do.

4. *Get support from real estate agents and brokers.* Many agents know of potential customers who do not qualify for conventional financing and/or may need time to save down payment funds. You may not want to pay a full commission, but it's worth a generous referral fee.

5. *Post signs in noticeable places.* Any specific property you control should have a rent-to-own sign in the front yard. Depending on your volume of business, you may wish to place signs at strategic locations within your community to encourage prospects.

Be dependable and consistent in your approach and it will pay off.

USE A LEASE/OPTION TO
TAKE A HOUSE WITH LITTLE EQUITY

Once in a while you run across a good takeover candidate that has little equity. The seller is willing to bail out by just letting you take over the mortgage. However, once you have investigated the value by a thorough comparable search, you may find that its value is not much more than the mortgage balance.

What do you do in a case like this? Many investors would walk away. But before you do, probe further. Is the house located in a good neighborhood? Are the surrounding houses appreciating? Are the repairs required minimal? If the answers are positive, consider taking over on a lease/option basis. This doesn't commit you to following through unless in a year or two the value has gone up a sufficient amount.

As the current owner was willing to let you take over the payments, you could still do so. Have the deed held in escrow with a firm agreement with the owner that lets you rent out now and take over at some time in the future at the then-current mortgage balance. This allows you to put a tenant-buyer in place and have a possible deal for the future.

A FINAL NOTE: KEEP A WORKING
RELATIONSHIP WITH YOUR AGENT

A lease/option doesn't give a real estate agent (if involved) any money until you close on your option. That could be several years from now. However, the seller could give the agent a sum such as $500 to $1,000 now against the full commission to be paid when the title is actually changed. It is in your interest to keep the agent happy, because you want to work with that agent in the future.

The next chapter presents more ideas on using the lease/option or rent-to-own strategy.

12

Lease/Options II: Arranging Contracts and Closings with Tenant-Buyers

This chapter discusses what should be in rent-to-own contracts with the owner and the buyer, how to proceed to a closing and ensure that the process runs smoothly, and how to apply advanced techniques for using lease/options to sell fixer-uppers.

STRUCTURING A SAFE LEASE/OPTION

The Property

You've been negotiating with an out-of-state owner on a possible lease/option. The single-family house is a 10-year-old three-bedroom, two-bath ranch that is not in need of repairs. It is vacant now, but the last tenant was paying $700 per month in rent. The seller had been asking $175,000 through a local sales agent. The house had been shown only five times, and now the time has expired for the listing. The owner has been trying to rent it himself by an advertisement in the local newspaper to which you responded. The assessed value is $150,000. Property taxes and insurance are approximately $200 per month.

The Deal

You start by structuring a deal with a hypothetical tenant-buyer. You want to know what to offer the seller, so you work backward by putting the customer first. If you rent it to someone who has committed to buy, you want to make the rent attractive. You surmise that what you'd like to offer would be $600 per month in rent with a $100 monthly rent credit that would be recovered by the tenant at the time of his or her purchase.

You find some comparable property that has sold within the past year. Each property had different-sized parcels of land but you find out from several sales agents the values each property would have sold for if on the same-sized parcel. Your estimate of value is $145,000. This amount is not far below the assessor's valuation for tax purposes.

Once you have discovered what would be attractive to a tenant-buyer and have valued the actual property, you can structure an offer to the owner. You decide your goal is $12,000 in profit on the sale. You will also attempt to get a $150 price differential each month between what the tenant-buyer pays and what you must pay the owner. Therefore, you offer the seller $125,000 based on a four-year option, guaranteeing the seller $450 monthly rent over that length of time or until the option is exercised.

Conclusion

Your seller balks and complains that this is less money in rent than he has been getting and the price is below what he was considering. You counter by explaining that the lease is for a longer time and concludes with an eventual sale. The seller concedes that if you will pay $500 per month and boost the price you offered by $5,000 to $130,000 he will agree. You, in turn, also agree as the arrangement gives you some profit on a monthly basis, as well as $15,000 in profit on the sale. This is more than your original profit projection of $12,000, although you will credit the tenant-buyer $100 per month at the eventual sale.

ADVANCED TECHNIQUES—
USE LEASE/PURCHASE/OPTION
TO SELL FIXER-UPPERS FOR BEST PRICE

One way to get a bigger markup is to pay cash in order to buy as cheaply as possible, fix up the house as needed, then sell to a tenant-

CASE STUDY: Lease/Option Closing

To encourage you to enhance your deals, we'll look at an exchange where you devise secondary financing from the seller that you will pass on to your tenant-buyer. You start by negotiating a lease/option with a seller. Then you find a tenant who gives you an option deposit and agrees to buy within the year. In your deal, the seller offers secondary financing that you can assign to the buyer.

The facts:

- You agree to pay the seller $126,000.
- Seller agrees to take back a $10,000 second mortgage that you can assign.
- Your tenant-buyer agrees to pay you $138,000.
- Tenant-buyer will use the $10,000 second mortgage from seller as part of down payment, with the balance in cash and conventional lender financing.
- Tenant-buyer has paid you $2,500 in option consideration, which will go toward purchase price.
- Tenant-buyer has earned $150 rent credit for 12 months, or $1,800.

At closing, the paperwork might look something like this:

First, the seller signs a deed to you, which is temporarily held in escrow by closing agent.

Second, you sign a deed to buyer, which is also held in escrow.

Third, the buyer's lender underwrites a check to closing agent for $116,000—your price to seller of $126,000 minus $10,000 second mortgage amount that will be passed on to tenant-buyer.

Fourth, tenant-buyer executes first mortgage with lender (80% of $138,000 purchase price, or $110,400).

Fifth, tenant-buyer gives to escrow holder balance of down payment of $23,300 (20% of purchase price, or $27,600, minus $2,500 option consideration and $1,800 rent credit).

Sixth, tenant-buyer executes second mortgage of $10,000, or is assigned second mortgage from you that comes from original seller.

CASE STUDY: Lease/Option Closing *(Continued)*

Seventh, escrow agent passes lender's check of $116,000 to seller.

Eighth, escrow agent gives you a check for the balance of proceeds from tenant-buyer of $7,700 (you've already received $2,500 option consideration and $1,800 rent credit).

Ninth, escrow agent passes title to tenant-buyer and records the two deeds and the first and second mortgage documents.

Note that some of these steps may be combined if the title passes directly to the tenant-buyer, or expanded if the second mortgage first goes to you before being reassigned. An experienced real estate attorney can make the paperwork flow.

buyer via a lease/purchase with a hefty consideration on an option limited to a one-year term. The profits are greater because by not requiring seller financing you've driven down the price considerably. This approach also generates more profit than wholesaling, where you wouldn't take title and would therefore gain only a small return. You may need to do some work if the house needs fixing up, but it's one of the best opportunities for profit. Once you build up a bit of cash it's an excellent method to follow.

In order to maximize your potential, you need to be adept at using several of the techniques described in this book. Someone with the right approach can turn any real estate problem into a money-making opportunity. Some of your first opportunities may be low-to-midrange fixer-uppers. They can take the most time, but until you get a reputation for handling real estate deals you may not have townfuls of property thrown at you. Once you have a pipeline of property opportunities, you can resort to wholesaling extensively for smaller profits but less of your time spent.

Perhaps the best key to using any of these techniques is to know the value of what you're acquiring and if it's a fixer-upper, what it will be worth once you've fixed it up. A word of warning: It's a lot easier to negotiate a discount than it is to sell it for more than it's worth. And there's no technique that will show you how to get more than market value. If it happens, it's a fluke. And even if you could work some miracle (from your point of view) and get some poor sap to agree to pay more than a house is worth, you're in trouble unless the entire price is paid in cash, because if it needs financing the deal is going to fall apart at the bank when the house is appraised. The same is true in a lease/option, where the overpaying tenant-buyer will wake up before it's takeover time.

The key to making a better-than-average profit is to buy at a discount if possible. And to do that you work hard to find an owner anxious to sell. Properties that fit this mold usually have some repairs needed that have scared away retail buyers. After fixing it up, you may wish to offer a lease/purchase to a prospective tenant-buyer rather than the straight sale discussed earlier.

On occasion you will run across a deal on a newer home where the financing is fairly substantial but the interest is at a relatively low, fixed rate and where the sellers need to get out, but there's not enough room for an agent's commission. Consider taking over the loan, putting it in trust if there's a nonassumption clause, and offering it the same way to outright buyers or through a lease/purchase.

WHAT IS THE DIFFERENCE BETWEEN AN OPTION AND AN AGREEMENT TO PURCHASE?

Before going into what should be in a lease/option contract, you should understand the difference between an "option to purchase" and an "offer or agreement to purchase." They are similar in that they both allow you to proceed to a closing and take title, but they're not exactly the same.

When you have an option to purchase, you can decide not to buy for any reason at all—to walk away when the option expires—or you can sell it or assign it to someone else for a fee. Normally, you would lose any option consideration. If on the other hand you decide to buy the property, you would present your option contract to the lender as your purchase offer.

An offer or agreement to purchase formally commits you to buy the property at some future time, subject to any escape clause you may have in your offer, such as subject to financing, partner's approval, and inspections.

If properly worded, both contracts allow assignability. For example, an owner has a property you would like to buy at some future date. You give the owner money as consideration on the option. You

CASE STUDY: Lease/Option on a Single-Family Fixer-Upper

This time you've found a single-family house with three bedrooms and two baths, in a low-income area, that you can buy for $65,000. Through comparable sales you estimate fair market value after repairs at between $75,000 and $78,000. The house needs minor repairs of $3,500. It currently has tenants paying $625 per month in rent. A problem is that the house is not located in a neighborhood that is rising in popularity or value. In fact, the area is slowly turning into a shopping park. You might write the seller an offer that allows you to have a short period of time in which to find a buyer or back out. However, since the existing tenants may be reluctant for you to show the property, you will probably have a difficult time trying to find a buyer quickly. And of course, the location of the neighborhood won't help.

Observations

As the area is not the best and is getting worse, you are limited. You probably should not consider a long-term ownership. And be suspicious of comparable sales you get from a neighborhood that is declining—next year those prices will be lower. You will have an uphill battle to find a buyer at a good price and provide financing for that buyer. This might normally stop you from moving forward.

The Upshot

You do not have a prime deal here. You must be creative. Without imagining the worst, you do have two prudent solutions: First, you could ask the existing tenants if they would like to buy from you on a lease/option; second, wholesale, or flip, the property to someone willing to deal with this neighborhood—which is not likely. To do either one of these you need a contract with the seller that allows a period of time in which to find a buyer or back out. Use the deteriorating neighborhood to drive down the seller's price and arrange for seller financing.

(Continued)

CASE STUDY: Lease/Option on a Single-Family Fixer-Upper (Continued)

This is a typical deal for many investors. On the negative side: tough neighborhood, lack of buyers, little conventional financing. On the plus side: low price, need for seller financing, pool of tenants. Whatever price you buy it at may be difficult to top in a timely manner, but you might find the right lease/purchase buyer where you can get a small down payment or option consideration and offer a rent credit that might be just the inducement needed to make a deal. And if you can get financing from the seller that can be assumed by the new tenant-buyer at a good interest rate, your chance of making the deal work improves. In this example, you might get a $1,000 option fee (down payment) from a tenant-buyer for a $69,000 selling price on a two-year option, with possible extension. You can credit $100 (or more) a month from the $625 rent toward the purchase price, plus, pay a bit less in rent to the owner (like $550) as you are guaranteeing a longer-term rental period. After about six months, you can direct a forgiving mortgage broker to them. Then, the right appraisal and an 80/20 mortgage should complete the deal.

have a written option to purchase in which you retain the right, but not the obligation, to buy the owner's property on or before a certain date. You also at any given time can buy, sell, or assign your rights in this contract to someone else on or before the date the option expires.

A lease/purchase or rent-to-own agreement for a tenant-buyer is similar to a sale with a deferred closing. The buyer leases the property before closing the sale. It's important that the lease/purchase agreement spell out the date of the closing, as well as other terms and conditions, such as who pays for what during the lease.

WHAT SHOULD BE IN LEASE/OPTION AND LEASE/PURCHASE AGREEMENTS

As you don't actually hold title to the property in a lease/option, you must have a well-planned contract. All contracts vary to some degree,

CASE STUDY: Higher-Value Fixer-Upper into Lease/Option

An investor finds a single-family home that was assessed at $135,000, but comparables of its current condition show that the value is nearer $125,000. The property needs $16,000 in repairs. After offering lower amounts, the investor settles with the seller for $115,000, all cash, no real estate commission. The investor is able to finance 75% at 9.25% with a mortgage company and takes in a 50–50 partner who pays the down payment of 25% ($28,750) and the repair cost.

The investor does the repairs, places a tenant-buyer in the property for a rent that covers costs, and gives the tenant-buyer a modest monthly credit toward a purchase of the newly fixed-up property at a price of $152,000, based on fresh comparables, $21,000 or 14% more than the partners' cost. On the strength of that arrangement, they refinance the 9.25% interest rate from the mortgage company with a 7.75% rate from a local savings bank, and at 80% of the new value! They thereby pull out $35,350 (75% of original $115,000 or $86,250 minus 80% of new value of $152,000, or $121,600) on refinancing, which goes a good way to reimburse much of the original down payment ($28,750) and repair cost ($16,000). At the future closing they anticipate another $30,400 (current mortgage of $121,600 minus selling price of $152,000). Note: Example disregards our amortization.

Profit before miscellaneous expenses will be:

Original cost:	$115,000
Repair cost:	$16,000
Subtotal:	$131,000
Selling price:	$152,000
Gross profit:	$21,000

Not bad, considering it's close to a "no money down" deal when the up-front money comes back on the refinancing. Experience shows that this type of deal works best when the property is in relatively good shape and is in the higher-value range that banks generally prefer to finance.

and your lawyer will have specific provisions designed to protect you in case of unforeseen adversity. Therefore, it's difficult to offer a boilerplate agreement. But it is worthwhile to bring up some of the main points that need to be addressed.

Some key contract provisions are:

- Use separate contracts with the owner (lease/option), with whom you have one set of issues, and another (lease/purchase) with your tenant who will buy the property.

- Have two contracts with tenant-buyer: one to lease and another to option (or buy).

- Identify the names of parties involved and the address of the property.

- Indicate length of term of each contract and specified extension clauses.

- Have a place for dates and signatures of all owners and partners, including spouses.

- In contract with owner, include particulars of option price, option consideration, lease price to owner, and ability to sublease as well as permission to rerent.

- In contract with investor, specify monthly rental price, security deposits, agreement to purchase consideration, and amount of rent credited to tenant-buyer.

- Specify closing costs, financing, and escrow provisions in all contracts.

- Keep term of option with seller as long and term with tenant to buy as short as possible, perhaps (in the case of the latter) one year, extendable with additional payment and higher purchase price.

KEEP YOUR RIGHT TO ASSIGN CONTRACT WITH OWNER

You want to make sure you can assign the contract you have negotiated with the owner without having to seek his or her permission. You could have a clause that reads, "This agreement shall be in force by the Seller and Buyer and/or Buyer's nominee or assigns." This in effect implies that the contract may be assigned or transferred without written consent from the seller.

As in wholesaling, where a key provision in the contract is to be able to assign agreement without having to take title, it's similar here in that it's the tenant-buyer who will actually take up the option and close.

You can, however, be more specific if you wish and state that it may be assigned without written or verbal consent from any parties to the agreement, or that it is fully assignable by you at any time. At the place where you sign your name there should be an "and/or assigns."

If for some reason your seller will not agree to your assigning the agreement, and wants you only to close, you will have to take title and resell in a simultaneous or later close. Another way is to state in the agreement that the details of how the title will be taken will be at the instruction of the closing attorney. For the exact wording, consult your attorney.

WHOM DO YOU MAKE RESPONSIBLE FOR REPAIRS?

No formal rules pertain to who pays for repairs and maintenance in a lease/option arrangement. However, it's a good idea to clearly spell out repair responsibilities—who is responsible for what—in your lease with the owner as well as in the one with the tenant.

Generally, the seller should be made responsible for any major repairs, such as breakdown of structural system, water supply, or furnace (i.e., those basics that make the house livable), as well as for any health and safety violations of the building code that might occur.

The tenant-buyer might be responsible for the minor upkeep relating to living in the house, such as faucet repairs, lawn care, and snow removal. It's a good idea to have in your contract with the tenant that he or she is responsible for all maintenance and general repair after a home inspection. However, if the repair exceeds a certain amount, say $150 or $200, you or the owner should pay for the repair. You can have a clause in the agreement that adds this excess amount of maintenance to the purchase price when the option is exercised.

WHEN YOUR TENANT-BUYER
WANTS TO CHANGE THE TERMS

You currently have a single-family house controlled by a lease with option contract with the owner. The lease time is for four years with a purchase price of $89,000. You get an offer from a tenant-buyer to rent with an option to buy for $100,000 to run the full four years.

Several problems may arise. First, perhaps the tenant-buyer wants more time than the one year you offer. Second, although her price will bring you a good profit, it is not guaranteed because the tenant-buyer's option with you does not mean she must close. The ideal condition for you is to have a tenant-buyer with a firm agreement for a short time commitment, say one year. Third, the tenant-buyer may not offer to pay for the option, but may request instead that it be included in the rental agreement (i.e., you pay for it, and she does not reimburse you).

What do you do? Is there a way for you to get your money out now? You have several courses of action to counter the tenant's offer. First, limit the time period in which the tenant-buyer must perform. In shortening the period you may need to lower the price, as your potential tenant-buyer's offer was to pay you top dollar or $100,000, but only four years from now. It may not have appreciated that much if you sell within a year and you may have to sell closer to today's market value. So, change the open-ended part of the option into a firm agreement on price where the tenant must close. As an alternative, make the tenant-buyer pay a nonrefundable deposit on the option itself, so that if she must back out you are not left holding an unsold property. Assign your whole position, which includes the option with the current owner, to the new buyer for cash and leave the deal.

MAKING SURE THE LENDER ACCEPTS RENT CREDITS

One of the problems you may run into in your area is that banks are sometimes reluctant to accept rent credit as a true value. What may be perfectly sensible to us may seem to bankers like subterfuge. As soon as the deal doesn't fit the mold, they become confused. From their point of view, they are lending, for example, 80% of the fair value of the property; they want to make sure the other 20%, either cash down or secondary financing, is also based on fair value.

Usually, the banker detects this fair value by seeing it listed on the purchase and sale agreement verified by the bank's appraisal. Normally this fair value is easily confirmed; however, if bankers in your area are not convinced and put their noses up at tenant-buyer option agreements, adapt by giving them what they want. That is, have a lease agreement with your tenant-buyer that states fair value rent (make sure it is) and stipulate that it be paid by one check. Then have a separate clause, perhaps in a separate option or sales agreement, that states that the monthly rent credit is paid by a separate check.

Now the banker sees a deal that better fits the bank's parameters—a more or less conventional agreement of sale that spells out selling price, deposit, and buildup of that deposit over time. Now the lender is likely to finance it, accepting rent credit as genuine.

If all else fails, in your option agreement with the tenant-buyer you can always have that you both will execute a firm buy–sell sales agreement a month prior to his or her taking over, for the purpose of clarifying the sale for the closing attorneys and bankers. In this agreement you would only need to state the selling price and how much is down on the deal, not how it got there. As long as your buyer is borrowing only 80% of the sales price as verified by a standard sales agreement, you have a workable deal.

DOES A LEASE/OPTION TRIGGER A DUE-ON-SALE CLAUSE IN THE MORTGAGE?

A question occasionally comes up about whether because a lease/option shifts much of the responsibility of a property away from an owner, it might trigger or activate the due-on-sale clause found in most mortgages.

Normally the lease/option does not cause the due-on-sale clause to come into play because the title to the property has not transferred until you close on the deal—at the end of the lease term or prior to that point if you choose to close early on the property. Furthermore, the lender has no formal way of knowing of any control change since the lease is generally not recorded.

However, in certain states a lease of more than three years can be considered a violation of the due-on-sale clause. Different states have different lengths of time before a technical violation occurs. In fact, in today's modern world where the concept of ownership has become more complex, some wary bankers are writing mortgages that cite lease/options as a violation.

As the investor, you should examine two avenues in any deal. First, does your state have any such law whereby lease/option agreements violate the due-on-sale clause within mortgages? Second, is there any language within the specific mortgage of an owner with whom you wish to do business that would trigger a payoff of the mortgage if the property were controlled by a lease/option? If there is, in the latter case it's best to see if the problem can be avoided by depending on the wording of the mortgage, separate agreements or any specific wording changes within your agreement with the owner that might be recommended by your attorney.

If no solution seems to appear, before you let go of the deal you can always go to the bank or mortgage company in question and entreat them to overlook the arrangement. The whole idea of a lease/option agreement triggering a due-on-sale clause within a mortgage has dubious legality, but you don't want to be the test case.

WORKING OUT A SIMULTANEOUS CLOSING

When you close a lease/option you will often use a procedure called a simultaneous close. And, specifically, how do you close the sale without taking title? Without using your own money? Here are some of the nuts and bolts: In a lease/option you get an option to take title to the property at some future time. Ideally, the title never gets signed over until your tenant-buyer is ready to take over. Your name may never appear on the title or official record of the transaction. Your goal in a lease/option with a seller is simply to have a claim to the title, which you exercise only at the time you sell the property to your customer, usually to a tenant-buyer to whom you are renting the property. There is no need for you to hold title, as you make sure your option and agreement papers signed with the seller are assignable to a buyer of your choice.

The simultaneous close with your tenant-buyer then hides your price arrangement with the seller.

Note that when you wholesale you usually pass the deal on to another business-investor for a modest gain, but when you pass on a lease/option, you usually chalk up a substantial profit, and you're dealing with a retail customer whom you should treat gently—if for no other reason than because that individual is paying you more!

So, you may feel it's wise to take title even though it's only for a few minutes. In other words, two separate transactions happen at the same time. You could set up a trust with a limited liability corporation (LLC) as the beneficiary of the trust and take title in this manner if you are concerned about your personal name being used.

As with many of the legal aspects in transferring property, consult with your attorney for the best arrangement.

WITH SELLERS YOU'VE GOT MORE
THAN ONE ARROW IN YOUR QUIVER

Let's say you contacted a couple dozen owners of rental properties in your area that you located from ads in your local newspaper, but few were interested in doing a lease/option. You think something is wrong with your approach and you want to know how to change it.

First, don't limit yourself to just one approach. Be flexible. Besides, if you come across a deal you yourself don't want at the present time, maybe you can wholesale it to another investor.

Second, don't let anything get in the way of your listening to the seller when he or she talks about the nature of his or her problem. Use a little salesmanship, take your time, and find out what you can do to help. Experience in talking with owners will help you in handling objections—and that's what selling is all about.

After all, with lease/options you will encounter owners who don't want to sell, just rent. Another objection is that owners are wary of having you sublease to someone else. And of course, the biggest objection for some owners is that they don't want you to make money off their property. But you'll never be able to counter owners' objections if you don't listen to what their needs are and what in particular bothers them. Try to see the owner's plight from his or her point of view. The idea is to draw the owner out, discover his or her needs, and see if you can offer assistance—in that order.

Once you begin getting some substantive information from the owner in your initial conversation, it's time to move beyond the telephone. Your use of the telephone should be little more than to establish contact and get a sense of whether your way of doing business might appeal to the owner. Once you get the bare bones of the deal, go directly to a personal meeting, at the property if possible. People aren't going to discuss their needs over the telephone, but once you extend the courtesy of meeting them, you have a chance of establishing a worthwhile relationship. And only then can you effectively work out the details of a deal that might solve their problem as well as make you money.

The next chapter will show you how to shift gears and switch from a buy-and-sell approach to one where you buy and hold, thereby enlarging your equity for an extended length of time.

13

Buy-and-Hold I:
The Single-Family

This chapter leaves the short-term ownership strategies of buying and selling to consider the advantage of buying and holding for a longer term for greater profits.

BUY AND SELL, OR BUY AND HOLD

Many self-styled real estate gurus question the concept of buying and holding, saying that renting out is not as attractive or financially viable as it has been in the past. Their argument is that tax laws have changed, and the economy is no longer as favorable as it was in the 1980s when rapidly rising inflation made the buy-and-hold strategy extremely profitable.

These naysayers further state that there is less risk in strategies that allow one to jump in and out of the market for short periods. They also raise the old bugaboo of being a landlord, implying it is too great a hassle to repair toilets and deal with tenants and such.

To some degree they have a point: There are fewer headaches in buying and selling, or buying and exchanging, or wholesaling or using lease/options. After all, who wants to have 25 units spread out all over, each with an average monthly gain after expenses of $100? That's only $30,000 per year! A lot of risk, to say nothing of bother, for only a modest amount. It's hard to get rich that way.

If, of course, that's all there were to it. But, to put the argument in perspective, the naysayers are right, but only one-half right. What they fail to put into their argument is that each local marketplace is different. And you as a practitioner of real estate investing must work within the parameters of what opportunities are most profitable. If you don't have as many opportunities for using lease/options, or buying and rehabbing fixer-uppers, the better opportunity may lie in, yes, buying and holding. And what would you buy-and-hold? In many areas, and this surely varies even within each city, it may be a single-family house or the small apartment or commercial building.

So, the answer is to keep all strategies in perspective. Let's quote a poem:

> *The pessimist complains about the wind,*
> *the optimist expects it to change,*
> *and the realist adjusts the sails.*
> —Anonymous

THE BUY-AND-HOLD STRATEGY

The buy-and-hold strategy you follow might be to buy property in improving neighborhoods, rehab them up to the level of other homes, get unblemished tenants (credit check, time on job, previous residence, etc.). Further, you should have positive cash flow with the thought of selling or wholesaling the rest. You don't just have to be a landlord to make money in real estate. It is wise to be aware of all techniques—lease/options, buying and selling rather than holding, wholesaling, rehabs, exchanging.

In contrast to a primary focus on fixing up and reselling single-family houses, you might opt to use the buy-and-hold strategy with a two- or three-family residence. The key is for each investor to have multiple strategies in his or her toolbox.

BUYING AND RENTING OUT THE SINGLE-FAMILY

Sometimes in looking for a fixer-upper you run across a deal in a single-family home that you can't pass up and that doesn't require repair work at all. If you check the prices of comparable (in current condition) property and find that what you're buying is 15% less, it's a good deal. You can buy and resell it or keep it as a rental. In today's market the acquisition cost of a single-family doesn't normally allow for a positive cash flow, but let's say it's two houses away from your family home and you don't want the confusion to the other neighbors of an immediate sale. Perhaps you want to wait a year or two before selling.

One of the first considerations is what you can rent it for. Start by checking rents, if any, in the neighborhood. How does yours compare with those? You need to stay in line with the market *and* keep a positive cash flow. In this case, because you're paying less than market value, your more modest mortgage allows you to rent at favorable prices that will bring in a modest amount of cash.

USING QUICK RATIOS TO VALUE THE SINGLE-FAMILY RENTAL

The next three chapters talk more about valuing a stream of income, but here's a quick way to do it in addition to the comparable sale analysis explained in the fixer-upper section on valuing single-family houses (Chapter 6).

Sometimes in a high-priced housing market it can be tough to get the rental price you need to cover mortgage and expenses on a single-family house. Here are a couple of ideas that will help you analyze your local market. Do an informal survey of your rental market by buying the Sunday newspaper and making a list of rentals. List the rental amounts in two columns of all three- and four-bedroom homes. Then, average the rents for both home sizes.

For purposes of an example, let's assume that the average rental for a three-bedroom home is $1,150; for a four-bedroom home, $1,400. Now let's make a very rough estimate of what the value of these rental homes might be. It's inaccurate to use the same method as is used to value an apartment property, but let's at least borrow some of that thinking. We can also make an inexact assumption that up to one-half of rental income goes to paying taxes, insurance, and so on. So for the three-bedroom house its annual rent would be $13,800, one-half of which is $6,900, from which you would pay your mortgage and receive profit. Note that this remaining amount is called the net operating income (NOI) as explained in detail in

CASE STUDY: Getting Started in Buying and Holding a Single-Family Rental

A young married couple called me and asked about buying a house that they might rent out. They said they were looking for some extra income and also wanted to know whether, if they owned it for a long time, it might be able to finance the college education of their soon-to-be-born child. They confessed they had saved only $1,500, but said they would be willing to work at fixing something up. I suggested they take a look at some of the homes in a particular neighborhood where there were some For Sale by Owner signs. They did the groundwork and a few weeks later called to tell me that they had met a seller who showed them his house and that he seemed to be asking a fair price. Would I come and look at it for them?

The owner himself hadn't lived there for several years and had been renting it out. But because he had moved out of state he no longer wanted to be a landlord. He gave the young couple a key, and with the permission of the tenants I went in to inspect while they were at work. I did a careful room-by-room evaluation and investigated what I could see of the electrical, plumbing, and heating systems. From my inspection I made up a list of what had to be done immediately and what could be deferred until the next year.

If the present tenants remained, the interior would not have to be cleaned and painted until some time into the future. The home needed some minor plumbing repairs along with a new furnace. Exterior painting and roof repair were critical—they needed to be done as soon as possible.

My need-to-do list came to just over $8,000, which indicated the seller wanted too much for the property. Based on my estimate for repairs I negotiated for the young couple a lower sale price and a small second mortgage, allowing them to buy the house.

For the work they and their moderately skilled friends and relatives couldn't do, they hired tradespeople and were able to finish the work in a few months while they kept the existing tenants. In three years their second mortgage was paid off and they were ready to buy another house.

Chapter 14 on multifamily housing. If you now suppose that this $6,900 is your return on an investment that gained you 7%, then the supposed investment of the three-bedroom house might be worth $98,570. This latter amount is a rough guess and should never be used to replace the comparable sales analysis as explained in the fixer-upper section, but here I wanted to show you a shorthand method to value single-family rentals.

To continue this example further, to profitably rent out a single-family house you must effectively get at least 1% to 1.25% of the home's selling price in monthly rent to support its landlord-related operating expenses and mortgage. In our example of the three-bedroom, the $1,150 monthly rent on a $98,570 selling price is 1.17%.

Note that figures can vary depending on your area, even the specific neighborhood in which you are investigating. In some areas the percent by which you can multiply the rental cash after expenses may be 5%, while in other areas it might be well over 8%. The same holds true for the percent of selling price; it could be less than 1% in one neighborhood and almost 2% in another. What you want to do is establish these percentages ("quick ratios") in each subarea or neighborhood in which you wish to deal in property. One way to tie them down for subject neighborhoods is to check at your local assessor's office for the monthly rents, and selling and operating costs for houses that have sold.

As you just saw in the quick ratio that related monthly rent to property value, you wish to boost up the ratio as much as possible to increase your monthly profits. Obviously, to do this you don't want to lower the property value but rather to raise rent. For example, a house that has a value of $90,000 and rents for $900 per month has a rent-to-value ratio of 1. If the same house were rented for a monthly rent of $1,100, the ratio would be 1.2.

Now that you have this tool, take a look at how the ratio might change at different house values. A house in the same neighborhood as the one in the preceding example that has a value of $140,000 and rents for $1,200 has a rent-to-value ratio of only 0.9.

Correspondingly, a nearby house that is valued at $50,000 and has monthly rent of $800 has a ratio of 1.6. What's going on here? We can complain all we want, but in many markets it happens to be a fact of life that the higher-valued homes don't receive the same proportion of rental income as do their cheaper brethren.

Check this out in your own local market. Your understanding of different rent-to-value quick ratios will give you a better idea of how to price property. Certainly, if you are going to buy and rent out groups of homes, you might opt for lower-priced property. With their higher ratios there's simply a larger proportion of money left over for expenses, mortgage, and profit.

Just realize that eventually you may want to sell those lower-priced homes. If your marketplace has sufficient sales activity in these homes, then you're covered. If, however, the active market is in the more appealing, middle-to-upper-priced homes with three or four bedrooms and two or two and one-half baths, you would be advised to use your buy-and-hold strategy in the latter area, as often in many markets these homes are the most desirable.

However, the topping off of rental prices in the higher-value homes is one of the reasons the buy-and-hold technique is not as popular as a get-in-and-get-out technique, such as fixing up and re-selling, where an investor does not get caught with monthly rents that fail to offer a reasonable return.

So, if you desire to buy-and-hold homes, seek rent-to-value ratios that are relatively high so that there will be enough money left over for profit. And profit should come before pleasing your ego with glamorous property.

THE FIVE TOOLS THAT LEAD TO WEALTH

What is the buy-and-hold investment all about? Here are some explanations:

1. *Cash flow.* Cash flow is the difference between rental income and operating expenses (taxes, insurance, maintenance, management, etc.), including mortgage payments (interest and principal). Obviously, in buying a property you want to make sure there is enough rental income to cover what it costs to run the building as well as the mortgage debt. In the negotiation of a mortgage you may want to stretch out the term so that your monthly payments will easily be taken care of by cash flow. A close ally of cash flow is net operating income (NOI), which is the cash remaining after expenses but before debt service. Net operating income is important as it is often used to help determine the property's value. More on cash flow and NOI in the next two chapters.

2. *Amortization.* Generally your mortgage payment is comprised of an interest amount and a principal amount. As long as you have a conventional mortgage and not an interest-only loan, your loan balance will be reduced by the amount of each principal payment you make. This principal reduction is called amortization and your equity is correspondingly increased by the amount of each principal payment. Although many properties are not held for the full time of the mortgage term, if they were the entire mortgage would have been paid off and recouped on sale. As you can see, amortization over time is a series of small steps making you rich.

3. *Leverage.* Leverage generally refers to the percent amount you can borrow on the value of a property. For example, a property that is 90% financed is said to have a high degree of leverage. In other words, leverage is how much of a property you can control with a minimal amount of money down. Certainly, risk comes with high leverage. And what is discussed in this book has much to do with making sure that the property you secure can pay off the indebtedness incurred. Remember, as you just saw with amortization, borrowed money can be a huge benefit when paid off over time and when paid for by rental income. The lesson is to make sure you don't overleverage property with a mortgage that cannot be paid for by tenant income.

4. *Appreciation.* Appreciation is the growth in value of a property. Appreciation in value is often the result of inflation causing a move to ever higher prices. In the past, many investment decisions were made solely on the potential for appreciation. Appreciation should not be your only reason for buying, but undoubtedly it has made more people wealthy than any other benefit. In today's market you must balance the possibility for appreciation with the desire for cash flow, amortization, and tax shelter.

Appreciation can also be enhanced by improvements made to the property. These could be what you do to a fixer-upper, or even the building of additional apartments in a multiunit building. In all cases you end up with a more valuable property, hence more appreciation.

5. *Tax advantages.* One of the benefits within the federal tax code is that you can depreciate (bookkeeping-wise) the building (i.e., so-called improved portion, not land) on your property over a period of time. For all practical purposes this allows tax on amortization (i.e., principal payments) as well as on cash flow to be deferred to a later time. Further, by exchanging, you can defer the tax until a future settlement if you transfer your current equity in the proper manner into a larger, and potentially more lucrative, property.

Any one of these five benefits would make investment in real estate outweigh most other opportunities. And when they are all available in one investment of choice, they are dynamite. Nowhere else can you gain the most potential amount of cash while amortizing a loan with other people's money, have a capital asset of sizable proportion that grows in value, and defer to a future time the tax on current cash income as well as the gain on sale.

A CAPITAL GAINS TAX REVIEW

How does your tax situation change and what advantages do you have in being taxed on the profits of an investment you hold for a longer time? Specifically, now that you're no longer a short-term investor where your income is treated as ordinary income, you must consider the special treatment of the capital gains tax.

Our federal tax laws seem to change constantly. Once we get used to one set of regulations new ones appear. In the early 1990s, a new law made the maximum tax on capital gains 28%, but now we have the Jobs and Growth Tax Relief Reconciliation Act of 2003. (See other rates in Chapter 20 on the new tax laws.)

To begin with, the new law on capital gains has reduced the tax to 15%, but like many aspects of the tax code, that's not true all the time. Let's try to list some of the basics. First of all, there is one set of rules for taxpayers in the 15% or less marginal tax bracket and another percentage for taxpayers at 15% or higher. Both groups of taxpayers who hold their property 12 months or less pay tax on capital gains at ordinary income rates. So far so good. Now it gets trickier. For a property sold after being held for 12 months, the gain is considered long-term. In this case, the lower-taxed group, the 15% or less taxpayers, pay a maximum of 5% on a long-term gain.

However, if the taxpayer in the higher-taxed group, more than 15% (marginal tax bracket), has held the property for 12 months, he or she will pay a maximum of 15% on a long-term gain.

Afraid that they were making the tax code appear simple, Congress opted for a special rule for investment real estate: The portion of a long-term capital gain ascribed to prior deductions for depreciation may be recaptured as ordinary income. In other words, if you are a 15% (or more) taxpayer, you will pay minimum capital gains rate of 15%, but when adjusted for prior depreciation deductions, a proportionately higher amount.

Note that capital losses may be deducted up to the extent of capital gains, with unused capital losses carried forward. Furthermore, up to $3,000 of capital losses may be deducted against ordinary income. On a joint return, the $3,000 limit applies to the combined losses of both spouses; the limit is reduced to $1,500 for married persons filing separately. Further note that losses are not allowed on sales between the taxpayer and brothers or sisters, parents, grandparents, children, or grandchildren. In addition, no loss may be claimed on a sale to your spouse, although the tax-free exchange rules may apply.

Thus investors whose gain is mostly attributable to the depreciation deduction will have to pay the higher ordinary income rate while those whose gain is from a low purchase price to a higher selling price benefit by having only a 15% tax. For an investor who held his or her property through the decline of the late eighties and had to keep taking a depreciation deduction but did not get the advantage of price appreciation, the higher bracket applies, while those who bought during the dip and whose gain is mostly price appreciation have the lower tax rate.

The good news is that for those buying now and in the future, a modestly lower tax rate of the maximum 15% will apply . . . as long as Congress doesn't meet again.

MAINTAINING INVESTOR STATUS WITH THE IRS

For investors who buy and hold property it's important to maintain "investor" status and thereby keep the lower capital gains tax. In contrast, "dealer" status requires any gains to be taxed at ordinary income rates, even if a property is held longer than 12 months. Keeping an investor status isn't usually a problem for those who buy and hold property for extended periods. But if you buy and sell continually on a regular basis you may become classified as a dealer.

The actual determination of whether you are a dealer or an investor depends on the details in each particular transaction. For example, the continual development of large parcels of land into smaller ones might very well trigger the IRS to regard your status to be that of a dealer. However, you are not likely to come under the IRS's scrutiny if you buy and hold single-family houses or apartment buildings for at least several years. Note that profits from short-term techniques like fixer-uppers, lease/option, and wholesaling will be taxed at ordinary rates as they are not passive but active investments.

Normally, property held as an investment for passive income does not trigger dealer status. If what you do rises to the level of a trade or business, then dealer status is more likely. Your real estate operation is subject to a number of tests, including the nature and purpose of the acquisition of the property, the duration of ownership, the extent of development or improvement on the property, the solicitation of customers through advertising, the volume and frequency of sales, and the continuity of sales and sales-related activities over time. Status is also affected by the comparison of sales with other sources of income.

To further complicate matters, even if you are classified as a dealer for some properties, it doesn't mean that you will be treated as a dealer for all properties. For example, you may have a development firm where you pay taxes at ordinary rates and also own separate parcels of property as passive investments.

Your objective should be to maintain investor status. And, generally, to buy and hold a property for an extended time as an investment will not trigger the IRS to classify you as a dealer. Further, you can insulate investment assets in separate entities from those that could be called active businesses. For example, development activities could be conducted in an S corporation while investment property could be held in your personal name or in a partnership.

EXCHANGE OF PROPERTY
TO PRESERVE LONG-TERM GAINS

You should be aware of the opportunity provided by the tax laws to defer payment of a capital gains tax by exchanging property, thereby allowing the amount of the tax to remain as an equity down payment for the purchase of a larger property.

If you've held a property for a few years, particularly an apartment building, you need to protect the equity you have built up. The only way you can avoid a large tax upon sale is to shift this equity through an exchange into another property. In fact, tax-free, or more accurately tax-deferred, exchanging is one of the major ways to create wealth in real estate. The ability to do this comes under the Internal Revenue Code's Section 1031, which lays down the ground rules for the greatest tax deferral available with regard to property. In fact, its net effect is that the government gives you an interest-free loan for the amount of money you would have paid in tax when you sold the property, and you do not have to repay it until you sell the property you've acquired in the exchange.

Exchanging preserves your equity even as you leverage it into a new, larger property. This situation occurs because Section 1031 of the Internal Revenue Code holds that an exchange is not a sale but a transfer of equity from one property (either personal or real property) to another, and is therefore not taxable. The exchange, then, is more than simply a way of preserving equity by sheltering taxes; by allowing you to use monies that would otherwise have been lost to taxes it creates even greater equity and profits. Exchanging, then, should be considered if you want to achieve your investment goals. The technique is not matched for saving you tax dollars and enlarging your equity. So don't hide an additional profit that you could gain by compounding through ownership in a new property. It is the ultimate way to maximize the performance of your assets.

ONE INDISPENSABLE TOOL— THE FINANCIAL CALCULATOR

Dealing with fixer-uppers doesn't require higher-order mathematics— just simple arithmetic. With multifamily units we up the ante—not to the point of calculus, thank goodness. But we do need to unlock the formulas that show how money increases in value over time.

To make money in real estate your needs are modest. You don't need a college degree, you don't need to inherit property, and you don't even need much money (although some helps). One thing you do need is a financial calculator. It's not for adding and subtracting, although you will use it to do that; what you will really use it for is to show you the "magic numbers"—how money increases over time, how a dollar today has a distinctly altered value in the future. It is your key to unlocking wealth, the foundation on which your investment career will be built.

In the old days (when we were still on the gold standard) investors figured numbers out on paper by hand (I had the formulas of the following memorized—ugh!), and afterward (but before Silicon Valley) they used mortgage tables where the answers were in long columns of numbers (knowing the formulas still bypassed the tables), and now finally, in contemporary times, we have the financial calculator. Now that mortgage tables are extinct, we can, with a few deft keystrokes, discover some incredible truths of what happens to money. (Note that although calculators are inexpensive and hand-held, computers can do the work faster and more comprehensively with elaborate printouts.)

Specifically, we learn:

- The cost to finance a property.
- The distinctions between various mortgages.
- The yield on a mortgage.
- The present and future value of a series of cash flows.
- The yield on a series of payments.
- The effect of early payments on mortgage loans.
- How to finance discounted mortgages.

These new calculators allow investors to see at a glance what mortgage costs will be under different criteria. For example, you can instantly change the term of a proposed 30-year loan to one of 15 years, you can change interest rates sooner than the banks, you can calculate the return on investment, or the internal rate of return, on a group of uneven cash flows—all with a small electronic gadget that costs between $20 and $100! Back in the old days it was an involved process of looking in books and tables for the payoff on a mortgage or the remaining interest on a loan. Now you reap the benefits of the changes from vacuum tube to transistor to microchip and can change rates, time periods, and payment amounts in no more time than it takes to push a button—all with the goal of reaching more profitable decisions more quickly.

Let's look at some typical uses of a financial calculator.

EXAMPLE A: THE TIME VALUE OF MONEY

One of the major ways a calculator is used in financial analysis is to measure how the value of a specific amount of money changes over time. For example, let's see how the principal balance of a mortgage changes over time. If you took out a mortgage of $120,000 on a single-family house you bought for investment that had a 7.5% interest rate (higher interest rate because it's not your residence) for a period of 30 years, your monthly payment would be $839.06. Your $839.06 includes an interest payment as well as an amount for the principal every month for 30 years to reduce the $120,000 you borrowed to zero.

Most financial calculators have the ability to show how much you would have paid in interest at the end of a year as well as the remaining principal balance.

End of first year:

Interest paid: $ 8,962.47
Principal paid: $ 1,106.25
Remaining balance: $118,893.75

End of second year:

Interest paid: $ 8,876.62
Principal paid: $ 1,192.10
Remaining balance: $117,701.65

End of third year:

Interest paid: $ 8,784.07
Principal paid: $ 1,284.65
Remaining balance: $116,417.00

Notice that as time goes on the remaining principal owed declines, while the amount of the principal paid each year is higher and the amount of interest is less—always totalling $10,068.72 annually ($839.06 per month × 12).

End of tenth year:

Interest paid: $ 7,900.61
Principal paid: $ 2,168.11
Remaining balance: $104,153.49

Notice how by the end of the tenth year the amount of principal that gets paid off during the year has almost doubled since the first year.

You have to wait until just after the twenty-second year for one-half of the principal balance to be paid off.

End of twenty-second year:

Interest paid:	$ 4,751.04
Principal paid:	$ 5,317.64
Remaining balance:	$60,433.97

And, also in the twenty-second year, observe how the interest and principal portions of the monthly payment are relatively equal.
The following is a variation of this example.

EXAMPLE B: ACCUMULATED INTEREST AND LOAN BALANCE AFTER A SPECIFIED PAYMENT

You are financing with a seller $92,000 at 7.75% annual interest, amortized over a 30-year term but with a balloon payment due after five years.
   You want to know the amount of the monthly payment, the amount of interest you will pay, and the amount of the balloon payment.

Monthly payment:	$ 659.10
Interest over the five years:	$34,805.88
Balloon payment at end of five years:	$87,259.92

Easy work for an inexpensive calculator!

EXAMPLE C: BUYING A RENTAL HOUSE

In deciding whether you should buy a single-family rental house, you will want to know if the house will produce a positive cash flow and if it will have a large enough rate of return to justify the investment.
   The seller is asking $120,000. The house is leased for the next year at $1,100 per month or $13,200 for the year. You believe you can continue to rent the house at that rate for the next five years.

Property taxes, insurance, and maintenance average about $3,600 per year.

You will manage the property yourself. You have $24,000 for a down payment and can get a mortgage for $96,000 at a 7.25% (not your primary residence) annual interest rate with monthly payments amortized over 25 years.

You want to know if the rent will cover the expenses, including the monthly mortgate payments, taxes, insurance, and maintenance, and what rate of return you will earn on your money if you sell the property after five years for $140,000.

As most financial calculators work, you first determine the monthly payments for the first five years. Then you calculate the amount paid annually on the mortgage and add this amount to the maintenance expenses. Then subtract the total expenses from the rental income.

Here's the cash flow for the first five years:

The calculator finds the amount of the monthly payment to be $654.89, and annually $7,858.68. Now you account for annual expenses of $3,600 and rental income of $13,200 for a profit each year of $1,741.32.

Next you calculate the loan balance after five years of $90,603.63 and subtract it from the expected selling price of $140,000 of the property. You find the equity to be $49,396.37.

Finally, you enter the down payment of $24,000, the yearly profit of $1,741.32 for the first four years, and the fifth year's profit plus the equity from the sale of the property, which equals $49,396.37. Then you calculate the internal rate of return (IRR), which in this example is 21.16%.

Among some of the financial calculator's applications are:

- Monthly payments to P&I (principal and interest) and to PITI (principal, interest, taxes, and insurance).
- Monthly payments on a mortgage with a balloon payment.
- Accumulated interest and loan balance after a specified payment.
- Annual percentage rate (APR) of an adjustable rate mortgage (ARM).
- Comparative data for making a refinancing mortgage decision.
- Interest and time saved with biweekly mortgage payments.
- Payment schedule on a graduated payment mortgage.

- Home improvement loan—second mortgage versus larger first mortgage.

- Present value of income-producing property.

- Internal rate of return.

- Trend line—or continuation of an existing trend—analysis.

- Term required to reduce a loan to a specific amount.

- Yield of a discounted mortgage.

- Points required to obtain a specific yield.

- Yield of a wraparound (or all-encompassing that includes all others) mortgage.

- Present value of a lease with even payments.

- Yield on a lease with advance payments.

- Depreciation of an asset using standardized methods.

THE PRESENT VALUE OF AN INVESTMENT

One of the reasons for the discussion on using a financial calculator is that you are now going to start studying investment analysis, the cornerstone of which is an understanding of the present value of future cash flows.

Specifically, in considering a new property investment, you'll want to quantify the benefits you expect to receive and you'll want to compare the expected returns of several possible investments. One way to do that is to use time-value-of-money calculations to find the present value of the expected cash inflows from the investment.

The time value of money is basically the concept that a dollar received today is worth more than a dollar received at some point in the future, because the dollar received today can be invested to earn interest. Time value of money problems generally involve the relationship between a certain amount of money, a certain period of time, and a certain rate of compound interest.

The next chapter continues the discussion of investment analysis, specifically in multifamily ownership.

14

Buy-and-Hold II:
The Multifamily

After we've studied how we can generate cash through the in-and-out techniques of buying, fixing up, and reselling single-family homes, wholesaling property to other investors, arranging rent-to-own with tenant-buyers, and then in the preceding chapter looking at buying-and-holding the single-family property, we now turn our attention to another buy-and-hold strategy: the longer-term ownership of the small apartment building.

WHY THE MULTIFAMILY IS A
GREAT LONG-TERM INVESTMENT

The traditional real estate investment of buying and holding a multi-unit property has consistently yielded success for decades. Among the reasons are a lower cost per unit, less competition in buying, less time per tenant in management responsibility, and several tenants to cover potential vacancy loss.

Part of the idea behind an apartment building is that if one house is a good investment, would not two, four, six, or eight houses be even better? Of course. Now let's put them all into one box and we've got an apartment building (or small office building)—a grouping of single-family residential units into one physical structure.

Here are some more advantages of multiple units:

Each individual apartment costs less than its equivalent in a single detached house. For example, a three-family apartment building might cost $180,000. That's $60,000 per unit. In some areas it can be hard to get a house in that price range. And yet, if the units are rented out, each will bring about the same amount of rental income as three separate houses. Since the per-unit operating expenses and mortgage cost are less, you have a better chance of collecting rent to cover these costs and produce a profit.

A multiple-unit building needs less in operating expenses per unit. Your costs are fewer and they are less. Landlord costs like property taxes and lawn care are much less, saving you a tremendous amount of money per tenant.

Multiunit buildings generally cost less per square foot than single-family homes. If a house costs $75,000 but you can purchase a four-unit building at $225,000, the units in the apartment building are each almost $19,000 cheaper. And although it may be more of a concern to a tenant, the utilities are often more expensive for a single-family house than the relative amount for an apartment. The same is true for the amount of mortgage attributable to each, which, in the case of the aforementioned multiunit, is being paid down by four families, not one.

Multiple units offer an improved vacancy factor. When a single-family home is vacant, it's fully vacant. You have to pay all the bills until you find a new tenant. However, if you have a four-unit building and one of the units becomes vacant, it's only a 25% vacancy factor. In fact, the more units you have, the less shock the vacancy factor will have on your cash flow. If one is vacant in a 12-unit building, your vacancy rate is less than 9%.

As vacancy, operating expenses, management, and financing costs are lower per unit, you are more likely to maintain a positive cash flow and have money left over to use any way you want. More units point you in the direction of building more wealth than you can obtain at any other activity—giving you time to pursue your dreams.

Further, you are often able to negotiate better financing on a building with several units in it than a single-family. This is in part because rather than having the financing rely on your income, the building itself yields money to pay back the financing, often on much better terms. And financing is frequently available from the seller.

In comparison to managing single-family houses, a multiple-apartment building is much easier. As the units are all at one location you don't need to travel all over the place to arrange for maintenance to be done, collect rent, or otherwise visit tenants. Furthermore, it is less costly to hire this work out than it would be if the work were spread out. And having others do the work allows you time to find new property.

The cash flow in an apartment building is substantially greater. If your cost per unit is less, your vacancy factor is less, and your management saves you time and expenses, then there's going to be more money left over.

As we've seen, one multiunit building creates synergy; it is cheaper per unit and easier to manage. You won't always be able to buy and resell apartment properties in the same way you can with single-family houses, but when you make a profit, it's big. It just takes more time—the average holding period for a multiunit is about 10 years.

Multiunits are easier to finance on a per-unit basis. It's not that banks are not cautious about lending money on multifamily units—they are. But it's a lot easier to make a positive financial statement for 10 units in one building than for 10 separate houses. As apartment ownership is a business investment, it is often possible to get seller financing, whereas in the case of single-family homes, usually lived in by the owner, secondary financing is harder to arrange.

Apartments are more durable over time than single-family houses in terms of compactness of design and solidity of structure, and in part for this reason are rentable to a wider variety of tenants.

Note that the relative profitability of homes versus multifamily units (risks and returns) must be judged according to the opportunities and characteristics of each local market.

TARGET PROPERTIES THAT THROW OFF CASH

Just as with fixer-uppers, most of the multifamily properties you will buy may not be handsome—in fact, some may be downright ragged. Indeed, when you look at a beautiful property you had better reckon that you won't be able to make the price work and that there are probably plenty of retail buyers who will pay a premium for elegant, "ready-to-wear" properties. Even if the comparable sales indicate a good price, sometimes you can't go forward unless there is a dramatically rising market in your area, because you won't have enough cash generated from rents to make it pay.

There must be agreement among overall value, cash generated after expenses, financing costs, and repairs. It's not good enough just for a property to be what you think is well priced if the cash after expenses doesn't justify the price. Similarly, if a property needs extensive repairs, the lowest price can be too much. Even lofty rents make the value of a property debatable if there's not enough money to cover financing. Consequently, properties that throw off cash and are not necessarily the most attractive are the ones that can best pay the expenses and meet financing obligations.

CREATE AN ACCURATE INCOME
AND EXPENSE STATEMENT

Now that you know some of the reasons why you should consider multifamily properties, we've got to get down to the nitty-gritty of how you determine what's a good deal and how you make it work. So, get out your calculator and let's learn how to find out if a property is a good investment. You saw the primary method of valuing fixer-uppers by matching one property to recent sales of similar property. That method can also be used to value income property, but here we'll focus on a more commonly used (and a lot easier) technique of matching a property's net income with that of a similar property's net income and its respective selling price.

START BY RESEARCHING RENTS,
VACANCY RATE, AND EXPENSES

Rental Income

As a buyer of investment property, one of your most important considerations is how much rent a property is generating. Specifically, when you are evaluating the rents of a particular building, you must ask yourself if these rents are consistent with what is being charged in comparable apartments. Or are they higher than the average, or lower? If this information is not commonly known, you can find the answers by asking apartment managers and owners. You want to evaluate your subject building with rental amounts found in the marketplace of comparable rental apartments. In most cases you will be able to evaluate the rental income from a particular property as it stands. But keep a wary eye out for apartments that may be renting at above-market value, as well as below-market value. Once you have made the determination of fair value rents, you will use this amount for the analysis of your subject property.

Let's start with some definitions. The rent roll or total rents charged is called the "gross scheduled income"; the word "scheduled" means that if all apartments were rented and monies collected that's what you should get. But in reality a certain amount of vacancy may occur that must be accounted for, as well as credit loss for tenants who for one reason or another fail to pay. When you subtract this vacancy and credit loss amount from the rent roll or gross scheduled income, the remaining amount is called the "gross operating income," meaning that this money is what you actually operate the building on.

Vacancy Allowance

Always investigate the vacancy rate for your particular area by inquiring directly of investment property owners. Ask the local landlords' association or investor group. Also take into account the vacancy rate for the specific building you are considering. Even though rates may be low at any one time, always figure in some reasonable rate, as over time they go up and down. Often, mortgage banks will require that a rate between 5% and 10% be used in any property analysis. Although the vacancy factor will greatly affect your overall expense criteria and effective revenue, never eliminate it to make a deal look good. When in doubt use 8% to 10%. Note that a vacancy rate of 7.5% means that all units are expected to sit empty for over 27 days (365 × .075), almost a month. It seems like a lot, and you must protect yourself against this downside risk. Many formerly happy landlords lost their ardor when overbuilding in the 1980s made apartments plentiful. As there is very little outside control in the construction industry besides zoning, expect these excesses to happen again.

Operating Expenses

Operating expenses are any cost that supports a property's capacity for producing income as well as any expense needed to maintain the property. This includes property taxes, insurance, utilities, maintenance, management, and supplies. It does not include financing payments such as interest or principal on any loans, nor does it include capital expenditures that improve property. It does not include personal income tax liabilities whether related to the property or not, nor does it include depreciation or cost recovery, which you will see in the next chapter.

In estimating operating expenses, be accurate. Know exactly what's going on in the building in which you are interested. Exact income and expenses lead to an accurate determination of value and financing. Don't compare last year's expenses to this coming year's supposedly higher revenue. Do the opposite: Compare the existing schedule of rents to this coming year's expenses. To do this you must ignore the figures provided by the owner. Do your own research using the examples here as a guideline. Never assume the units will rent for more unless you get definite confirmation in the marketplace. Any precipitous rise in rent is extremely rare as existing tenants may be legally able to resist. And units must usually be improved before a significant rental rise is justified.

Here are some of the typical operating expenses and how you might research them:

Advertising. You may need to advertise for new tenants as apartments become available. It's a small cost but must still be attributed to the building.

Management. Whether you do it yourself or hire a management company, the expense will be the same. Make sure you figure 7% to 10%. Even if you find a live-in resident manager who will keep the tenants happy and collect the rent, it still costs. If the building you are considering buying is big enough—six units or more—it may need a resident manager on-site whose cost should be figured separately from management.

Property taxes. Verify next year's property taxes at the assessor's and tax collector's offices. Note that property assessments on which taxes are based do not normally change upon selling price, but it's better to check now than be sorry later. In some tax jurisdictions property taxes can run from 2% to over 10% of rental income.

Heating costs. These oil, gas, or electric costs are attributable to the landlord when the building is commonly heated or cooled. Check with service companies for estimate of next year's prices.

Water and sewerage. Again, inquire with local authorities whether costs will be rising. If a new sewerage plant has to be financed starting this coming year, you can count on your cost going up.

Trash removal. Check what reasonable cost should be for either private or public contractor. If the owner does this now, use reasonable figures for outside hiring.

Lawn care and snow removal. Even if this work is currently done by the owner, you must figure it as though you plan to contract it out.

Pest control. Many modern multiresident apartment buildings must periodically deal with insect and other pest invasions.

Maintenance. Don't rely on maintenance figures used by the current owner. Make your own, more realistic estimate. Note upkeep that has been deferred. Study the building's weaknesses, especially in an older structure, that could lead to a larger-than-normal ongoing maintenance cost. A building inspection report will give you a better idea of both work that has been deferred and what would be normal operational maintenance.

Supplies. This may seem minor, but lightbulbs, sand for icy driveways, and other modest items can add up.

Remember, while it's true that every dollar you save on ongoing, year-in-and-year-out expenses drives up the apparent investment value of your building, cutting corners on money that should be spent on operating the building does nothing but deceive you about the building's true economic status. Be absolutely objective when constructing an income and expense statement.

Commonly, you begin an evaluation of an income property by constructing two statements: one by the information given to you by the owner, and, more importantly, a so-called reconstructed statement that shows your best estimate of what the income and espenses will be under new ownership.

You can see from the two statements that when you subtract the operating expense from the gross operating income, you get what is known as the "net operating income." This net operating income, or NOI as it is commonly known, is crucial to understanding investment real estate. It is the operational monies you have available after you have collected rents and paid your property-related expenses; you can then use it to pay financing costs, income taxes, or just put in

WORKSHEET: Annual Income and Expense Analysis

Reconstructed Statement
(Best estimate under your new ownership)

Gross Scheduled Income: $_____

Less __% Vacancy: $_____

Gross Operating Income: $_____

Operating Expenses:

    Advertising: $_____

    Management: _____

    Heat/AC: _____

    Gas/Electricity: _____

    Insurance: _____

    Rubbish: _____

    Property Taxes: _____

    Water and Sewer: _____

    Lawn and Snow: _____

    Maintenance: _____

    Pest Control: _____

    Supplies: _____

    Other: _____

Total Operating Expenses: $_____

Net Operating Income: $_____

your pocket. And although NOI is simply the rental income less the operating expenses, as an investor you can think of it as the money that would be returned to you each year if the property were bought for all cash and prior to the payment of any income taxes or regaining of investment capital. The NOI is then a stream of income—the economic benefit you expect when you buy an income property—produced by the property and separate from financing and income taxes.

CASE STUDY: 44 Taylor Court

Here is an example of organizing an investment analysis. The first step is to take down the information the owner gives you. The rental list prices must be matched with comparable rentals in your community. If they appear to be fair, as in this example, use them in your analysis.

Rental List, or Gross Scheduled Income

Apartment #1, three-bedroom:	$1,200
Apartment #2, one-bedroom:	575
Apartment #3, one-bedroom:	495
Apartment #4, two-bedroom:	700
Apartment #5, one-bedroom:	625
Apartment #6, two-bedroom:	725
Total monthly:	$4,320

Owner's Statement

(Information given to you by owner or owner's agent)

Existing scheduled rental income:	$51,840
Operating Expenses:	
Heat and Light:	$7,051
Insurance:	3,703
Property Taxes:	4,340
Rubbish:	757
Water and Sewer:	990
Repairs and Maintenance:	1,256
Total Operating Expenses:	$18,097
Net Operating Income (owner's):	$33,743

Keep in mind that most owner's statements are biased because of the seller's desire to sell and must be reconstructed for what income and expenses would be under your ownership for the following year. In this example, the income shows no vacancy, which is not likely unless the rents are significantly under market rent. Owners' expenses are always skinned to the bone when they report them to a prospective buyer. Rarely is maintenance or management accounted for. Typically, an owner will boost the rent and

CASE STUDY: 44 Taylor Court *(Continued)*

minimize the expenses in order to artificially inflate the net operating income. Now reconstruct the statement for your new ownership:

Reconstructed Statement

(Best estimate under your new ownership)

Gross Scheduled Income:	$51,840
Less 10% Vacancy:	$5,184
Gross Operating Income:	$46,656
Operating Expenses:	
Advertising:	$300
Management:	3,000
Heat/AC:	4,000
Gas/Electricity:	500
Insurance:	4,000
Property Taxes:	4,500
Rubbish:	850
Water and Sewer:	1,100
Lawn and Snow:	1,500
Maintenance:	2,300
Total Operating Expenses:	$22,050
Net Operating Income:	$24,606

You have reconstructed the owner's optimistic figures and replaced them with figures that more accurately reflect what will actually happen under your new ownership. You have judged the rents to be fair. But one of the first changes was to estimate a nominal vacancy rate. Expenses have been fleshed out to reflect the increase for the next year in operating expenses, as well as the addition of those expenses the owner overlooked: advertising for apartments, true maintenance figures, and management. You must compute property management when buying, because whether you have someone else do it or you do it yourself, it is a true cost against the property.

NET OPERATING INCOME IS
BASIS FOR ESTABLISHING VALUE

One of the reasons you go through the process of establishing accurate figures for income and expenses is to determine a base figure that you can use for comparison purposes. In your case, this base figure is the remaining rent after expenses, or NOI. The NOI is one of the most important economic figures on your property, certainly in terms of making a buying decision. The NOI is similar to cash flow except that it doesn't take into account mortgage payments—it is the subtraction of operating expenses from rental income prior to the payment of mortgage. This stream of income can be valued, and this value, in turn, is used to determine the worth of multifamily apartment or commercial property.

Because the NOI does not show mortgage costs it represents a stable figure, whether owned by poor or rich, heavily mortgaged or not. Once the net operating income is determined, it can be weighed against the selling price of a property to come up with the capitalization rate. This capitalization rate is the overall rate of return or yield made by a particular capital investment. And you get this "cap rate" by dividing the net operating income by the price of the property. Thus it is the direct ratio between NOI and selling price.

Once you establish the net operating income for an apartment or commercial property you—using cap rates for comparable property—can project its value. Critical to confirming the NOI is verifying accurate income and expenses.

WORKING WITH THE CAPITALIZATION RATE

Now that you have a carefully researched income and expense statement and therefore an accurate net operating income (NOI), let's look at how we can use the latter to your benefit. The capitalization of income is the most reliable method of estimating value in an income-producing building. Commonly known as the "cap rate," it measures the relationship between the income a building produces and its value. In other words, it indicates what the NOI or stream of income is valued at in the marketplace. And, remember, the NOI is the net income you would have if you bought a building for all cash.

We can show this relationship in a formula of simple arithmetic:

$$\text{Cap rate} = \frac{\text{NOI}}{\text{Present value}}$$

Or, to find present value:

$$\text{Present value} = \frac{\text{NOI}}{\text{Cap rate}}$$

Okay, you now know how to get the NOI, but what you really need to know is the present value; so how do you find the cap rate?

It's not as difficult as it may seem. In fact, you've done the hard part by coming up with a realistic NOI. If you bought an income-producing property for $250,000 and it had an NOI of $25,000, it would have a cap rate of 10%. Or, stated another way, you were willing to pay $250,000 for a $25,000 stream of income because you sought a 10% rate of return on your invested cash (i.e., you looked for a return of 10% on your $250,000 investment, which is $25,000).

Cap rates change as the expected rate of return on invested capital changes. In the marketplace, stocks, bonds, money markets, and other opportunities compete for the real estate investor's dollar, thereby changing the expectations or rate of return required from any particular investment. Investors are pleased to invest in real estate at a low rate of return of 8% when the stock market is moribund.

Further, in your own locality, apartment buildings sell for different cap rates or rates of return based on their overall quality or desirability. For example, buildings of a lower quality that produce NOIs of $25,000 may require a higher cap rate or rate of return in order to sell. Cap rates, then, change in an inverse relationship: The higher the cap rate, the lower the value, and vice versa. For example, investors may expect a higher cap rate (11% to 13%) on wood-frame apartment buildings in middle-range neighborhoods than they would (8% to 9%) for smart-looking brick buildings in classy neighborhoods. Let's see how these numbers work out in your formula:

$$\frac{\text{NOI}}{\text{Cap rate}} = \text{Present value}$$

Wood-frame building of moderate quality:

$$\frac{\$25,000}{12\%} = \$208,333$$

Smart, classy brick building:

$$\frac{\$25,000}{8\%} = \$312,500$$

That's over $100,000 more for the snappier building! In other words, investors are willing to pay more for a high-quality stream of income.

What's also important here is that you will find the cap rate for a building you are investigating by the comparison with similar apartment properties that have recently sold and their cap rates.

A similar event occurs with the fluctuation of interest rates. If rates are relatively low, investors tend to agree to a lower cap rate for real estate purchases as the competition for their investment dollar in the general marketplace has lessened. Note that by using the capitalization formula this lower cap rate means a higher price.

Understanding the principles behind the cap rate process is crucial to your being able to value income-producing property. It is the most reliable and primary way used in the investment real estate business. In an extreme example (which I don't recommend), investors have traded apartment properties in different areas of the country without having seen them solely on the basis of cap rate. Here we'll be far more judicious.

CAP RATE IS A FUNCTION OF BUILDING'S AGE AND CONDITION

The cap rate is a function of the building's location, age, and the amount of deferred maintenance. Older buildings in need of repair have a higher cap rate. This is because these building have more risk, and therefore they require a higher rate of return to the investor—a higher cap rate making the property's price tag less. For example, a newer building in a good location with little maintenance required would have a relatively low cap rate. When measured against the net operating income, this lower cap rate would indicate a higher price. The key is to research the income and expenses to obtain an accurate NOI.

For example, a classy building might have a cap rate of 8.4%, which, when measured against an NOI of $50,000, indicates a value of over $595,238. An older building of the same type but showing deferred maintenance might have a higher cap rate of 9.7%, which would indicate a value of less than $515,464—almost an $80,000 difference!—all because the better-quality, newer building involves less work and risk; hence it sells for more than its older and more worn counterpart.

Investors are willing to pay a premium for the same stream of income if it involves less risk. Less risk equals lower cap rate; more risk equals higher cap rate.

So, if you learn nothing else from this book, learn how to estimate an accurate net operating income. And then learn how to compare this NOI to actual selling prices of comparable property in your marketplace. The most common mistake new investors make is to ignore the importance of these calculations. Knowing the NOI of property and the cap rates of comparable property is what long-term investment is all about. It's not difficult—it's eighth-grade math. Just learn to do your own research and never trust an owner's figure!

For example, let's say you're considering a six-unit apartment property whose rent roll you have verified at $84,000 a year. It is 25 years old and in reasonably good condition. The current owners want to retire and move out of town. They are asking $450,000 for the property. Your investigation of the rental market in your area reveals that over the past 10 years vacancy rates have averaged 5% for this type of property. You confirm that all expenses—taxes, insurance, utilities, maintenance, management—for the coming year will be 45% of gross rent. You have a trustworthy estimate of net operating income of $42,000, in this case 50% of gross rent.

Asking price:	$450,000
Rent roll (gross scheduled income):	$84,000
Vacancy (5%):	−4,200
Operating expenses (45%):	−37,800
Net operating income (50%):	$42,000

Now you make a list of all other six-family apartment buildings that are in relatively the same age and condition and have sold within the past year. You look into the rent and expenses of each and, as accurately as you can, you estimate their net operating incomes. You then divide each property's selling price into its respective NOI to give you a capitalization rate. You find that these cap rates average 9.4%.

When you apply this cap rate against the verified NOI on your subject property you get a value of just under $447,000 (NOI of $42,000 divided by 9.4% equals $446,808).

In other words, investors buying apartment buildings of a similar age and condition were willing to pay $447,000 for the $42,000 stream of income, thereby gaining a return of 9.4%. Note this cap rate is not necessarily the overall rate of return over a period of time, but simply the rate at which the NOI of $42,000 is valued at the time of purchase.

With this information you judge that the $450,000 the seller is asking is reasonable in your marketplace.

Investment pros determine the NOI for numerous multiunit properties in their market area. They update this information yearly in order to take quick but prudent action as property becomes available.

The next chapter talks more about the financial dynamics of an apartment purchase, specifically how to compute the worth of the future income your property will generate.

15

Finding the Value of an Income Property

This chapter continues our examples of using the NOI and cap rate to establish value and to value future cash flow.

A FIRST DEAL: USING CAP RATE TO PEG VALUE

A beginning investor was eager to succeed in her first real estate venture. She found a three-unit property offered through an agent for $169,800. The agent told her the seller had refused an offer for $155,000. The apartments grossed $2,400 per month. The agent told her the property tax was $6,400 per year, heat cost $2,200, and insurance $1,600. The seller lived in one unit, which, when rented out by the investor, would add $800 a month to the gross rent.

Statement from the seller:

Gross rent (including owner's apartment): $38,400

Expenses:

   Taxes: $6,400

   Heat: 2,200

   Insurance: 1,600

Total expenses:	$10,200
Operating income:	$28,200

Looking at the unrealistic amount of operating expenses—sellers rarely count up all expenses—the investor immediately knew that she needed to research figures that would more accurately reflect costs under new ownership.

The fact that it had been on the market for five months seemed to indicate that it was overpriced. Our investor knew she would have to estimate more in operating expenses. She knew it would be best to figure on a 10% vacancy rate and about 12% of gross rent for maintenance. She also knew there was deferred maintenance, such as repairs to the water heaters and furnace, that needed to be dealt with. She suspected other capital repairs might also be needed, such as replacement of carpeting. Although she intended to manage the building herself, she knew that for the purposes of determining the current value, she should calculate a fee for outside management of 10%.

On investigation, she determined her full and most likely income and expenses would be:

Rent roll (gross scheduled income including owner's apartment):	$38,400
Less 10% vacancy:	–3,840
Actual gross rent:	$34,560
Property taxes:	6,800
Heat/oil:	2,400
Trash removal:	800
Lawn/snow:	1,000
Maintenance:	4,140
Management:	3,400
Total operating expenses:	–$18,540
Net operating income:	$16,020 ($34,560 – $18,540)

Now she had an accurate NOI with which to make a value judgment.

She would handle the deferred maintenance of needed carpet and furnace repairs within the first few months of owning the building.

She and her agent determined that the rents were under the market rate for the size of the apartments and that they could gradually be moved up over the next three years. In net cash after expenses she would have $1,335 per month to service financing payments. Her vacancy and operating expenses of $18,540 were 51.9% of the scheduled rent roll, or 46.4% when figured on actual rent received.

With the help of her agent the investor determined that other comparable three-unit apartment buildings that sold within the previous year had relatively the same proportion of expenses to income as those of this property. Furthermore, when she linked the rent after expenses (net operating income) of these properties to their selling prices, they averaged 9.5%. When she took this 9.5% and capitalized it against her net operating income of $16,020, she came up with just over $168,600.

This led her to make an offer of $160,000 if the seller would take back a second mortgage of 20%. The seller, after a few days of studying the income and expense figures that pointed to this lower price, agreed with the investor to finalize at $162,000 including the 20% second mortgage.

Here is the income and expense statement including the mortgages:

Rent roll (gross scheduled income including owner's apartment):	$38,400
Less 10% vacancy:	–3,840
Actual gross rent:	$34,560
Total operating expenses:	–18,540
Net operating income:	$16,020
First mortgage (70% of $162,000 or $113,400 at 7.75% for 20 years):	$11,172 (yearly)
Second mortgage (20% of $162,000 or $32,400 at 9% for 15 years):	$ 3,943 (yearly)
Total mortgage cost:	$15,115
Remaining amount or "gross spendable":	$ 905

What is significant here is that, after she pays all her expenses and then subtracts her first and second mortgage payments from the net operating income, she has cash left over—cash that should grow over the years as rents increase.

CASE STUDY: Another Example of Using the Capitalization Rate

You find a small building with four one-bedroom apartments and monthly rents of $750. Currently one apartment is empty. The seller is asking $195,000. The building needs work, primarily carpeting and new paint. Outside it could use some siding and roof repair. You're not sure what the market value is.

You begin inquiring. First, you find several other similar small apartment buildings that have sold this past year. You find that the rents in your proposed building seem lower than the average of the other one-bedroom apartments. You check what the operating expenses are likely to be under your ownership for the coming year. You calculate that after a vacancy factor and operating costs including a management fee, your net operating income (NOI) is just less than one-half of gross rent. In talking with the buyers of the other apartment properties, you find that their ratio of expenses to income is also close to one-half. Furthermore, when their net incomes are related to the price at which they bought their buildings, they average about 10%.

Armed with a capitalization rate of 10% for this type of small apartment building in your area, you see how that applies to your subject property. The annual rent roll is $36,000, from which you subtract an estimated vacancy rate of 10% or $3,600, leaving you $32,400. You've determined that your operating expenses (under your projected first year of ownership) would be $14,400, leaving you a balance of $18,000. Note that this NOI is after deductions of operating costs but before subtracting financing costs; therefore, the NOI is the same regardless of who owns the property or what his or her mortgage payments are.

Rent:	$36,000
Vacancy:	−3,600
Rental balance:	$32,400
Operating expenses:	−14,400
Net operating income:	$18,000

When you compare this net operating income amount to the capitalization rate of 10% set by the selling prices of similar property, you find it points to a value of $180,000. This does not mean you offer that amount, but it does give you an idea that whatever amount you pay on the low side of $180,000 will be comparatively less than the selling prices of other similar properties in the marketplace.

YOU REALLY WANT TO KNOW
HOW MUCH CASH IS LEFT OVER

Whatever you own in terms of income property, whether it's 100 units spread out in 12 buildings or a quadruplex around the corner from your own residence, the standards are the same. You collect rent from tenants, and pay it out for operating expenses, improvements to the property, and mortgage payments. You hope at the end of each year you will have some cash left over and that as little as possible will go to the IRS.

What you want to know at the end of the year is the same as what you wanted to know at the beginning: Did you make any money? You find the answer in determining exactly what your cash flow will be now and in the future and the value of those future cash flows. You also want to know what will be your taxable income.

VALUING FUTURE INCOME—
DISCOUNTED CASH FLOW ANALYSIS

Now let's carry the NOI/cap rate model to the next step and look at how to evaluate income that is received in the future, which is called discounted cash flow (DCF) analysis. It is not the purpose of this book to go into an exhaustive inquiry into the various ways of analyzing investment property. But we will try to give you a basic understanding to pursue this topic further in numerous books and computer software available.

So far we have looked at monies taken in and disbursed within the same year. Now let's concern ourselves about the future. In our discussion on calculators we introduced the time value of money. Now we have another way in which we can use that principle. Simply stated, we would like to have a dollar today rather than the same dollar tomorrow. In other words, if we are going to get that same dollar back in the future we expect some profits should be added to it. This is called the "opportunity cost," which allows us the possibility that if we invest wisely, that dollar will grow over time. Another way of looking at this scenario is that if we don't have the use of that dollar until some time in the future we have lost the opportunity to put that dollar to use until we do receive it.

Here's a simple example: Let's say you wanted $1,000 to grow by 6% a year over the next five years (note monthly computation is rounded).

Starting today: $1,000
End of year 1:   1,056
End of year 2:   1,122
End of year 3:   1,191
End of year 4:   1,264
End of year 5:   1,342

As you can see, your $1,000 has grown by one-third. Isn't that better than merely a return of your $1,000? Of course. Now let's look at what happens in reverse. Supposing you knew you were going to receive $1,342 in five years; what would it be worth today? It wouldn't be worth the $1,342 because you don't have it now, losing the opportunity to use or invest it for another five years. But it's still worth something, and if you discount it back over the same five years at the 6% that you used to grow it, it is $1,000.

And this is what you do in real estate. You anticipate future income that you discount back to present-day value. As you've just seen, you receive a stream of income called the NOI. It's logical to assume if you get that the first year, you will continue to receive it into future years. In fact, you can even anticipate it will grow slightly each year. And finally, depending on your holding period, you will sell the property, bringing yourself another chunk of cash.

For example, for simplicity's sake let's assume you own a property without any financing so that the NOI is your cash flow. Our example also assumes you live in Colonial days before the IRS and therefore your net income is not taxed. The NOI of our subject property starts at $15,000.

The cash flows are:

End of year 1: $15,000
End of year 2:   16,500
End of year 3:   18,000
End of year 4:   20,000
End of year 5:   65,000 (NOI plus sales proceeds)

The total of all this money, or $134,500, is not what you actually get, at least not in terms of today's dollars. So in order to find today's value, you need to discount these amounts over the period in which they've been received. For purposes of our example let's apply a discount rate of 10.5%, which you might reasonably expect for a real estate return.

With your trusty calculator you find that at a discount rate of 10.5% the future incomes are worth only $93,300 today. You'll also notice that, as in real life, these incomes are all unequal. The $93,300 is less money than the $134,500, but you have to wait to receive the latter; therefore, in today's dollars it is worth less. And at a discount rate of 10.5% it is worth exactly $93,300.

Let's assume this property was bought for $160,000 (cap rate of 9.4%), and the money received at the end of the five-year holding period in today's dollars is $93,300. In other words, it cost $160,000 to receive $134,500 in the future, which today is worth $93,300. We'll return to this in a minute.

Note that if you applied a higher discount rate—that is, you expected a higher return—the value of these future income flows drops. And of course the value increases if your rate of return is less. This rate then is important. The one in the example is chosen to reflect a moment in time when one investor felt he or she could reasonably expect to achieve such a return by investing in comparable investments of similar risk. In this case comparable properties commonly returned 10.5%.

DISCOUNTING CASH FLOW AFTER FINANCING

In reality, investors use the discounted cash flow method to discount, or find today's value of future income, by using cash flow left over after financing charges have been subtracted.

To continue the preceding example, let's assume you bought the property for $160,000 and you have a 70% mortgage loan of $112,000 with payments of $883 per month, or $10,597 per year, at 8.25% interest for 25 years. You will start by seeking the "gross spendable," also known as "cash flow before taxes."

The cash flows are:

End of year 1:	$15,000
P&I:	−10,597
Gross spendable:	$4,403

End of year 2:	$16,500
P&I:	−10,597
Gross spendable:	$5,903

End of year 3:	$18,000
P&I:	−10,597
Gross spendable:	$7,403

End of year 4:	$20,000
P&I:	−10,597
Gross spendable:	$9,403

End of year 5:	$65,000	(cash flow plus sales proceeds)
P&I:	−10,597	
Principal return:	8,192	(principal paid off over five years now returned on sale)
Gross spendable:	$62,595	
Discounted value of above cash flows at 10.5%:	$58,608	

In this last example we presented the cash flow before taxes for each year of the holding period, including the sales proceeds and principal payoff for the year of sale—the NOI less mortgage payments with principal gain added back on resale. Specifically, the example shows financing subtracted from the NOI, which leaves the gross spendable of each year, which is discounted by 10.5% to a present value of $58,608. Now, remember, in the previous example you didn't have any financing, so you were "buying" the $93,300 present value of cash flow with the full price of the property of $160,000. Here, with mortgage financing of 70%, your down payment is only 30%, or $48,000. Therefore, in this second example you put down $48,000 to buy these future cash flows valued today at just over $58,500. A little better relationship after financing imposed some leverage on your down payment.

Note that these cash flows do not relate to the value of the property; they do, however, estimate the value of the stream of income, which shows what you actually bought with the cash you invested. That is, by discounting those amounts of cash you will receive in the future, you can, at a chosen discount rate, measure what they are worth. It takes into account the time value of money, continual cash flows, financing, recapture of principal amortization, and eventual resale. It can also take into account taxation if so computed.

You will notice that the less down payment—that is, the more financing—you invest, the less value you have in terms of future cash flow ($58,608 versus $93,300); however, you benefit by having to put down substantially less to receive that benefit. You can then use the discounted cash flow technique to get the right balance between down payment and mortgage to fit your individual requirements.

Note that if you applied your individual tax bracket for each year you would get a discounted cash flow "after tax."

INTERNAL RATE OF RETURN

Like the other methods you have studied here, the internal rate of return (IRR) method takes into account the time value of money. Basically, it allows you to find the interest rate that is equivalent to the dollar returns you expect from your investment. Or, stated another way, the IRR is the discount rate that equates the present value of the project's future net cash flows with the project's initial outlay. Once you know the rate, you can compare it to the rates you could earn by investing your money in other investments.

Formally, the IRR, also known as the average annual total return, is the rate at which the present value of an investment's future cash flows equals the cost of the investment. The IRR, then, is calculated at the point when the net present value of cash outflows (the cost of the investment) and cash inflows (returns on the investment) equals zero. In its simplest form the IRR is similar to the interest rate on a savings account; that is, the IRR is the interest rate the savings account pays to give you the same return on your investment for the same time frame.

Note that if the internal rate of return is less than the cost of mortgaging, it doesn't bode well for the investment. Generally, in order to compensate for time and risk, investors desire to earn an IRR that is at least several percentage points higher than the cost of borrowing. The IRR's most common use is to compare one investment with another.

Let's turn to a simple example:

You are considering a $60,000 investment in an income-producing property that after expenses and financing charges gives you each year the following gains:

Initial investment:	$70,000
End of year 1:	$ 6,500
End of year 2:	7,400
End of year 3:	8,700
End of year 4:	10,850
End of year 5:	87,800 (annual cash flow, principal return, and sale proceeds)

Using your financial calculator you arrive at an IRR of 13.72.

This example is similar to the discounted cash flow illustration; that is, each year, including the final year of sale, a series of uneven cash flows is received. What's different is that you will take into account the initial investment, which in this case is $60,000. Funds going into the investment are the initial down payment and monies for capital repairs over the period of ownership, or, if needed, cash infusion to support any deficits should they occur. Cash coming back to you includes a series of annual gross spendables (after financing), principal return on sale, and sale proceeds. This example is before yearly income taxes or tax on capital gains.

As you can see by this example, an investment produces a number of cash flows over time, and the discount rate by which the present value of those cash flows equals the investment is the internal rate of return.

Technically, IRR is a discount rate: the rate at which the present value of a series of investments is equal to the present value of the returns on those investments. As such, it can be found not only for equal, periodic investments but for any unequal series of investments and returns such as those considered here. Further, you could make a series of investments as well as gain a series of returns in a particular building and the IRR will give you a picture of your overall rate of return. As you can see by this example, an important thing to remember is that since IRR involves calculations of present value (and therefore the time value of money), the sequence of investments and returns is crucial.

DEPRECIATION AND INTEREST
DEDUCTIONS DETERMINE YOUR TAXABLE INCOME

It is not the purpose of this book to go too deeply into investment analysis, but rather to give you a rudimentary understanding of where the profits come from. And certainly we'd like to stay away from arcane matters of Internal Revenue taxation. But here let's deal with some basics of how taxes relate to cash flow.

First, understand that any cash you make—nominally from any endeavor—is taxed. However, as you probably know, any expense paid to help produce that cash is usually deductible. All operating expenses are deductible; that is, rental income minus expenses is subject to taxation.

Second, understand that some but not all financing cost is deductible. Specifically, you may deduct the interest portion of your loan payments. The principal portion (the paydown of the loan) of the loan payment is taxed—even though you don't get this amount in cash! It's taxed because it goes to reduce the amount of your indebtedness.

Another financing cost that's deductible is the points you may have been charged for the privilege of being granted the loan. These, unfortunately, cannot be deducted during the year you paid them, but only over the period of the loan. So, if you took the 25-year, or 300-payment, loan for $500,000 that requires payment of one and a half points (1.5%, or $7,500), you can deduct only $25 per month, or $300 per year.

You can also deduct from your taxes what's known as depreciation, or "cost recovery," on the assumption that the asset in question is slowly losing value. Here is how it works: Generally, when you buy a computer for business use, the total cost of that computer can be deducted from income in the year you bought it. Can you do that with a $500,000 building? I'm afraid not; at least not in the year you bought it. What you can do, however, is deduct a portion of the building over a period of years until such time in the future when you have deducted the whole amount. With real estate, where the entire property consists of a building on the land, only the building portion is a depreciable asset.

Although the rules of the IRS tax code do change periodically, at present you could depreciate a residential income property over $27\frac{1}{2}$ years, and an office or other commercial building over 39 years.

The chief benefit of being able to deduct the depreciation each year is that it often shelters, or protects from taxation, your yearly cash spendable and the principal payoff on your loan, which you don't receive in cash.

Here's how it might work:

First, the facts: You buy an income-producing property for $600,000. You finance it by a 70% conventional loan of $420,000 at a fixed rate of 8.25% for 25 years and for which you paid two points at the closing. You also have a second mortgage with the seller for 20% or $120,000 at a fixed rate for 9.5% for 15 years. A reasonable division between building and land for your $600,000 property is $450,000 for the building and $150,000 for the land. Note that this ratio between building and land could be ascertained from actual sales or taken from the property tax assessor's division, or be estimated by an independent appraisal. The building will be depreciated over $27^1/_2$ years.

Purchase price:	$600,000	(value of overall property)
Building value:	$450,000	
Depreciation yearly:	$16,364	($450,000 building portion of overall property spread over $27^1/_2$ years)
Land value:	$150,000	(unable to depreciate)
First mortgage:	$420,000	(8.5%, 25 years)
Payments:	$3,311	per month, $39,738 annually
Second mortgage:	$120,000	(9.5%, 15 years)
Payments:	$1,253	per month, $15,037 annually
Points:	$8,400	
Point deduction:	$336	($8,400 spread over the 25-year life of first mortgage; no points charged for second mortgage)

Computations:

Gross scheduled income (schedule rent roll):	$124,800
Vacancy/credit loss (4%):	−4,992
Gross operating rent:	$119,808

Operating expenses (46%):   −57,408

Net operating income (NOI): $62,400 (cap rate of 10.4% based on $600,000 purchase price)

First mortgage: $39,738 (annual P&I)

Second mortgage: 15,037 (annual P&I)

Total mortgage payment: −$54,775

Gross spendable (cash flow): $7,625 (12.7% return on $60,000 down payment)

Principal payoff first mortgage: $4,828 (amortization first year—taxable)

Principal payoff second mortgage: $3,469 (amortization first year—taxable)

Total mortgage principal: $8,297 (balance paid down on mortgages but taxable)

Potential taxable: $15,922 (total cash and mortgage payoff)

Point deduction: −336 (1/25 of $8,400 point charge)

Depreciation: −$16,364 (1/27.5 of $450,000 building)

Taxable income: −$778

To summarize, after subtracting vacancy and operating expenses from rental income to determine net operating income, you then deduct mortgage payments to arrive at gross spendable. To ascertain the taxable income you add to the gross spendable the principal portion of any mortgages, finally subtracting the appropriate annual amount for your original points charge and the amount of allowable depreciation on the building or "improved" portion of your investment. In this example, the deductions for depreciation and the point charge are more than the monies potentially taxable, so there is a negative amount of taxable income. Depending on your individual tax status, you might be able to use this negative taxable income to shelter income from other sources tax-free.

At first glance cash flow and taxable income may seem similar, but major differences exist: cash flow is actual money you can spend, while taxable income is subject to the whims of interest deductibility and guidelines for allowable depreciation periods.

YOUR CASH FLOW AFTER TAXES

The taxable income arrived at in the preceding example would be the same regardless of an individual investor's tax status. Since people are in different marginal tax brackets, what would this last concept mean for a typical investor? To start with, notice in that example that not all taxable incomes are positive. In fact, it usually is desirable for a property to throw off a negative taxable income so as to shelter (protect from taxes) income from other sources. (Limitations on the use of excess taxable income may vary among individual investors.)

In the example, the cash flow before taxes was $7,625, and after accounting for mortgage amortization and depreciation deductions, the taxable income was a negative $778.

If, for example, the property was bought for all cash without mortgages, the net operating income of $62,400 was also cash spendable, and the depreciation of $16,364 remained the same, the taxable income would be $46,036.

Net operating income (NOI):	$62,400
Gross spendable (cash flow):	$62,400 (10.4% return on all-cash investment of $600,000)
Depreciation:	−$16,364 (1/27.5 of $450,000 building)
Taxable income:	$46,036

If we presume an investor with a 26% marginal tax bracket, the tax liability would be $11,969, leaving a cash flow after taxes of $34,067. For an investor in a 30% bracket, liability would be $13,811, leaving a cash flow after taxes of $32,225.

As you can see by the example, the two mortgages in the last example not only produce a higher return before taxes on cash invested ($7,625 or 12.7% return on $60,000 down payment), but deductible interest in addition to depreciation creates a negative tax liability (−$778). In this latter example, the return before taxes on cash is less

(10.4% return on $600,000 investment), while creating a taxable income of $46,036, up to one-third of which may be paid out in tax!

In this section of the book we have tried to do our best to introduce you to some of the basics of real estate investment analysis. However, computations of individual tax liability can be complex, comprising postponed losses carried forward and passive loss limitations, among other intricacies of the tax code. It requires computer software to resolve the complexity of sophisticated tax analysis, particularly in terms of showing ownership over a period of years, and is therefore beyond the scope of this introduction on investment strategy.

The next chapter investigates using the NOI/cap rate method to determine what you can offer on an income property.

16

Making the Offer
on the Multifamily

Now that you've got a sense of how to establish value for an income property, we'll look at deciding when to buy and how to make the offer. But first we'll start with a warning about one of the more popular, but less accurate, methods of fixing value.

BEWARE OF GROSS RENT MULTIPLIER

Before we go on and show how financing and remaining cash enters into the real estate equation, we must mention, if only to warn you about its unreliability, another method investors often use to value income property: the gross rent multiplier, or GRM.

The GRM matches the gross or total rent from a building with the building's value. It is similar to valuing homes in that the subject property's gross rent is matched against the relationship of gross rent and selling price of comparable property, thereby establishing the unknown value of the subject property. For example, suppose you want to find the value of a six-family that has a rent roll of $65,000. You find at least three similar buildings in terms of size, location, and quality.

First comparable:	Annual rents of $58,000
	Sold for $320,000
	GRM: 5.5
Second comparable:	Annual rents of $69,000
	Sold for $428,000
	GRM: 6.2
Third comparable:	Annual rents of $72,000
	Sold for $418,000
	GRM: 5.8

Applying the average GRM of 5.8 of these comparable properties against the subject property whose annual rent is $65,000 points to a value of $377,000. Hey, that's a lot easier than doing all that work evaluating vacancy and expenses—no wonder so many use it. Never mind this "hey" business; let's wake up. Many investors who have bought without ever looking further than the GRM have made some disastrous decisions. Why? It doesn't take into account a property's operating expenses, which can vary widely from property to property.

This method can sometimes be used as a shorthand way to determine value for the single-family property, but only if similar houses in the same neighborhood are customarily rented. Further, it seems to work better with single-family houses, as operating expenses can vary greatly with multifamily properties.

So, for income property, be warned. Do it the right way and capitalize the NOI at the average rate of comparable property. A little more work will keep your investment portfolio healthy.

USING THE CAPITALIZATION
RATE TO KNOW WHAT TO OFFER

Imagine that you are approached by a seller who offers you a six-family apartment building for $360,000. The seller says the market value of the property is over $420,000, but the apartments are only 50% rented. How might you tackle this problem? What are the building's possibilities?

Obviously, you need more information to effectively make an evaluation. First, you need to find out what this seller's needs are and why. Will he do any financing? Does he have to have all his money now? Once you know this, you can start working up some creative offers. Second, you must also determine the property's true value and find out why three of the apartments remain unrented.

The big question is why he wants to sell a property supposedly worth $420,000 for $360,000. Is the property really worth $420,000? You will need to evaluate the true net operating income of the building, find comparable properties, ascertain what they sold for, and calculate their NOIs, to be able to determine a comparable cap rate (each NOI divided by its respective selling price).

Let's suppose you find out that the three units are unrented because major repairs are needed inside each. You also determine that if the building were fully rented, the annual gross amount would be $72,000. From this you subtract a vacancy rate of 6% (the average for the last five years in your marketplace) and operating expenses of 44%, leaving you an NOI of $36,000.

Capitalization rates of other comparable properties that have sold average 9.8%. When you relate the comparable cap rate to the NOI ($36,000 divided by 9.8%) you get only a bit more than $367,500, confirming the offering price but somewhat less than the supposed bargain of $420,000. Of course, this assumes the apartments are fully occupied. You also determine that the repairs to the three unrented apartments will cost $30,000. Realistically, you've got to talk to the seller about a price shy of $330,000 ($360,000 minus $30,000), perhaps starting at $310,000.

AGAIN, ONCE YOU DECIDE TO BUY, MAKE TWO OFFERS

Making two offers can help a seller make up his mind. Here's another example with more numbers that will show you how the NOI is used to find value.

To start, let's do a little problem solving. Here are some of the particulars of a possible deal. Assess the following information. You are offered a four-unit rental property for $170,000. It has a monthly gross rent of $3,350 and a net to the seller of $2,500 after $850 in expenses. There are leases on all units and $2,800 in security deposits. The building is 12 years old and in better-than-average shape. The neighborhood is not the best, but it's not the worst, either. The seller has come down with an illness and must move to his son's home in another state. The investor is considering offering 10% cash down with the seller carrying a mortgage for the balance.

The seller's motivation does not appear to be a problem here. It's close to a must-sell situation. You start looking at price. First, are the rents in line with the market? You call your local rental agent and confirm that they are slightly under market value. Second, you find that the vacancy rate over the past five years has been 6% in your area. Third, you find a major hurdle with the owner's expenses. The seller's stated operating expenses are almost all property taxes and oil for heat; the rest of the expenses, such as lawn care and mainte- nance, he took care of himself. You refigure his expenses as if you, or any other investor, were going to operate the property. You estimate that your expenses would be at least 43% of the rental income. That leaves on an annual basis (rent of $40,200 minus vacancy of $2,412 minus operating expenses of $17,286) a balance of $20,502 as oper- ating income. You find out from the sales of other similar properties that a capitalization rate ranges between 11.5% and 13%, with most near the higher end, around 12.5%. When you measure the $20,502 NOI by the 12.5% cap rate, you come up with just over $164,000. The asking price of $170,000 is not unreasonable. The next step is to endeavor to buy it at the best price you can negotiate.

You now know your upper limit. The next step is to drive a better bargain.

You check the building with a contractor and an inspector and do not find it requires any repairs beyond general maintenance. You've assured yourself that the roof isn't going to cave in next year. Even though the seller appears anxious but not greedy, your goal is to fo- cus on getting the building at the best price and terms. You start by constructing two offers: The first is for $150,000 with the seller tak- ing back 90% financing and splitting the 10% down payment into one half at closing and the other half 30 days after closing; the sec- ond offer is for $140,000 with the seller providing a second mortgage of 20%, and the same splitting of the 10% down payment and a con- tingency agreement that you are able to procure 70% conventional financing for the balance.

First offer: $150,000 with seller taking back 90% first mortgage of $135,000 at 8.5% for 20 years.

Net operating income:	$20,502
Mortgage payments (principal and interest yearly):	14,059
Gross spendable:	$6,443

Note that gross spendable of $6,443 is a 43% return for the first year on the down payment of $15,000.

Second offer: $140,000 with seller taking back second mortgage of 20% or $28,000 at 9.5% interest for 10 years. First mortgage of 70% will be gotten from a local lending institution.

Net operating income:	$20,502	
Mortgage payments:		
First mortgage (70%):	10,206	($98,000 at 8.5% for 20 years)
Second mortgage (20%):	4,348	($28,000 at 9.5% for 10 years)
Gross spendable:	$5,948	

Note that in this second offer the gross spendable of $5,948 is just under a 43% return for the first year on the down payment of $14,000.

The strategy behind these two offers is to give the seller two choices from which to choose rather than just one that might be easy to dismiss. The financing requirements are likely to get the seller to decide whether he desires to give full financing but get a higher price, or help in a smaller way with a second mortgage for a lower price. For the investor the down payment is similar, as is the percentage return on the down payment—the advantage of the second offer being, however, that the property is bought for $10,000 less.

DECIDING TO BUY OR NOT TO BUY

Let's look at some typical information you might have gathered on the potential purchase of a small apartment building.

The Basics

The building is six converted one-bedroom apartments in an older house. The apartments are in reasonable condition but not of high quality. They are low-income and bring in total rent of $2,600 per month. There is little opportunity to raise the rental level. The owner says her operating expenses are about $1,000 per month. She has

CASE STUDY: Making Simultaneous Offers

A short while ago I made two offers at the same time on a turn-of-the-century Victorian that had been converted to a six-family. The property was in reasonably good condition, near the center of town, and had a good record of student and young professional tenants. I was dealing directly with the owner. One offer was for all cash where I was going to get the first mortgage from my local bank. The second offer was for a higher price but the seller would take back the financing. The seller was a successful businessman who had had the property for 20 years and was anxious to sell as he was leaving the area. He was asking $450,000. The property was free and clear of financing or liens.

I gave the seller two offers. Sometimes when a seller can decide between a "yes" and a "yes" you've got a better chance than when he's choosing between a "yes" and a "no." One offer was for $420,000 all cash, the second for $440,000 and the seller would take back an 80% mortgage, while the bank offered 70%. The seller would receive an interest rate one-half percentage point above what I could get at the bank—the bank charged 8.25%, while the seller's rate would be 8.75%.

I also had a private lender who would lend as a second mortgage 50% of the $126,000 down payment, or $63,000, if I could buy at $420,000 or less. I wanted to give the seller all cash and attempt to drive down the price.

Offer #1

All-cash price to seller:	$420,000
Mortgage from bank (70%):	$294,000
Balance:	$126,000
Private second mortgage (15%):	$63,000
Down payment (15%):	$63,000

In offer #1, the first mortgage with the bank of $294,000 at an interest rate of 8.25% on a 25-year term is $2,318 per month, or $27,816 annually. The second mortgage with a private party of $63,000 at 9.75% for 15 years is $667 per month or $2,985 annually.

(Continued)

CASE STUDY: Making Simultaneous Offers
(Continued)

Offer #2

Price with seller financing:	$440,000
Mortgage from seller (80%):	$352,000
Balance:	$88,000
Down payment (20%):	$88,000

In offer #2, the first mortgage with seller of $352,000 at 8.75% for 25 years is $2,894 per month or $34,728 annually.

The owner grappled with the two choices. He decided on all cash as he had other expenses that would offset his gain. And since he was leaving the area he did not want to be tied to the property the way he would've been with a long-term mortgage commitment to the new buyer. He took the cash offer, and although I would have liked to get the financing from him, I was able to do better in price, and finance part of the down payment.

It probably worked to my benefit for the seller to consider one of two alternatives rather than just one or none at all.

---

had this property for sale for a brief period after owning it only a year and a half. The assessed value is $285,000.

She will sell you the property for $260,000 and is willing to assume a first mortgage of $220,000. In addition, she will give you a second mortgage of $30,000 at 8.5% over 15 years. You will only have to put down $10,000.

Your Investigation

Because the building is an older house converted to apartments, there are few comparable sales of similar buildings in your area. You have an inspection done and no major physical problems are present. The termite test shows that no wood-boring insects are present. You check further and find there's some deferred maintenance for refurbishing the floors and repainting the walls in the hallways. You estimate that this and other smaller expenses inside the apartments will cost $12,000.

You call the previous owner, who holds the first mortgage, to ask what he would take if his mortgage were cashed out. Because the current owner has owned it for less than two years, you feel there may be a problem with the property. However, you verify and find out she is correct when she says that she must move with her husband who has taken a job out of state.

You examine the records at your local tax assessor's office, and although the assessments of most single-family houses seem to average about 80% of selling prices, when you try to match up assessments and actual selling prices of rental property, there is very little relationship.

You know that the income the property generates can determine its value. You first determine how much net operating income (income minus all expenses but before debt service/payments) the building generates over the course of a year.

You start by constructing your own income and expense statement. You've been given one by the seller but know you need to construct one as if it were under your ownership. You check rents of similar one-bedroom units in the local rental market and find that the current rents are typical of what is being charged. You also find that the building has had a vacancy from time to time that you must account for. After you check with the utility suppliers and make your own estimate of what maintenance will cost under your ownership, you conclude that the minimal amount you will account for operating expenses is 45% of rents, not the 35% used by the seller (seller's statements are rarely accurate). You further determine that you will use a vacancy rate of 5% as you want to protect yourself in case you do have vacancies. Your new income and expense statement seems more reasonable:

Rental income:	$31,200 (annually)
Vacancy rate (5%)	−1,560
Remaining after vacancy expense:	$29,640
Operating expenses:	−14,040
Net operating income:	$15,600 (before debt service)

From the owners and managers of other small apartment buildings with the same size and quality of apartments, you obtain rental income and operating expenses and determine net operating income for these properties. You find that those buildings with units similar to yours sold at an average capitalization rate of 10%. That is, the properties sold for 10 times the net operating income. You apply this capitalization rate against the NOI of the building you are investigating: A cap rate of 10% converts the NOI of $15,600 to a selling price of $156,000.

You also found that buildings with larger and better-quality apartments, hence more rent, still had about the same ratio of operating expenses to rental income of 50%, but that investors were willing to pay more for the remaining net operating income. These buildings with better-quality apartments had capitalization rates of 8% to 8.5%. If you applied an 8% cap rate to the $15,600 NOI of your subject building, it would indicate a valuation of $195,000 ($15,600 divided by 8%)—entirely inaccurate for the quality and type of apartment property you are investigating.

Don't confuse this method of valuation with a percentage return from the property. Use it as a technique to determine an income property's value. And while it's true the property is generating cash in relation to value of the capitalization rate, you as an owner further benefit by amortization on loans, tax shelter through book-keeping depreciation, and appreciation of value. The combination of these latter factors easily makes the overall return to you considerably higher.

Your Conclusion

You now know why the current owner is trying to sell after having owned the property for such a short time. She probably already knows it when you explain that the property is worth considerably less than the $260,000 asking price and that without any margin to raise rents or trim expenses, no one is likely to pay more than $156,000 for the $15,600 stream of income. This example is typical of the numerous deals you will investigate before you find one that is sufficiently safe and profitable.

IF IT'S NOT WORTH SELLING, IT'S NOT WORTH BUYING

Although you may not know a property's exact worth 10 years in the future, you should plan for the eventual sale at the time of purchase, and that's one of the reasons you have you look very carefully at a building and its income and expenses before you commit yourself. In short, the investor who will buy from you in the future is someone who will look as hard at basic analysis as you do today.

In ascertaining a capitalization rate by dividing the net income and selling price of comparable properties, you may find that the marketplace demands, for example, a 10% return on the comparable properties to the one you are investigating. You then can divide your subject's $50,000 NOI by 10% and arrive at a present value of $500,000. In other words, the marketplace has said that it will pay $500,000 for a net income of $50,000. Or stated another way, the marketplace expects a rate of return of $50,000 for a $500,000 investment.

For the purposes of analyzing a future sale, you now take this cap rate and NOI to project a future selling price. For example, you know that the present value of a dollar is worth more today than in the future due to its lack of use until a future time. To compensate for this in the marketplace, an upward drift (disregarding an economic catastrophe) is allowed in rents as well as expenses. For the purposes of our example we'll assume a modest 2% growth rate. That is, if your net operating income or NOI at the beginning of ownership is $50,000, at the end of the first year (beginning of second) your NOI has increased by $1,000 to $51,000, and so on until the end of the ninth year (10-year holding period), when your NOI has risen to $61,060, or just over $61,000. Capitalization rates themselves may change over a future 10-year period, but without proof of future change, you apply the same rate that you and other investors have at present applied to property of this type—10%. Therefore, when you divide your increased 10-years-into-the-future NOI of $61,060 by 10% you get a future value of $610,600.

This increase in value may seem modest due to practical evidence that many investors have made higher gains over a 10-year holding period. But here it's more important for you to understand the principle, if not the actual numbers, of how a future selling price is projected.

Next, you need to figure the gain after taxes over that period of time. In the preceding chapter you saw that you calculated depreciation for a first year of ownership (one year of a 27$\frac{1}{2}$-year depreciation period) and showed how this amount assists in sheltering cash flow from taxes. Here we will show you how to project that depreciation out for a 10-year holding period.

Before we proceed, we need to introduce one more concept: "cost basis." Recall in the last chapter when we applied the allowable depreciation to the "building" portion, or $450,000, of the whole (land and buildings) $600,000 property. In that example we took 1/27.5 of the $450,000 the first year for depreciation. As your example didn't go forward beyond the first year, we didn't tell you the obvious: that at the end of that first year the $450,000 has decreased by said depreciation to $433,636 ($450,000 minus $16,364). In its simplest form, the property's depreciated amount, or "cost basis," declines each year by the amount of the depreciation. The land portion, as in the previous example, of $150,000 does not get depreciated; therefore the current cost basis of the property at any one time is the starting value of the building minus the amount of depreciation taken with the land added back. Here the cost basis after the first year would be $433,636 plus the $150,000 or $583,636. Notice that for the first year this amount is the total value of the property ($600,000) minus the depreciation ($16,363). At the end of five years the depreciated amount of the building would be $368,180, or $450,000 minus depreciation of $81,820 ($16,363 times 5); adding back the undepreciated land cost of $150,000, you arrive at a five-year-out cost basis of $518,180. Note that because you can depreciate only the building (or so-called improvements) you must make the calculation on the building, then add back the land. To conclude, you have taken $81,820 of depreciation over five years and have a current cost basis of $581,180.

Now let's look at how cost basis works on your current example of the $500,000 property. Here you will divide up the land and building as simply as possible: $100,000 for the land, $400,000 for the building. Again, you choose a depreciation schedule of 27½ years.

Basic facts:

Purchase price:	$500,000	(value of overall property)
Down payment:	$125,000	
Building value:	$400,000	
Depreciation yearly:	$ 14,560	($400,000 building portion of overall property spread over 27½ years, or 3.64% per year)
Land value:	$100,000	(unable to depreciate)
Mortgage (75%):	$375,000	(8.25%, 25 years)
Payments:	$ 2,957	per month ($35,480 annually)

Computations (first year):

Net operating income (NOI):	$50,000 (cap rate of 10% based on $500,000 purchase price)
Mortgage payment:	$35,480 (annual P&I)
Gross spendable (cash flow):	$14,520 (11.6% return on $60,000 down payment)
Principal payoff first mortgage:	$4,719 (amortization first year—taxable)
Potential taxable:	$19,239 (total cash after mortgage payment)
Depreciation:	−$14,560 (1/27.5 of $400,000 building)
Taxable income:	$4,679

So far your example is similar to the one in the previous chapter except that now you will look into the future 10 years:

Net operating income (NOI at 2% per year):	$59,852
Mortgage payment:	$35,480 (annual P&I)
Gross spendable (cash flow):	$24,372
Principal payoff first mortgage:	$9,822 (amortization tenth year—taxable)
Potential taxable:	$34,194 (total cash after mortgage payment)
Depreciation:	−$14,560 (1/27.5 of $400,000 building—constant amount each year)
Taxable income during tenth year:	$19,634

Now let's calculate your cost basis at the end of the tenth year. Our yearly amount of depreciation is $14,560. After 10 years this amount is cumulatively $145,600. Subtracting this amount from the $400,000 cost basis you originally attributed to the building, you arrive at $254,400. Add back the land value of $100,000 and you get a current adjusted cost basis of $354,400.

Purchase price:	$500,000 (value of overall property)
Building value:	$400,000
Land value:	$100,000 (unable to depreciate)
Depreciation yearly:	$ 14,560
Depreciation at end of 10 years:	$145,600
Cost basis building:	$254,400 (after 10 years)
Cost land:	$100,000
Total adjusted cost basis:	$354,400

When you apply a 2% growth rate against your $50,000 net operating income, after 10 years the NOI has increased almost $10,000 to $60,958. You apply the current capitalization rate of 10% against the new NOI, and you find a future value of $609,580, or rounded to $610,000. When you subtract the adjusted cost basis of $354,400 from your 10-year-out selling price of $610,000, you get a remaining taxable amount of $255,600.

Future selling price:	$610,000
Adjusted cost basis:	$354,400
Taxable sales proceeds:	$255,600

To review, your adjusted cost basis is the property's original cost, plus any capital improvements, minus accrued depreciation. In other words, it is what you paid for the property, including capital improvements, minus the depreciation you have written off. The tax liability subject to a long-term capital gains tax is the difference between the new selling price and the adjusted cost basis. Note that the sale will also take into account any selling costs as well as recapturing operating losses from prior years that you were not allowed to take because they exceeded your "passive loss allowance." Any remaining loan points that you were writing off over time can be deducted when you sell.

In this example, assume that it cost you an extra $28,000 at the time of sale for commissions and legal cost. This would reduce your taxable sales proceeds to $127,600.

An investor's marginal tax bracket is applied to taxable income at ordinary taxing rates. In the case of a sale, however, as the proceeds are a capital gain, an upper limit is imposed.

If you assume that during the year of sale your ordinary income is taxed at 28%, you will pay a maximum of 20% on your long-term gain. Note that an exception is allowed for property acquired after the year 2000 and held for five years or more, where the maximum tax drops to 18%. However, a slight hitch exists in that the portion of the long-term gain referring to prior deductions for depreciation would be taxed at a rate of not more than 25%. In this example, since the depreciation taken was $145,600 and is more than the taxable gain of $127,600, this latter gain will be taxed at 25%; the tax liability, then, will be $31,900.

Now to your cash standing on sale. After 10 years your original mortgage of $375,000 has been paid down by $69,376 in principal and now stands at $305,624.

Future selling price:	$610,000
Mortgage payoff (after 10 years):	305,624
Sales proceeds (gross):	$304,376
Commissions/fees:	28,000
Before-tax sales proceeds:	$276,376
Tax liability:	31,900
After-tax sales proceeds:	$244,476

What have you done so far? You have taken the future selling price and subtracted the outstanding balance of the mortgage and selling costs to arrive at your before-tax sales proceeds. When you subtract the tax liability as noted above, you have your after-tax sale proceeds.

Now let's look at some returns based on the information you have gathered. First, let's look at the overall rate of return, or IRR, before taxes, on your initial investment ($125,000 down payment):

Year	Gross Spendable (Money Coming Out of Investment)
1	$14,520
2	15,529
3	16,559
4	17,609
5	18,681
6	19,774

7	20,889
8	22,027
9	23,188
10	$300,748 (spendable $24,372 plus before-tax sales proceeds $276,376)

Ignoring taxes, the internal rate of return is 19.13%. Note that you use the 2% rate of price increase, which affects rental income and expenses, specifically the net operating income (NOI).

Now, similar to the preceding, but using the after-tax returns, let's see how your $125,000 investment fares. The example uses the ordinary marginal tax rate of 28% applied to the taxable income of years 1 through 10.

Year	After-Tax Income (Money Coming Out of Investment)	
1	$ 3,369	
2	4,361	
3	5,417	
4	6,513	
5	7,655	
6	8,844	
7	10,083	
8	11,376	
9	12,726	
10	$258,612	(after-tax income $14,136 plus before-tax sales proceeds $276,376 minus tax of $31,900, or $244,476)

The 25% tax on the $127,600 taxable gain makes the tax liability $31,900, which was subtracted from the before-tax sales proceeds of $276,376, equaling the remaining amount of $244,476. Considering a 2% growth in prices, the after-tax internal rate of return is 11.5%.

So now you can go back to your original premise and ask yourself whether, if it has this value in the future, it is worth considering today. Understand that the IRR can be looked at as the degree of risk any one individual takes and that it varies with the unique match of an investor and a property.

This section on investment analysis, spanning several chapters, has tried to give you the basics of analyzing an investment property. And although I have slogged through these calculations with a financial calculator to show you that you can do it by hand, many of you will use a computer program, as the ease of use and the opportunity to run divers scenarios repetitively have great advantages. However, using the calculator for the first few times does give you an understanding of how this process works in a way that the computer does not, and it fits in your pocket. Regarding tax matters, these chapters have only touched on the basics. Make sure you rely on qualified tax advice in participating in an actual transaction, as each investor's financial situation is different.

RAISING RENTS LEADS TO MORE VALUE

Two basic principles dominate the raising of rental income in multi-family property. The first is never to project higher rents on a property you are contemplating buying just to make the numbers work out better. The second is that for a property you already own, any dollar you can increase the rent by will increase the value of your property up to five times.

Like all shorthand methods of evaluation this one should not be relied on except to corroborate other methods. Let's look more closely at how this principle works. An apartment building has six two-bedroom units all renting at $950 per month. That's $5,700 per month, or $68,400 per year; operating expenses run 50% of the rent.

Rental income:	$68,400
Operating expenses:	−34,200
Net operating income:	$34,200

For this example we'll assume that the NOI is capitalized at 10%; that is, other similar apartment buildings that have sold within the past year have a 1 to 10 relationship of NOI to selling price. That means that your $34,200 in NOI capitalizes to $342,000 in value.

This method is called the income approach and is the standard method used by appraisers, assessors, and brokers as well as yourself in evaluating apartment properties.

Now let's go back to our original premise: every $1 in additional rent jumps five times to $5 in value. In our example, each $1 in rent becomes 50 cents after expenses and is capitalized at 10% to $5. So, every $1 becomes $5.

Instead of $1, let's suppose the market in your area allowed you to raise your rents by 5%. In the above example your annual rental income is $68,400 of which 5% is $3,420, making your new rent $71,820. Assuming your operating expenses remain at 50% of total rents, your new NOI is $35,910. When you capitalize this at 10% you get $359,100—a rise in property value of $17,100!

WORKING WITH AGENTS ON MULTIUNIT DEALS

When looking for apartment properties you will often be negotiating with agents. Don't let this intimidate you. In contrast to fixer-uppers, not only do agents list some of the best multiunit properties, but they can help you make some of the best deals.

It's true that when a real estate agent is involved, your ability to discuss the seller's situation is going to be limited. In fact, you may have a hard time even meeting with the seller. However, after you show your seriousness by making your first offer, you may have an opportunity. Even if you can be there when an offer is presented, the listing agent is also going to be there. And although it's difficult to accurately gauge the seller's motivation at this time, you can probably offer an explanation regarding the details of your offer. At the very least you may be able to sense the seller's true needs.

After assuring yourself that this property is financially a good deal, make an offer that has the seller carrying a second mortgage for 20%, subject to your getting approved for an 80% mortgage. This fully financed offer is a safe way for you to get the ball rolling with a seller who is represented by an agent. Have a clause in your contract that allows you to be there when it is presented to the seller. Use this opportunity to learn about the seller's motivation. If you are encouraged, make other offers that come closer to appeasing the seller's wants and fulfilling your goals.

You can always ask the agent for a partial refund of his or her

CASE STUDY: Buying Duplexes as a Group

An owner has four duplex rentals he wants to sell as a group. The owner is motivated by increased family responsibilities and work commitments. The properties are located next to one another in a stable rental neighborhood. He is asking $320,000 for all. For a 10% premium the owner will sell any one of the duplexes individually. The owner bought the properties 10 years ago for $190,000 with a starting mortgage of $140,000 at 9.5% for 25 years and now has a mortgage balance of less than $117,136. The owner has not made any capital improvements, but the properties have been well kept up and are not in need of any significant repair. Your investigation shows that rents are fair market value for comparable rentals. Combined rental income is $5,680 per month, or $67,000 per year. Your projected vacancy and operating expenses are 45% of rental income or $30,150, thereby making the remaining net operating income $36,850. You find that the capitalization rate of comparable sold properties with similar age and condition is 11.5%. You also find that the selling prices of comparable duplexes are the same as the owner's asking price.

Observations

The owner's taxable gain is the original purchase price of $190,000 minus depreciation of $35,000 (taken over 10 years at 2.5% per year on improvement portion of $140,000), which equals current tax basis of $155,000; when subtracted from today's selling price of $320,000, this equals a taxable gain of $165,000. So, if the owner is in a typical overall federal and state tax bracket of 40% during the year of sale, he will pay $66,000 in taxes and be left with only $99,000.

The price needs to be negotiated down. But when you project the owner's NOI by capitalization rate found in the marketplace of similar rental property, you find the value of $320,000 ($36,850 divided by 11.5%), the same as the owner's asking price. Also market analysis of comparable sales of individual duplexes also indicates no discount in asking price from fair value.

(Continued)

CASE STUDY: Buying Duplexes as a Group
(Continued)

Optimal Strategy

You need to know how much room there is for negotiation. Only if he is motivated will you be able to deal at a better price. It appears the key to his motivation may be that he faces a huge taxable gain. Aim to bring about a deal with him that will minimize his tax. One way would be to work out an installment sale where he won't pay tax on his gain until the year in which he receives the profit. For this benefit to him he may be willing to reduce his selling price to you. This arrangement also benefits you as it provides the financing, and if at a favorable interest rate, it makes his price more acceptable.

commission toward your down payment. This works best if you're dealing with the owner of the agency who is also the listing as well as the selling agent. Not having more than one agent involved allows the best possibility for a fee arrangement of this kind.

The next chapter investigates some of the ways to finance the multi-family purchase.

17

Financing the Multifamily

In this chapter we'll address the two primary types of mortgage loans for income-producing property: the fixed rate loan and the adjustable rate mortgage, or ARM. We will also discuss leverage and FHA loan programs. In addition, we'll explore the various alternatives for financing your apartment purchase.

In essence, there are three basic steps investors need to follow: First, ask seller to fully finance; second, ask seller for a second mortgage or taking over subject to existing mortgage; and third, look for conventional financing. The latter, however, often allows a small discount in price as, without the seller's help, the seller is more at the mercy of the buyer's offer. In fact, to put the financing discussion in context, most times you will be relying on outside lender financing, such as a loan from a mortgage bank. However, it is advisable strategy to at least ask the seller to participate as you may be able to negotiate a better rate and no points.

CASH AND SKILLS HELP GAIN A CONVENTIONAL LOAN

Income and management skills are required to obtain financing. However, qualifying for an investment mortgage is similar to buying a single-family home. You often have to have a reasonable amount of income and show you have the capacity to meet the monthly payments. You must also be able to make the required down payment. If you have had some past credit problems, they are often overlooked.

Other requirements for the multifamily include management experience, or evidence that you can provide a manager for the property. Further, you are responsible for the upkeep and maintenance. Some lenders require that additional capital be set aside for property repairs.

Your choice among loan programs is likely to be limited. Many lenders want to finance on adjustable rates running about five years before changing. The strategy many investors choose is to finance at a long term for a fixed rate.

Some borrowers have opted for the 203(k) rehabilitation loan program (see Chapter 9), which is insured by the Federal Housing Administration (FHA). If you are looking at property that is in need of repairs before it can be used as a dwelling, you might want to consider the 203(k). The 203(k) loan can be used to purchase and repair most existing residential dwellings for residential purposes up to four units. Fixed rates over 30 years are available through the 203(k). Note at present the program requires the borrower to be a resident of the building.

The 203(k) loan can be used to finance most structural improvements, as well as for most work outside the dwelling, such as landscaping, repairing patios/terraces, or fencing. The loan amount is based on the property's after-renovation value and cannot exceed the current FHA maximum mortgage amount in the borrower's area. Your down payment is 15%, but you can finance closing costs and fees. You can also wait on any payments for six months while repairs are being made and the property is unoccupied.

KNOWING THE LENDER'S
GUIDELINE—THE DEBT COVERAGE RATIO

The debt coverage ratio is often used by lenders as a benchmark in multifamily real estate lending (over four residential units). In order to affirm that the borrower has sufficient cash flow to cover vacancy rate and operating expenses, financial institutions usually require that the net operating income (NOI—income less all expenses before debt service) exceeds the cost of debt service by a certain amount—generally a minimum of 30%. For example, if the net operating income after expenses is $150,000 and the principal and interest payments for all loans is $100,000, there would be a debt coverage ratio of 1.5.

As you can see, a ratio this high leaves plenty of funds with which to pay expenses and meet any rent loss that may occur. In the savings and loan crisis of the mid-1980s many newly originated mortgages had debt coverage ratios close to 1.0, leaving little margin for error. If a tenant defaults or an unforeseen operating expense arises, the borrower may not have enough monies from the property to meet his or her obligations.

GETTING THE SELLER TO FINANCE

As you saw in financing the single-family, it is always wise to explore the possibility of financing the multifamily with the help of the seller. Often the terms or interest rate can be better than what is available with conventional lenders. It may not always be a full first mortgage, but it is not uncommon in the transfer of income-producing property for a seller to give a second mortgage to help with the required down payment.

In fact, many investors start negotiations by presuming the seller is willing to finance. This could take many forms. A first mortgage on the entire amount may appear unrealistic, and, true, it doesn't happen often. But you do see this enough to pose that it's worth asking the seller. A common alternative for financing investment property is to have some mixture of seller financing and funds from a conventional lender. Although both the seller and the bank may insist on some monies as a down payment, the nature of a competitive marketplace has caused most sellers to expect to provide secondary financing. In the section on fixer-uppers we discussed some ways to use a second mortgage, but here we'll show you one of the more popular ways to get the seller to finance—one that benefits both you and the seller.

AFTER A CONVENTIONAL LENDER TAKES THE FIRST MORTGAGE

Typically, for most real estate you are able to get a 70% first mortgage from a bank. You and the seller dance around with offer and counteroffer on the makeup of the remaining 30%. As a buyer you may want to put down 10% and have the seller carry the remaining 20%; the seller may want you to put down 20% and only offer you 10% as a second mortgage.

Your strategy should be to get as much of a second mortgage as possible. However, the seller usually wants some limitations. Many wish to avoid giving a second mortgage at all. The reality is that a seller often needs to give secondary financing to get a reasonable price, or even to sell the property. The seller also knows, or should know, that buyers rarely walk away from deals after they've taken title. Plus, should the worst happen and the buyer defaults, the seller can either buy out the first loan or acquire the equity at foreclosure.

We're also seeing more and more banks doing 70/20/10 loans. It's great for us as investors. The bank provides 70%, the seller 20%, and the investor 10%. The banks don't even look too closely at where we, as investors, get the money.

The value of the second mortgage, and its interest rate, will have much to do with the placement of the mortgage in the equity pecking order: If the second mortgage is after a very small down payment it will be less secure, hence have less value, and may therefore carry a higher interest rate than a second mortgage that comes after a full 20% to 25% equity (assuming true, fair market value). The reason that this is important is that the seller may wish to sell the second mortgage to make up for a lower down payment from you.

Correspondingly, the value will be worth more if the interest rate is high. While it's typical for rates on second mortgages to be one to three points above the interest rate on the first mortgage, it is likely to take a rate higher than that (check legal limits in your state) for the seller to sell it for par value in the marketplace. In fact, the salability of the second mortgage plummets when there is less than 20% equity, as in the minds of some mortgage note buyers it is inadequately secure.

TAX LAW PROMOTES SELLER
FINANCING WITH AN INSTALLMENT SALE

In an installment sale the seller carries back financing and you, as the investor, pay for the property over a period of time. Popularity of installment sales is not as great under current tax law as it was prior to the last major tax revision. Perhaps the reason is that the overall tax rates are lower than in the past, therefore lessening the need to

CASE STUDY: An Installment Sale with Seller Carrying Back Financing

A seller owns an investment property free and clear with a current tax basis of $100,000. If he sells this property for $300,000, his taxable profit, or capital gain, is $200,000 (not considering any selling expense). Depending on the seller's tax bracket he might be paying $40,000 to $60,000 in taxes during the year of sale. That sort of bite will preclude him from accepting anything but a hefty down payment.

However, consider what happens if he sells using the installment method and the buyer pays $50,000 down. The seller then carries back the remaining $250,000, payable and amortized over 25 years with interest at 8.75%; monthly payments are $2,055.36. Suppose a midyear closing of June 1; the first payment is due July 1.

During the remainder of the year, the buyer makes six payments of $2,055, in addition to $50,000 down.

Seller reports the sale on his 1040 (IRS Form 6252).

The payments are taxed in three components: return of capital, capital gain, and interest.

To report the sale in his 1040 he uses IRS Form 6252 to find the "gross profit ratio" of 67% by dividing the "gross profit" by the "contract price."

Contract price:	$300,000
Cost basis:	−100,000
Taxable profit:	$200,000
Gross profit ratio:	$200,000 divided by $300,000 = 67%

This means that 67% of every dollar of principal is profit, subject to capital gains tax whenever it is received; 33% of every dollar of principal is a tax-free return of principal. (Note that all interest is taxable any time it is received.)

In the first year, the seller gets $50,000 down, plus $12,330 (six payments of $2,055): $10,912 is interest; $1,420 is principal.

(Continued)

CASE STUDY: An Installment Sale with Seller Carrying Back Financing *(Continued)*

On Form 6252, the seller reports the down payment plus principal as 67% taxable as capital gain; 33% is a tax-free return of capital, while $10,912 is taxable interest.

Eventually, the seller will get $300,000 of principal, 67% of which ($200,000) is taxable, the same as if he had made an outright sale. However, the rules governing installment sales allow the seller to spread the tax liability over an extended period of time. In this example, he spreads it over the 25-year period of the mortgage.

spread the tax out. However, regardless of a seller's marginal tax bracket, installment sale financing does allow a seller to defer the payment of tax to the year in which he or she receives funds and makes a profit. It also allows taxes to be paid in the future with, one hopes, cheaper dollars. And, of course, it allows the use of that money until those deferred taxes must be paid. As the columnist Robert Bruss has pointed out, installment sale financing does help get properties sold faster and at a better price.

An installment sale is one of the best ways for a seller to minimize capital gains taxes. That opportunity is available under the current federal tax law. By way of example, let's say you were trying to buy a small apartment building. The owner no longer wants to own the building but is afraid of what her taxes might be. You've investigated rental income and determined what your operating expenses would be under your ownership, and you've had the building thoroughly inspected. Both investigations have given this building a clean bill of health. Now, if only you could get the seller to budge.

The seller is concerned about paying this huge tax on her profit. She has owned the property for many years and has very little tax basis left. The question is, how can she structure this sale so she can avoid this tax consequence and have more manageable tax liability?

The answer is in the current application of the tax code. Specifically, as long as the seller does not receive all her money in the year of sale, seller financing qualifies as an installment sale. It is possible that even with an installment sale, she might still have to recapture her depreciation in the year of sale, but it would be at the maximum rate of 25%. Note that if she does not do an installment sale and any mortgage balance she has is higher than her tax basis, she will have a tax problem. Note too that seller financing is an installment sale because it spreads the tax over the years of the financing. Thus, the less cash she takes up front, the better. The longer the amortization, the lower the taxes.

Now that you have the idea that a seller can defer paying taxes until the year he or she receives the profit, let's see how you and your seller can use the installment sale to benefit you both. We'll start by estimating a modest selling cost and that the seller's current mortgage is assumed. For tax purposes, when you assume the seller's mortgage, the contract price is reduced. Here you assume the remaining balance of $435,000 on the seller's mortgage, and you make a down payment of $20,000. The seller's closing costs are $9,000. The seller nets at closing $11,000.

The seller's gross profit ratio is found by dividing the gross profit by the contract price. For example:

Sales price:	$300,000
Existing mortgage:	–$5,000
Contract price:	$255,000
Cost basis:	–$100,000
Expenses:	–$9,000
Gross profit:	$191,000
Gross profit ratio:	$191,000 divided by $255,000

Seller pays tax on 75% of every principal payment (excluding the mortgage assumed). Seller's first year profit is $15,000 (75% of $20,000), even though he nets $11,000.

Just a word of warning: Certainly the installment sale benefits both sellers and buyers. But as a buying investor make sure you are not paying a premium for the property just for the benefits of a pay-as-you-go installment plan. Furthermore, in your mortgage agreement with the seller, include a prepayment discount that brings down your effective cost if you arrange other financing in the future. Also, negotiate that the installment sale financing is assumable so that you can pass it along when you sell or exchange.

In any sale, particularly one of this nature, be sure to consult with a certified public accountant (CPA). You must make sure that both you and the seller structure the deal to mutual tax advantage. In addition, but not exclusively, you could use one of the popular tax software programs where you can run through a variety of outcomes using the installment sale income tax Form 6252.

The big rival to the installment sale is the "1031 exchange," which also allows for the deferral of all or part of the seller's tax.

USING A LAND CONTRACT TO BYPASS THE BANK

Here's a variation of the installment sale called a "land contract." A land contract or "installment contract" (different from an installment sale where the term is referring to a tax deferral) is a legal document for the sale of real estate whereby the purchase price is paid in periodic installments by the buyer, who is in possession of the property, even though title is retained by the seller until a future date or until the final payment is made. It is, then, simply an agreement where the seller finances the purchase of his or her property without a bank or outside financing. The seller takes a down payment and receives monthly principal and interest payments directly from the buyer for the rest of the purchase price.

An important aspect of this "land contract" or similar "contract of sale" is that the sale is not complete until the contract is satisfied. This means that title does not transfer to the buyer until he or she pays the contract in full. In some states a "notice of interest" can be recorded on behalf of the buyer to show he or she has an interest in the property.

If you are an owner, this strategy can be helpful in making a deal. For example, you may get a better price by financing a less than gold-plated buyer. And the title remains in your name in case of default. However, unless there is some advantage in terms of price or lack of mortgage financing, you would generally seek all cash. You would also want to make sure you worked out an installment sale whereby you would pay tax only on your taxable gain as you received monies.

If you're buying, the land contract can allow you control of a property (though without holding the deed) without having to go the formal financing route. It can be particularly helpful if you are currently stretched creditwise with other fully financed properties. Note that in many states the terminology for different agreements may vary. In some it is called a "contract for deed," "trust deed," or "articles of agreement for warranty deed." You should always check the laws in your state if you wish to do this type of contract.

TAKE OVER A LARGE MORTGAGE

Another way to take over with no money down is to look for someone with a large mortgage. Negotiate to assume this loan with a deferral of the remaining equity payment for a short period of time. This allows you time after you gain title to obtain a loan on the remaining equity to pay the seller. The seller may require the equity loan be further secured beyond the property itself by other assets. The amount of time could be at some near time in the future, and even the payoff date would be waived if good-faith efforts did not allow equity or refinancing.

Essentially, this is a deferred down payment, or second mortgage loan from the seller that you as the buyer are obligated to exchange with cash proceeds from an additional loan. This deal is workable because it gives the seller hope that payment will come in sooner than the normal terms of a second mortgage. As a buyer it gets you into the property for no cash and gives you a limited time in which to find a secondary mortgage.

Making some modest repairs or capital improvements can be a justification for additional mortgage funds. It's also a valid technique for a seller who is in a hurry to sell and would like to maximize his or her profit while deferring a portion of the proceeds (down payment) for the short term.

In Chapters 11 and 12 on lease/options you saw another way to take over this property that works for a seller who does not need to receive the cash from the sale immediately. You lease the property for a period of time and rent it out for equal or more than your carrying costs to a tenant who agrees to purchase in future.

The purpose here is to give you a simple example of how a first and second mortgage fit into the financial structure of a property. And although this example may not exactly fit your local marketplace, the principles are the same.

Is this a good deal? Of course. There are not many other investments where you put down $33,500 and get an 8% tax-sheltered return the first year (and as rents rise, this is bound to escalate!) with someone else making principal payments on your loans, in a market

CASE STUDY: First and Second Mortgage Payment Structure

Let's look at a five-unit apartment building to see details of a first and second mortgage structure. Assume that you have investigated income and have an expense statement setting the net operating income, which in turn determines what you have left over to pay for financing.

To summarize:

Reconstructed Statement
(Best estimate under your ownership)

Scheduled rental income:	$73,000
Less 9.7% vacancy	$7,100
Gross operating income:	$65,900
Total operating expenses (42.5%):	$31,025
Net operating income:	$34,875

Here are mortgage details, assuming a $335,000 purchase price with $33,500 down:

First mortgage—70% of purchase price
Principal: $234,500
Interest: 8.5%
Term: 20 years
            = $2,035 per month or $24,421 per year

Second mortgage—20% of purchase price
Principal: $67,000
Interest: 10%
Term: 20 years (balloon at end of five years)
            = $647 per month or $7,759 per year

Note: At the end of five years the balance will be $66,168. Principal of $6,832 and interest of $31,962 will have been paid over the five-year term.

CASE STUDY: First and Second Mortgage Payment Structure *(Continued)*

In any agreement you should keep open the opportunity to continue with the second mortgage for another five years should you, for some unforeseen reason, not be able to refinance and pay off the balloon payment.

Let's recapitulate and set these figures against your NOI:

NOI:	$34,875
First mortgage (P&I):	24,421
Second mortgage (P&I):	7,759
Mortgage subtotal:	$32,180
Remaining balance:	$ 2,695

Therefore, $2,695 is the gross spendable, or what you have left over after paying operating expenses and debt service. This gross spendable is the cash return on your actual money invested, the 10% down payment.

of growing rental prices and value. Some investors would complain that you should've worked the deal so you put less down. Well, perhaps so. Here, I wanted to show a typical example of a modest down payment deal.

HOW LONG DO YOU WANT YOUR MORTGAGE TO RUN?

One of the aspects continually debated among real estate investors is the length of the term on a mortgage. Do you shoot for a long-term or a short-term payoff? The arguments on each side abound. Those arguing for a short term pronounce:

■ *"After paying 15 years on your 30-year mortgage, you'll still owe 90% of the amount you borrowed!"*

This is true only if your interest rate is a whopping 14.75%; and you would owe less than 82% if your rate was only 10%, for example.

■ *"After paying nearly 25 years, you'll still owe over 50%!"*
True, but only at the hefty 14.75%; if at 10%, you'd pay off almost the same amount in 23 years.

■ *"You will pay over three and a half times the amount you originally borrowed before paying off your mortgage!"*
At the high rate of 14.75%, that's true. However, at 10%, it's only a bit more than two times.

Wow! Heavy stuff. As you can see, what you will pay is in part a function of interest rate, and borrowing money over 30 years is expensive. It certainly is an argument for paying off mortgages as soon as possible. However, those suspicious of paying off early argue:

■ *"Paying off a mortgage early is harmful unless you are able to find an investment paying more than your current mortgage."*
True, if you saved $200 per month on the difference between a 30-year and a 20-year mortgage and were able to invest that $200 at a rate paying off more than the mortgage interest, you would benefit. However, it may be difficult to find an investment with a consistently higher rate over the mortgage for the full 30-year term.

■ *"A shorter-term loan may sometimes crimp your cash flow during the period of your ownership."*
Cash does periodically get tight, particularly during the first few years of ownership. However, as principal on the loan gets paid down there is a better chance for an equity loan when or if difficulties arise. Besides, with a longer-term loan you can always accelerate payments if your investment is paying better.

■ *"As interest is deductible, each dollar paid in interest is, in reality, worth somewhat less."*
True, a nominal 10% interest for practical purposes is closer to 7% after deducting for state and federal taxes. Nonetheless, money is money, and tax deductibility is not so great that you want to pay $3 to save $1!

ACCELERATED MORTGAGE PAYMENTS IN PERSPECTIVE

Although there are some advantages to paying off a mortgage in more rapid payments than scheduled, let's put this in perspective. An agreed-upon accelerated, or biweekly mortgage plan, sometimes called a "banker's secret," has disadvantages. First, you don't need a rigid plan that forces you to make extra payments when you simply can make an extra payment, even at a higher or lesser amount, and instruct the bank to apply the extra payment to your principal.

Whether you do this or not has much to do with the interest rate on the mortgage in question. If the interest rate on the loan is a modest-for-these-times 5%, your true rate is somewhat less, as this interest is deductible from your income tax. If your rate is a hefty 12%, even after an average deductibility of 30%, your rate is still almost 8.5%, and you may want to make extra payments to bring down the principal.

Another way of making a decision is that if you can find an investment paying more than your current mortgage costs, the funds that go to buy that investment make a higher return, helping to pay the lesser cost of your current mortgage.

For example, if you had a $100,000, 7.5% mortgage amortized over 25 years, or 300 months, with payments of $738.99, you could pay an additional $138.35 or a total of $877.34 per month, and pay off that mortgage in only 200 months and save $46,229. This may seem like a substantial savings, but let's look further.

If you invested that $138.35 in a quality (no-load) mutual fund paying 10% per year, at the end of 200 months you would have $70,692.17. At this time you sell the mutual fund and pay off your $100,000 loan, which now has a balance of only $54,827.23, and you save $15,864.94. And if you started with a mortgage that was for a longer period or higher interest rate, the savings are even more dramatic.

As an even better choice, don't pay off your house. At the end of 25 years you will have paid for your house and your fund balance will be around $183,567.40 (before taxes).

Plainly, you must put the early payoff of your mortgage in perspective. If you want to have your personal home debt-free, that's understandable. But as an investor you need to apply the example of the time value of money to your investment loans to maximize your return.

SOME FINANCING GUIDELINES

Difficulties arise in attempting to give advice that may work in any particular marketplace because there are usually three varying trade-offs: interest rate, term, and cash flow. The following are guidelines only and must be adapted to your particular circumstances of marketplace and property.

First, for a long-term loan (one or more years), understand that interest rate is more important than term. Our examples have shown that if you negotiate a lower interest rate and/or shorter term you dramatically bring down the overall mortgage costs as well as accelerate the principal payoff.

Second, match the term of your mortgage to the type of investment you are planning. An apartment building you are going to hold for 15 to 20 years could have a longer mortgage term than one you are only going to hold for a five-year term. In fact, the shorter your likely holding period, the more acceptable a longer term on the mortgage, because you aren't going to feel any wasting effects of payments spread out over many years.

A word of warning: Don't opt for a longer term such as 30 years over a shorter 20-year period to make a deal go. Always decide whether you go into a deal based on whether you are buying a favorable stream of income (i.e., NOI). Remember, investing in real estate is not about giving you the right to kick bricks and mortar, it's about buying (and maintaining) a stream of cash.

Suggestion: Stay within a 20-year term if you feel comfortable with making these payments, longer if you can get a greater return (such as another property) with the difference. Most of us who are in the property business—that is, into buying more property—want to be as highly leveraged as possible. Perhaps you only need to moderate that with the right purchase. The idea is to use the extra money for real estate (an appreciating asset) instead of a new car (a depreciating asset). You've got a better chance at becoming a millionaire if you don't let your ego get in the way by buying fancy cars, anyway. Don't show off, but just work on making your life exactly what you want it to be. That shows you really know the time value of money.

MORE CREATIVE TECHNIQUES TO MAKE A DEAL WORK

Sometimes what a seller wants is just beyond what you wish to pay. One common situation is when the seller wants more money as a down payment than you wish to put down. As an example, let's assume you've thoroughly checked out, physically and economically, a 10-unit apartment building. You and the seller have come to an agreement on price and the seller will give you the financing. The seller owns the property free and clear. The only obstacle is that if the seller is going to finance, she wants to limit her risk and require 20% down, but you feel the most you are willing to do is 10%.

You have a choice. You could set this deal aside and get back to the seller later to see if her motivation has increased, or work out something that might meet her needs while allowing you to stay within the 10% down.

Here are some solutions that will allow you to act:

- Allow the seller to keep the security deposits and assign her your first month's rents. Of course you can only do this if there is enough rental income to cover this initial cash drain.

- Give the seller more security—a blanket mortgage that includes other property you may have, land or a house, that is not heavily financed. This extra collateral may lessen the seller's wish for safety and assure her of your commitment.

- If the rental income is sufficient, offer the seller a shorter payoff on the mortgage (i.e., if she had agreed to a 20-year payout on the mortgage she is carrying back, propose a 15-year payback). In this way, equity in the property, hence security, is built up faster.

- Obtain bank financing for a portion of the loan and have the seller subordinate her mortgage to the bank loan. This means she could possibly get a lot more than her request of 20% cash and might make her more flexible on the terms of the mortgage with you. It is possible that if you get new financing and the seller agrees to subordinate her mortgage, you could even walk away with cash at closing.

- Let the seller refinance the property. Then you assume that mortgage, giving her a second for the balance. This allows her to draw out as much cash as she wants.

- Give the seller a short-term, second mortgage for the other 10% down payment. The seller will still carry the longer-term first mortgage of 80% along with the shorter-term second of 10%. In essence, it allows you to meet the seller's request for a larger down payment by paying the additional amount over a three-to-five-year period. Make sure the property's cash flow allows this.

- Bring in a partner who could put up 10% of the price. Combined with your 10% you would be able to meet the seller's down payment requirements.

- Find an investor who is willing to put up the entire 20% down payment and agree to split 50–50 all future equity.

- Explore with caution whether the characteristics of the property are such that minor or cosmetic repairs would allow you to raise rents, thereby putting you in a position to pay the other 10% down payment within a short period, such as a year.

- Instead of putting down the entire down payment, get the seller to agree to take half at the closing and half in 30 days. This allows you to use the incoming prorated rents (and in some states the security deposits) toward the second half of the down payment.

- Formally agree to make such improvements that will increase the market value of the property and assuage the owner's desire for security.

- Similarly, make improvements to drive the value of the property up and allow you to refinance and cover the additional 10% down.

- Give the seller 10% down, an 80% first mortgage, and a 10% second that she could sell to give her the additional cash she seeks. If the property financials look good, the seller should have no trouble selling the note.

- Get the seller to subordinate her first or second mortgage to you as an additional loan whose proceeds might be directed to returning the down payment or fixing up the property. If this provision were not used immediately, in the future it could supply funds for another project. Note that a seller who agrees to a provision of this nature will usually limit the amount of funds that may be borrowed and require that additional security be posted, at least until proof is provided that funds were spent on improving the property.

- Get a better deal on the interest rate and firm up your commitment by promising the bank you will deposit all the rent money into their bank.

- Like a single-family fixer-upper, any improvements you make to an apartment building will usually increase its value substantially beyond the cost to repair.

- Once value is improved, refinance to pay off short-term loans with seller at a discount or pay off funds or loans used to repair property. Or, as refinancing funds are tax-deferred, you could increase them by making a down payment on another property.

THE ROTH IRA

The Roth IRA is a special form of individual retirement account that may benefit you as a real estate investor. The Roth IRA helps individuals with annual incomes up to $110,000 (joint incomes $160,000) to create retirement income that is nearly but not entirely tax-free. That is, contributions made are taxed when you deposit them, but thereafter income will be tax-free. In fact, all the profits are tax-deferred until retirement.

You also have to keep the Roth IRA for five years. If you change a traditional IRA (the tax-deferred kind) to a Roth IRA you must pay the tax on the value of the assets. But again, the future income will be tax-free. This strategy will work well if you expect a significant rise in your capital. Investment real estate is an excellent candidate. Doing rehabs, wholesaling, even buy-and-hold strategies will benefit.

One of the rules for switching IRAs is that your income has to be $100,000 or less in the year you convert. Note that if you have previously paid taxes on contributions prior to converting to a Roth IRA, you don't have to pay taxes on the contributions again, just the income you earned on them. Converting is an easy process that will save you money over time.

You have more than 10 years to save before you take distributions—without mandatory distributions—from your IRA. And, you can make contributions as long as you continue to make less than the $100,000.

The Roth IRA can make your profit from a real estate deal tax-free. For example, an investor had $70,000 in a Keogh profit-sharing plan which he switched to a traditional IRA with the intent of converting to a Roth IRA. At the time of conversion he paid a tax of $15,000 from the $70,000, which left him $55,000. He used that to buy a fixer-upper and make the necessary improvements. Three months later he sold the property for $85,000, with a profit of $13,000 after taxes. He now has the $85,000 in the tax-free IRA to use again.

WHEN TAKING IN A PARTNER CAN MAKE MORE PROFIT

Sometimes, perhaps not often, you will need to take in a partner. The need for an all-cash deal, a hefty down payment, or the need for an extra signature on a mortgage can all be reasons for teaming up with another investor. Whether it's a fixer-upper where in addition to a need for capital funds, an investor throws in with you to work on the repairs; a multifamily where extra funds make the down payment easier; or a lease/option deal where two can cover more ground and make additional sales, here are some guidelines on where and how you might work out splits:

- Any deal where the partner is equal in cash and works with you 50–50.
- A deal on a fixer-upper where the partner fronts all money but doesn't participate further, also 50–50.
- A deal on a fixer-upper where the partner fronts one-half of the money but doesn't take part in the supervision or work: 30/70% to 40/60%.

Note that these suggestions are an attempt to balance out responsibilities between an active partner (you) and a passive money person (your partner). They may need to be modified to reflect your actual partnership relationship.

Most real estate investors buying and selling fixer-uppers are able to do it alone. Perhaps the reason for this is that working out a fixer-upper is, in part, operational—the key task is the execution of the repairs. And as two people can disagree on what may need to be done, it may work against having a partner. On the other hand, if you have worked well with someone, you may be able to accomplish more by teaming up with that person.

Multiple-unit buildings are often owned by two or more investors because of the larger down payment and equity-credit problems posed by a mortgage lender. Furthermore, multiunit properties are generally considered a passive rather than an active venture, due to the standard practices of landlording and the widespread use of management companies.

Partnerships have their value. Sometimes it is a matter of choice to go it alone. But many investors partner up when they haven't got the money for a bargain, so be thankful for the chance to benefit from a partner to make a profit.

If you are going to take in partners, make sure your choice is someone who is known to you and has some experience in business. Hopefully, this experience will have been in real estate but if not, then it should at least be someone of reputable business character; that is, the person has not purposely caused financial injury to anyone. Is this someone you can rely on for advice? Does the individual's experience complement or oppose yours?

You can also (tactfully) find out whether the person has had litigation filed against him or her. This doesn't mean that such litigation automatically indicates a bad partner, just that you should know what this matter was about and how it was settled.

The partner should have funds available to meet the obligations of the property. Does your potential partner understand the risks involved? The person should also have the same psychological commitment and financial goals as you do. For example, if you are going to hold an apartment building with your partner for an extended time, make sure he or she is in agreement on the general time period of holding. The same is true if you and your partner, or partners, are going to buy and resell fixer-uppers.

The next chapter deals with how to make the job of managing your apartment investment pleasant for both you and your tenants.

18

Managing Your Property

In this chapter you'll see how to stay on top of managing your apartments—specifically, how to make it a satisfying experience for both you and your tenants.

FIRST TIME OUT: BE YOUR OWN LANDLORD

For the first small apartment building you buy, you should act as your own landlord, experience supervising the physical ins and outs of your property, and have direct contact with your tenants. Exceptions to this might be a case where you took over a building that was already managed by a competent management company, or if your other duties did not allow for the time necessary to deal with maintenance and tenants. Learn from your own mistakes so that when you begin to use outside help, you will understand their job.

The best investment will fall short if your tenants don't pay their rent. And there is no easy way to evict a bad tenant. If a person gets behind in rent, try to find out what the nature of the problem is and see if it can be worked out. If tenants deceive you on a continual basis about paying, you should act legally to evict them and receive the

266

full payment of rent. These problems can best be addressed by doing your best from the beginning to get worthy and conscientious tenants. Whether you screen prospective tenants yourself or use a manager, it is an important job. You will make a major mistake if you do not do a thorough screening of prospective tenants and make sure you select the best-qualified ones.

The purpose of discussing property management here is to remind investors to protect their investments and to show that owning multiple units requires real management, either by yourself or an outside company.

Don't confuse a resident manager with property management. The former is simply an on-site contact for tenants, possible rent collection, and minor maintenance tasks. He or she does not perform the duty of executive management. If you arrange for a resident manager to live in the building and undertake these tasks, the overall responsibilities of management will still fall on your shoulders.

WHAT A PROPERTY MANAGER DOES

Property managers—whether that means you or an outside company—supervise property for the owner's financial benefit and peace of mind. They provide executive oversight of services that usually include:

1. A pretakeover inspection of the property, outlining what's expected and making proposals.

2. Finding and screening tenants, showing apartments, and securing and verifying rental applications. Management then selects tenants from applications taken and checked references, and negotiates and executes leases.

3. Designing and implementing tenant retention programs and assuring an ongoing, positive relationship with tenants. Goodwill with tenants can make or break an investment. Management will also evict offensive tenants when necessary.

4. Advertising as needed with local newspapers and rental magazines. Depending on the location of the property, management will also look at other venues of advertising based on response, effectiveness, and cost.

5. Performing normal duties of property management, including oversight on procedures regarding tenants moving out, identifying any problems the tenants leave behind, providing for regular apartment cleaning between tenants, and making inspections with new tenants.

6. Supervising property rent collection and bookkeeping, including the handling of property receipts, journal entries, records of account, bank deposits, and delinquent accounts; keeping an account summary of tenant activity, and detailed monthly reports of all expenditures and billings, including monthly reports/annual budget reports.

7. Collecting rents and security deposits, with funds forwarded either to the investor's specific business account for rents on that particular property or to the escrow account for that property.

8. Supervising property maintenance, ensuring that properties are inspected weekly and that any vacant units are brought into condition of immediate possession; supervising on-site resident managers as needed.

9. Keeping up adequate records. Having the right property management forms helps to keep you organized with the proper records. Prescribed form letters to tenants can address a number of problems, saving the time of writing letters for each different tenant problem.

10. Insurance, tax analysis, and management. Company will provide necessary certified accounting personnel and negotiate insurance packages, keep pertinent insurance up-to-date, and uphold fire safety and security regulations.

11. Increasing cash flow by being aware of market trends that allow for adjustment of rents and minimizing expenses in relation to work required.

12. Being responsible for the property's compliance with government and environmental regulations.

Management is all about efficiency—efficiency in controlling maintenance and dealing fairly but firmly with tenants. Your success in the real estate business will be based in part on how well you or the management company takes care of your property and your tenants.

GETTING GOOD TENANTS

One of the most important tasks of a property manager is to get good tenants. If you're doing the management work yourself, always meet, interview, and check references of your tenants. I can't stress enough that you must give the matter of tenant selection your personal attention.

If you have a good reputation as a landlord, you will have your choice of the better tenants. This does not mean that you have to meet every plea put forth by the tenant, but that you attend to reasonable problems. Immediate repairs to a clogged toilet, ripped carpet, or broken door hinge will let tenants know that you care about their living conditions.

Note that even with tenants who face you with a sticky problem, you should avoid a quarrel. The tenant may be in the wrong, but you should meet any reasonable request with respect and attention—and be even more careful with unreasonable requests! You never want to lose control of a problem.

The sample rental application could be altered to suit your particular needs. Just be sure you ask for the information that is likely to be important to you.

A LANDLORD'S PRIMER

The following is a primer on what you need to be aware of in capable property management in order to ensure quality tenants and increased profits.

Although maintenance is a critical responsibility for you, choosing the right tenants must vie in importance. Although you should never discriminate against a prospective tenant for race, religion, national origin, sex, marital status, or physical disabilities, you do have the right to choose your renter. And even if it seems you have a gold-plated tenant sitting at your desk, make sure you have him or her fill out a rental application form. It, among other basic information, would include the applicant's employer and current landlord, both of whom you should contact. For it is in these matters that you need to verify that you have a tenant who can afford the rent as well as make his or her payments on time.

To get good tenants ask your current tenants (if you have them) for recommendations of friends they might know who are looking to

SAMPLE FORM: Rental Application

Rental Application for (address)_____

Name _____ Home Phone _____ Work Phone _____

Social Security No. _____ Driver's Lic. No. _____

Date of Birth _____

Present Address _____

How long at this address? _____ Rent $_____

Reason for Moving _____

Current Owner/Manager _____ Phone _____

Previous Address _____

How long at this address? _____ Rent $_____

Reason for Moving_____

Current Owner/Manager _____ Phone _____

Names of people who live with you (include ages of minors): _____

_____

Any pets? _____ Describe _____ Waterbed? _____

Present Occupation _____ Employer _____

Phone_____

How long with this employer?_____ Immediate Supervisor _____

Phone _____

Previous Occupation _____ Employer _____

Phone _____

How long with this employer?_____ Immediate Supervisor _____

Phone _____

Current Gross Income per Month (before deductions) $_____

List sources of income (other than present employment listed above):

_____

_____

SAMPLE FORM: Rental Application *(Continued)*

Savings Account: Bank _____ Branch _____

Acct. No. _____

Checking Account: Bank _____ Branch_____

Acct. No. _____

Major Credit Card _____ Acct. No._____

Expires _____

First Credit Reference _____ Acct. No. _____

Bal. Owed _____ Mo. Pmt. _____

Second Credit Reference _____ Acct. No. _____

Bal. Owed_____ Mo. Pmt._____

Have you: ever filed for bankruptcy? _____ ever been evicted?_____

or ever been convicted of a felony? _____ Explain any "yes" answers on back.

Vehicle(s)

Make(s)_____ Model(s)_____ Year(s)_____ License(s) _____

Personal Reference _____ Address _____

Phone _____

Contact in Emergency _____ Address_____

Phone _____

Nearest Relative _____ Address_____

Phone _____

I declare that the statements above are true and correct. I authorize verification of my references and credit as they relate to my tenancy and future rent collections.

Date _____ Signed _____

Above Verified by_____ Date _____

rent. You may also need to advertise, but fair warning—this is not always the way to get the best tenants. So, you must screen them carefully. And always write a fully descriptive advertisement of what you are offering for rent—a full description of the unit, number of bathrooms, number of rooms overall, who pays for utilities, rent and security deposit, as well as any restrictions such as pets or number of occupants.

You should always receive a security deposit. You may also wish to collect the last month's rent in advance. Unfortunately, some tenants are likely to play fast and loose with payments unless there's a penalty to back up prompt rental payments. And should the worst happen, this deposit will help you defray damage that occurs while the tenant is occupying the unit, or cover the rent while you are trying to evict, if needed.

Note that deposits can only be kept for unpaid rent or damage, and damage does not include normal wear and tear. Deposits should be returned promptly, after a reasonable period of inspection, normally within 30 days after the tenant moves out, to ensure that word doesn't get around that you are slow in your obligations. An inspection should occur as soon as possible in the unit being vacated. Many landlords inspect on the last day the tenant occupies the unit. Some states and local municipalities have laws regarding the use and return of security deposits. In Massachusetts deposits have to be held in a separate escrow account that bears interest in favor of the tenant until they leave.

Make sure your tenants know exactly when the rent is due. Make sure they do not exceed that date for payment. And tell them you expect prompt payment. Try not to set a precedent of a grace period, or you'll find many tenants taking advantage.

Should tenants refuse to pay their rent, they must be removed as soon as possible. Even though you carefully selected your tenants from all the other applicants, the unforeseen can happen. Like everyone else, tenants can be affected by losing their job, illness, or divorce. You may want to work out a special payment plan with a tenant who otherwise has a good payment record but has temporarily met some hardship. A tenant who is constantly late needs no such help and should be evicted as soon as possible.

Many communities regulate the number of persons that can occupy a unit. As a landlord interested in preserving one's property you don't want to pack groups of tenants into any one unit, even though you may gain more funds. The extra wear and tear and noise will not be worth it. So you should always limit the number of tenants per unit. Have this stipulated in your rental agreement.

If you have student tenants, as I've had in the past, make sure they understand they can't have loud parties or music. Make this grounds for eviction. The key is to select the best tenants possible for the type of property you have for rent. This is the way you avoid problems.

No matter how many units you have, be prompt in dealing with maintenance. Whether you do it yourself or have a repairperson on call, just make sure that what needs to be addressed is done quickly and efficiently. Remember, you're not going to save any money by waiting, and it's more important to keep your tenants happy and continue that stream of payments each month.

A fact of life for most landlords is pest control. This is particularly true in multifamily units. Because of the specialized ways in which roaches and mice are exterminated, professional pest control is usually required. You can shop for the best price and service.

In conclusion, nothing can make your job easier as a landlord than an excellent tenant. Be prepared to spend some time finding the best, which will save you money (and time) in the long run.

WHEN ALL ELSE FAILS: REMOVING LATE-PAYING TENANTS

Nobody wants to throw out tenants. As a landlord you should do everything you can to avoid evicting someone. A prudent landlord knows that rent problems are minimized by the careful selection of a tenant—if you do your homework on checking a prospective tenant's references, income sources, and character before you rent, you've got the best chance at collecting timely rent from an ideal and satisfied tenant.

Unfortunately, the best-laid plans can go wrong and something can happen that causes the tenant to vary an otherwise exemplary pattern of payment and behavior. A tenant's rent problem usually starts with a typical warning flag of the rent being late, then simply ceasing. You can agonize over what has gone wrong. What did you miss when you interviewed the applicant for the apartment? This is a valid question for the future, but doesn't help solve the problem for now.

You can start by finding out why the rent began coming in late. If the tenant has a real problem and can't make the payment on the

CASE STUDY: Removing a Late-Paying Tenant

An investor and his tenant are in the sixth month of a one-year lease and the tenant has been consistently late on the rent for five of the months. The investor is not sure if he wants the tenant out or just wants him to keep more current on the payments. The tenant has no phone or mailbox, a sure sign of a problem. The investor has asked the tenant to give him a way he can communicate with him. At the moment the investor can reach the tenant only with a note left on the door. The investor wants to know what recourse he has. Should he tolerate it and not renew the lease? Or, because the tenant eventually pays the rent, should he ignore it? Besides the fact that not receiving rent in a timely manner is a big problem, there is also the fact that the investor cannot communicate with the tenant. Unfortunately, this is not within his control. He cannot force the tenant to get a phone or receive mail (although it should be in the lease that tenant accepts mail). Ultimately, if paying the rent late is the only real problem, then the investor might want to hold on for the remainder of the lease and decide then whether to renew.

On occasion you will learn about tenants the hard way. And when you have a tenant who can afford his or her rent but just doesn't pay on purpose, then you need to get rid of that person. One investor had a tenant who started being as late as he could get away with. The landlord had done all the background checks, credit report, and character references, but still ended up with a nonpaying tenant. After three months of unpaid rent the landlord went to the courthouse to start the eviction process. The tenant paid the rent the day before the court date. After doing this twice the tenant wanted to know if the investor would let him out of his lease, which he gladly did—however, by agreement, keeping the deposit.

first day of the month, ask what the best day is to pay on time. As long as it does not cause your payment for the mortgage to be late, perhaps you can restructure the lease. Also, what does your lease say about late rent payments? Perhaps there's something the tenant is misinterpreting as a grace period.

Communication with your tenants is crucial. If you can keep an active dialogue with them, you are most likely to understand their problems and be able to monitor their goals for keeping up-to-date with payments. One question you might deal with is whether your state allows you to require late fees or rent credits that might encourage early payment.

If all else fails, you could offer an unsatisfactory tenant money—a modest amount, such as $200, to leave in one day, or $100 in three days. Perhaps this is not professional, and you certainly don't want to set a precedent with the rest of your tenants, but it's less expensive than court.

You need to understand the tenant eviction process in your state. Eviction works in a similar fashion in all states, but there are differences in procedure and time periods with which you must become familiar. Even in the most tenant-oriented states, such as Massachusetts, a tenant, no matter how far behind, will always be responsible for paying the rent, and may ultimately be evicted.

Here is how the eviction process works in many states:

1. If the tenant is 15 days late with the rent, the landlord must send, via certified, return-receipt-requested mail, a "three-day notice" that demands that the rent be paid within three days.

2. If rent is still unpaid after the time limit, the landlord can file for eviction. He or she may need to serve the tenant with a summons 12 days before the court date. If after being served the tenant still has not paid, the landlord (or his or her lawyer) brings the necessary records and the verified summons to the court at the proper session. If everything is in order, the judge issues an order for eviction and the tenant has five days to vacate or the police will remove the tenant.

Note that the above procedure and time frame may vary for your area. Always consult an attorney and/or the court staff itself for the proper way to proceed.

No landlord likes to pursue tenants for rent. But eviction due to consistent late payment of rent is a judgment call you have to make yourself. Only you know *all* the relevant facts, and someone else's experience may or may not work in your situation. If you have a tenant who is not paying and is also ignoring you, you have little choice; you must evict. And be wiser on the next rental.

ON LOOKING FOR A GOOD
PROPERTY MANAGEMENT COMPANY

You will not always want to manage your own property. In fact, you may not wish to in the beginning, but you should manage your first few buildings if possible. Then once you gain in experience in relating to tenants, collecting rents, keeping records, supervising maintenance, and so on, you may want to turn those duties over to a professional management company. This is particularly true if you have employment commitments and have gathered too many apartments to keep track of them efficiently.

Start by looking for a company that has experience in managing the size and type of apartments that you have. The size of the company isn't so important, but it is important that they are ready to devote their efforts on your behalf. Do be wary if the company owns competing apartments, because this is a built-in conflict of interest. Furthermore, choose a management firm that is not a brokerage company. The company you choose should not be distracted by brokerage sales. By extension, never sign a management contract that gives any exclusive rights to sell your property. This could severely cripple a future sale. Your contract with the management company should also specify prompt terms for ending the relationship if needed.

In choosing a company, make sure they put an effort into selecting and relating to the tenants under their supervision. Specifically, the company should agree that in showing apartments they will have a skilled representative who will also have a second meeting with the prospective tenant and a thorough investigation into their references. Avoid a company that is geared to large apartment complexes. They are not likely to provide your building or your tenants proper consideration. And always interview the specific property manager who will be assigned to your property. You want to assure yourself of this manager's experience and competence.

YOUR LIABILITY AS A LANDLORD

How do you protect your assets in terms of liability? Do you incorporate? Do you inspect? Your liability concern is not with profit/loss but with protecting your personal assets should you be sued, such as in the typical "tenant-slipped-down-the-stairs" plight. In fact, it doesn't matter how well a property works financially if you are thumped by one outlandish claim—or (even) a well-founded one.

However dire it may sound, there are some practical ways to limit your liability. One of the first considerations is to make sure you and the property are properly insured for a tenant or visitor who might have an accident on your property. Although policies vary from company to company and state to state, you may have some coverage for liability for rental ownership under your homeowner's policy. Similarly, you may want to investigate a personal umbrella policy that would have some form of overall liability coverage for you at home as well as for your rental properties. Most major insurance carriers have landlord policies whereby a rental property can be endorsed onto your existing homeowner's policy. In planning for the worst case, you want the insurance company to pay for any suit.

LIMIT YOUR LOAN LIABILITY TO THE PROPERTY

The other kind of liability you need to concern yourself with is personal default on the loan. It's always best if you can limit the liability of any mortgages to the property itself and not cover them by your personal assets, such as your home. Unfortunately, you will not always be able to limit mortgage liability to the property being bought, but you can limit the breadth of your personal assets that provide security for your property loan.

Numerous ways of controlling property without personal liability have been discussed in this book: not signing mortgage personally, corporate signature, lease/option, management takeover, and so on. Another way is to cover your personal residence through a homestead exemption. Basically, as usually interpreted, should the worst happen, this law shelters your personal residence from certain forms of foreclosure. Homestead exemption laws vary from state to state and you should discuss this procedure with your attorney.

Generally, you can't buy direct insurance for default on a loan. One of the best protections against having a property fail is to buy it right in the beginning—and that's what this book is all about. If you find a deal and buy it right (read "at a bargain price," a price that would make it very difficult to lose money no matter what happens), then you have minimized your default liability. Buying right = lower risk = minimal liability. Note that a corporate structure, such as a limited liability corporation (LLC), isn't going to be much help if you make a poor choice structuring the deal on the property.

Consequently, always make sure that any property you buy is subject to a satisfactory physical inspection. However, you won't necessarily spend money on inspectors until you know that your offer is going to be accepted.

SHOULD YOU FORM A
CORPORATION OR LIMITED PARTNERSHIP?

Generally, when you are getting started in real estate investing you need not be concerned with how you take title. Most investors use their personal name because it allows them to pass on any tax loss as well as profits to themselves personally without being "double-taxed," as one is in a corporation. However, as you both gain and keep property over a period of time and increase your activity by accumulating more assets, you may want to consider some form of legal corporation or partnership.

One idea to consider is the limited liability partnership (LLP), which helps limit liability while allowing tax pass-through. The same is true if you form a limited partnership. Both of these are legal entities that help you limit liability. This way you have protection in case things go bad. They are also easier to maintain, or to dissolve should things not work out. Other alternatives are the limited corporation and the full corporation, or a land trust. Eventually you may wish to establish a family limited partnership and a living trust.

Although we all plan on conducting our business free of lawsuits, there have been precedents where courts have found that because personal and corporate assets have been mingled, all assets are liable to be seized. Talk to your attorney and accountant for the ramifications for you of different procedures, as well as for how these entities may vary in your particular state. Note that regardless of the legal entity or name in which you take title, a lender is probably not going to free you (unless you have a tremendous amount of assets) from signing the mortgage loan personally. In other words, the limited partnership or corporation is a way to minimize (not eliminate) liability from a tenant or a visitor, but it rarely protects you from exposure on a defaulting loan.

In the next chapter we remind you that planning ahead will give you the knowledge and confidence to win.

19

The Magic Formula
for Success:
Use Flexible Strategies

This final chapter concludes with how strategies work together and
what you have to do for success.

BE FLEXIBLE—PROFIT WITH DIFFERENT STRATEGIES

In order to make good money in real estate, let different strategies
work for you. Working one strategy is great, especially in the beginning, but don't tie yourself completely to just one. They work together. What you cannot do in one deal you can often do in another.

Now you know some of the long-term strategies for buying and
holding with the continual paydown of a mortgage combined with
rental cash flow and appreciation of value. You also know about
short-term strategies for buying low, fixing up, and reselling high,
where you seek profits now. Managed right, two or three deals a year
can keep you in cash. You can also buy and resell, or contract and assign your position to another investor. All of these strategies are discussed in this book. The real road to wealth is to put a combination of
them to work for you based on what's happening in your market
area. By this, I don't mean you should do a little of this, a little of

that, but that in choosing one strategy in which to specialize, you may on occasion find it advantageous to employ another strategy temporarily. For example, it's not unreasonable to concentrate on fixer-uppers while wholesaling a different fixer-upper to another investor, or running across a single-family house you can lease for an extended time, allowing you to rerent it to a tenant-buyer, ultimately putting some of the cash you earn into a single- or multifamily that you will hold for an extended time.

It's not the combined blending of all techniques into one single strategy, but the focus on borrowing one or two other strategies as opportunities become available.

Some complain about the long-term strategy and say that it compromises your borrowing power by having you hold a large liability, such as a mortgage on a multiunit building. They say, too, that the difficulties of renting and being a landlord are not worth the risk, and that some properties will not appreciate in value. True, accidents can happen. But in this book you saw how to buy right and manage expenses and tenants so that your financial future will not be compromised.

The fast in-and-out attention required for handling fixer-uppers and wholesaling needs to be balanced by the longer-term goals of holding onto something. Note that the property you might buy and resell may not be the same one that you would choose to hold for an extended period of time, such as multiple units. The cash-generation possibilities of repairing and reselling are fine for single-family homes. You can also lease a property with an option to purchase where you then lease out the house to someone with whom you execute a lease/purchase agreement.

So, each strategy—buying, fixing up, selling, leasing, optioning, exchanging—all these opportunities occur in the marketplace and all will work for your benefit when you know how to use them. You don't have to walk away from a deal just because a seller wants to defer a sale until next year. You don't have to say no to a fixer-upper because you've got too much on your plate. Being able to use each strategy to maximum benefit increases your efficiency and keeps you open to all possibilities.

CHOOSE THE BEST TECHNIQUE TO CREATE WEALTH

You have three two-family rental properties. One has $45,000 in equity, another has $15,000, and the third has only $7,000. The issue is the equity. If you sold the house with the largest equity, you could take the money (after taxes) and buy another with a higher ratio of equity to mortgage (i.e., you would have higher leverage).

You want to know whether it is better to leave the equity in the property accruing more equity and wait for it to be fully paid for, or sell now and buy something else. Sometimes it's better to stay with what you know. And it's true that your equity in the first property seems to balance the other two that have far less equity. Selling the first property also will create a large taxable gain. What are the possible solutions?

- Make an offer on a new property that includes a second mortgage on your high-equity property.

- Use the equity in the first property to refinance your three properties into one blanket mortgage. This would consolidate your equity and lead to better opportunities for further purchases.

- Find a suitable replacement property with which you could exchange. Although this alternative doesn't allow you to keep the first property, it does allow you to leverage its high equity tax-free.

Note that none of the three solutions recommends an outright sale. When dealing in real estate, one of the key attributes of wealth is to keep your equity moving forward with no or minimal tax consequence along the way. Therefore, in the example you can either refinance, leverage your present equity into additional property, or exchange equity into a larger, potentially more lucrative deal.

BEFORE THE FINISH—USE AN ATTORNEY

One other strong recommendation: If you are new to real estate it is prudent to have your offers reviewed by a competent real estate attorney. Never rely exclusively on a sales agent when it involves deposit money or interpretations of contract clauses. Agents may try to close deals on their own, telling you that you don't need a lawyer for settlement, that they will guide you for free. Be warned! A competent attorney can guide your real estate career and help you avoid costly mistakes. Paying for an attorney in a real estate transaction is well worth the few hundred dollars it will cost. They are your advocate, hired by you, and represent your interests. You can usually rely on them to give you the right answers to your questions. They will also ensure that closing documents are correctly prepared and that the title is recorded properly at the registry of deeds or county courthouse.

PLAN AHEAD TO REDUCE THE RISKS OF REAL ESTATE

Real estate investing has risk. Even those who have been in the business for many years always need to ask themselves what can be done to limit uncertainty.

What if you can't find tenants? You don't want to be left in the lurch paying a mortgage on a vacant property. Buildings can deteriorate, credit can be ruined, mistakes will happen. The answer lies in knowledge and learning from other people's mistakes.

It's always helpful to see how others do it. That's why you bought this book; that's why you need to keep up on the latest information— read the current books on each strategy, or log onto the Internet and participate in newsgroups that focus on investment real estate. Check out the Internet sites that specialize in investment real estate.

Learn everything you can about the particular specialty or specialties you wish to practice. Go out and see as much property as you can. The more you know about a property, the safer you are. Knowing the property can help you avoid pitfalls. Talk with other investors on how they acquired their property. Asking questions will elicit a surprising amount of information. Most investors are happy to relate the intricacies of how they bought and how it has worked out for them. Looking at real estate and talking with those who have traveled a similar route will give you the confidence to move forward. Remember to constantly stop and remind yourself of what you've learned.

KNOWLEDGE GIVES YOU CONFIDENCE

You may feel a bit of fear in getting started. I know I did, and I probably lost a few good deals until I gained confidence. In fact, confidence is the way to eliminate fear about anything. And the way to have confidence is to gain knowledge. Know more about that property you wish to buy than the present owner does, and become thoroughly familiar with the investment technique that you will use to make the purchase. So, face up to those fears and get started. Remember, the harder you work, the more opportunity you have to succeed.

Read! Read! Read! Read every fragment you can find on your chosen specialty. Then start putting that knowledge into action. Even if you think something does not pertain to you, if it is even marginally close to your area—read it! Start reading and looking at properties. This is the way to make fewer mistakes. Even when you are experienced, don't slow down on your reading.

Note that this book summarizes several strategies while other books focus on a single strategy or specific area of property investing.

Have you checked into investor clubs in your town? This is one of the best resources for networking and learning more about your market.

LET PEOPLE KNOW YOU DEAL IN PROPERTY

Just as though you were on your way to being a Hollywood star, you've got to let the world know what you're up to—that you buy houses (not that you're in the property investing business; that sounds too pompous). You don't want to appear arrogant. Besides, you've got to be clear with those with whom you may do business: *You buy houses!*

That's the basic thing you do. Don't confuse potential sellers with explanations about the different ways you might buy houses. You'll put them to sleep trying to explain lease/options or how they can benefit from exchanging with you. Besides, you don't want your potential customers to know you are implementing an investment technique. Keep it simple. You don't want them to think you are a professional who will take advantage of them financially; you want them to understand that you'd like to help them by finding a solution to their property question. The techniques you've learned—lease/option, wholesaling, installment sale financing—you keep to yourself and make known the details only when you present a seller with an offer that will solve his or her problem.

WORK HARD TO BECOME KNOWN

Work hard to get known as a real estate investor. Run classified advertisements for properties wanted. You are not wasting money; these ads work. You should run them constantly. Cooperate in activities that help you become recognized within your community as an investor. Deals will come to you when people know you're serious and that you follow through. Once you've been investing for a while you will find that deals start coming to you rather than having to find them yourself. Remember, you are assisting people with a basic dream—living in their own home—and in doing that you are pursuing your own dream of financial independence.

The magic in owning real estate comes from matching the right property with the right strategy. Whether it's fix up for resale, wholesale, lease/option and turn over, buy and hold—the aim is to profit. Don't let yourself lose track of that goal.

20

How You Benefit from the New Tax Law

In this final chapter you will see how you can take advantage of provisions in the new tax law. You will also see how the latest regulations in the personal residence exclusion as well as new rules on second homes can greatly increase the equity in your real estate portfolio. The chapter concludes with an update on how interest rates are made and why they may remain favorable for investing.

RECENT TAX LAWS KEEP DOLLARS IN YOUR POCKET

The major tax legislation for 2003, "Jobs and Growth Tax Relief Reconciliation Act of 2003," signed into law in May 2003, has modest benefits for real estate investors. Specifically, this law offers a lowering of capital gains taxes as well as an incentive for investing in qualified improvements. Although the new law leaves depreciation recapture rates untouched, it improves cash flow and bolsters investment in new property.

Let's start by looking at the bonus first-year depreciation inducement. Under the new law you are allowed to deduct an additional first-year depreciation amount equal to 50% of qualifying property on which you can then depreciate the balance according to the current depreciation schedule.

Note that bonus depreciation applies only to property improvement with a recovery period of less than 20 years. Although this rules out many real estate investments, you can still benefit from this bonus on the following: carpeting, electrical equipment, plumbing, movable partitions, office equipment, removable lighting fixtures, furniture, and computers. Qualified leasehold improvements may also qualify. However, to qualify, the building must be more than three years old when the improvement is made. Major items of improvement such as making a building larger, adding an elevator, or adding structural components are ineligible.

Unfortunately, the 50% additional depreciation deduction won't apply to property acquired or put under contract prior to May 5, 2003, nor will it apply to property bought after the end of 2004. To qualify, you must have acquired the property after May 5, 2003 and before January 1, 2005. Property does not qualify if there was a binding written contract for the acquisition in effect before May 6, 2003.

Note that prior to 2003 the law provided for a 30% bonus first-year depreciation. You can elect to claim the normal 30% instead of 50% bonus first-year depreciation, or elect not to claim bonus first-year depreciation. If you claim the 50% first-year depreciation deduction, you are not eligible for the 30% additional first-year depreciation deduction added in 2001. Three reasons you might not want a larger bonus depreciation (or to elect out of it entirely) are where you have about-to-expire net operating losses, you anticipate being in a higher tax bracket in future years, or you wish to maximize the size of deductions when marginal rates are higher.

SHELTERING TAXABLE GAINS FROM YOUR HOME

Under current tax law, you can shelter up to $500,000 (maximum exemption for a married couple filing jointly; up to $250,000 filing individually) in gain from the sale of your principal residence. However, you must have owned and used the home as your principal residence for at least two of the five years prior to selling. Normally this exemption is not allowed if you have not owned the property or lived in it for the two years or 730 days. If the home being sold is a second or vacation home, then you must have owned and used your second home as your principal residence for the required two-year period.

Some narrow exceptions to the two-year rule exist that allow you to reduce the taxes. In certain circumstances, when the two-year rule is not followed completely you may be permitted a reduced maximum allowable exclusion, but only when the tax on the gain from the sale of a property cannot be entirely avoided, or when the gain exceeds the exclusion amount. Under regulations issued by the IRS in 2002, you may qualify for a partial exclusion if you sell your home because of a change in employment requiring a move of more than 50 miles. You can also gain a lower exclusion due to poor health or to unanticipated factors such as legal separation, divorce, death, or other unforeseen circumstances. In this case the amount of the exclusion depends on how long you owned and lived in the home before selling it. For example, if you were forced to sell your home after one year, you would qualify for half the maximum exclusion.

Note that the ownership period does not have to be at the same time as the occupancy period, nor does it have to be uninterrupted. However, two years or 730 days must amass within the five years prior to the sale.

Furthermore, you may use the exclusion no more than once every two years. Therefore, you could qualify for the maximum exclusion for a four-year period for both your primary home in which you lived for two years and your second home in which you also lived for two years. If you gain the exclusion in this manner, plan on providing proof of actual occupancy, such as your respective addresses used on tax returns, street lists, driver's license, and so forth.

Do note that if you fail to qualify for either the full or reduced exclusion, your taxable gain will still benefit from the federal capital gains tax rates and, in most cases, from state and local income taxes as well. However, if you have held your property for less than one year, your taxable gain will be treated as ordinary income. Under most circumstances, when you hold a property longer than one year, you qualify for the current capital gains rate of 15%.

In any case, you want to do everything possible to minimize the taxable gain on a sale. As a reminder, "taxable gain" is the sale price less expenses of the sale subtracted from the original cost of the home plus expenses for the purchase and the cost of improvements of that home made over the years. In other words, to reduce the "amount realized," make sure you deduct current expenses, real estate commissions, legal and title fees, and advertising expenses, as well as add to the original acquisition price, or "adjusted basis," expenses such as attorney fees, inspection fees, surveyor fees, mortgage and application fees, and document taxes. Don't forget to factor in capital improvements, including additions to the building, roof replacement, attic or basement conversion, driveway repaving, addition of a deck, replacing gutters, installing air-conditioning, heating system improvements, and any other improvements that add value to your home or improve its usefulness. Although ordinary repair and maintenance costs cannot be used to increase your adjusted basis, genuine capital improvements can amount to a considerable amount of money over time—all of which can increase your adjusted basis, thereby reducing your taxable gain. The key is to keep good records of what you've done to improve your house over the years. When you total up what you've done you may be surprised.

A final note: Many states typically treat a gain that is not covered by the federal exclusion as ordinary taxable income; therefore, you want to do everything possible to minimize your taxable gain on a sale.

USING THE GAIN EXCLUSION WITH MULTIPLE RESIDENCES

As just discussed, the gain exclusion for sales of primary residences ($250,000 for singles; $500,000 for married couples) is handsome. Now let's look at what you can do to benefit even more. Let's say you have several holiday residences. How can you save up to $500,000 on each property? First let's look at the basic rule: You must have owned and used the home as your main residence (a second home qualifies too—see following section) for at least two years out of the five-year period just prior to the date of sale. Let's look at an example. You and your spouse own four homes. You sell your primary home in which you have lived for two of the last five years, which qualifies for the $500,000 gain. You then move into your second home on Grand Isle, Maine, where you stay for another two years before selling and excluding a substantial gain from this sale as well. Then you move to your third property in Orlando, Florida, and live there for two years. I think you understand.

You could also replace each home after it's sold with another. So the exclusion law as it's currently written allows you to do the "live and move" cycle repeatedly, excluding gains on each sale.

Now, most of us don't have the funds or have the time to enjoy multiple homes, but even if you're not rich, you can still take full advantage of the tax laws by having an overlapping ownership of several "potential" residences—that is, if you and your spouse have a strong sense of wanderlust!

TAX RULES FOR SECOND-HOME OWNERSHIP

Assume you have a second home that you rent out as well as use yourself for part of the year. The IRS allows you to deduct interest on up to $1 million of mortgage debt on two personal residences. In addition you may also deduct up to an additional $100,000 for home equity loans. The key is how you qualify your second home as a personal residence. Specifically, to qualify, your second home must be rented more than 14 days a year and have personal use (family members and anyone else who pays less than market rental rates) of more than 14 days or 10% of the rental days, whichever is greater.

As always, no matter how many homes you own, property taxes are usually deductible. And if you own three or more homes, you can pick the two with the most mortgage interest that qualify.

You do need to account for rental income and interest and taxes separately, one accounting for when you or family members occupy the house (vacant time included), and another for when you rent it out. The personal portion of interest and taxes can be listed as itemized deductions on your year-end income tax filing Schedule A.

Beyond deducting interest and taxes you can also deduct a percentage of operating expenses—utilities, insurance, association fees, rubbish removal, maintenance, depreciation—to the extent you don't go over the rental income (carryover operating expenses can go against rental income of future years). Note that the percent calculation used for operating expenses is the time rented in proportion to the time for personal use, not including vacant time. You will account for this on Schedule E (Supplemental Income and Loss). Your goal is to completely deduct interest and taxes (part on Schedule A and the rest on Schedule E) and have enough operating expenses to sweep away your rental income.

The big payoff here is that if you follow the guidelines above for qualifying your second home, essentially the primary investment after your main residence, and you arrange to occupy it for at least two weeks, you may take advantage of the $500,000 residence exclusion when you do sell.

Now, what happens when you rent your second home out most of the time and use it yourself, or with family members, very little? Well, quite frankly, if you rent more than 14 days a year and if your personal use doesn't exceed 14 days or 10% of the rental days, whichever is greater, your second home falls under the tax rules for rental properties and not personal residences. For example, if you rent for 190 days and use it yourself for holidays for 19 days, it's rental property. The obvious strategy is to make sure you use it for 20 days to take advantage of the personal residence rules just explained. If for some reason you do not match the "more than 14 days or 10%" rule, your plight is not that onerous, at least not on a year-to-year basis. You will still have a rental property in which interest, property taxes, and operating expenses can be accounted for on the total number of days the house was used as a rental.

In fact, if you don't have enough rent to cover your cost, you may be able to post a taxable loss on Schedule E. However, to do the latter you must meet certain IRS "passive-loss" rules where you can deduct passive losses in a given tax year only to the extent of passive income from other sources (such as other rental properties that produce gains).

The latter situation inevitably leads to another exception: You can write off up to $25,000 of passive rental real estate losses if you "actively participate" in the management of the property, and have adjusted gross income under $100,000. Furthermore, for this exemption to apply, the IRS says your average rental period must be eight days or more. So beware: If you normally rent out for a week or less, the write-off under the passive-loss rules doesn't apply. Note that if you do qualify, but your passive loss can't be taken in one year (because the loss is more than $25,000), the IRS allows you to take it in future years.

Note that the interest during your personal use (19/190 days in our example) is nondeductible, because your home doesn't qualify as a personal residence. (The personal-use portion of property taxes is still deductible on Schedule A.) So make sure you take residence yourself for more than 14 days or 10% of the period in which you rent out. Then you can keep the property in personal residence classification where you can deduct interest and taxes, as well as protect the $500,000 exclusion.

Sound bewildering? It is, at least the first time you look at it. Once understood, it's not difficult to follow.

The final tax rule you need to be aware of is when a second home is rented for fewer than 15 days a year and used by you for more than 14 days. For investors who are familiar with renting out property this may seem like a rarity. Fortunately for those of you in this category, your second home is considered a personal residence: You deduct the interest and property taxes in the same way you would for your primary residence. You don't have to worry about splitting operating expenses and depreciation. You aren't allowed any. But under the rule you also don't have to declare any income—still not bad considering you clearly are keeping your second home within the exclusion ($500,000/$250,000) guidelines.

SHOULD YOU TURN YOUR OWN HOME INTO AN INVESTMENT PROPERTY OR SELL IT?

The first and often primary investment in our lives is our home. Let's take a look at how the new tax law affects us as we decide whether to rent it out or to sell it. This decision often confronts young investors who live in a primary residence but think about adding another residence to their portfolio. Should one buy something bigger by leveraging the equity in one's present home? Or should one take the profit and put the cash directly into a new residence, perhaps a three- or four-family?

So let's take a look at whether you should sell your home or rent it out. Let's assume you have a home you bought some years ago for $100,000 that is now worth an estimated $325,000—a potential $225,000 gain not counting fees. Part of the dilemma is that if you sell now you will lock in a sizable gain, but if you wait you might gain more money later. But as usual it's not even that simple. Let's see how the tax situation can influence your decision.

As we've discussed, you can gain a sizable tax benefit—married couples can enjoy up to $500,000 and singles $250,000 in capital gains tax-free—if you've lived in your home for two of the last five years. In fact, you could rent out your home for a total of just under three years while you are making up your mind—just don't complete a full third year of renting. If you do sell more than three years after you started renting out, you lose the tax exclusion—your gain then will be taxed at long-term capital gains rates, now currently well under rates for ordinary income.

But let's go ahead and assume you sell after renting out for four years. In our example above you've already rented out for just under three years and now you need to make a decision to sell, protecting your exclusion, or to continue to rent out. You project out that after a full four years your current $225,000 in taxable gain may have increased (3% average rate of inflation on current value of $325,000) slightly more than $40,000, to $265,000. If you sold after the four years you would apply a 15% capital gains rate against the $265,000 gain and pay a $39,750 tax.

Does it make sense to pay $39,750 for a $40,000 gain in appreciation? Of course not. Wouldn't you have done better to have reinvested the tax-free $225,000 in another property that presumably would have benefited from the same appreciation rate? For example, what would happen if you sold at $325,000 (tax-free due to the exclusion) and bought a $500,000 house and then sold it in four years? Assuming the same 3% appreciation rate, your $500,000 investment will have increased to $562,500 (rounded). But this time because your cost basis is your purchase price of $500,000, your taxable gain is $62,500 and when 15% capital gains rate is applied, your actual tax will be only $9,375! And, if this is a residence meeting the two-out-of-five-year test, the gain is tax-free.

The following chart shows some of the positive and negative reasons for renting out or selling:

Pros and Cons for Renting Out

FOR	AGAINST
■ Mortgage and operating expenses like taxes and insurance payments paid by rental income	■ Possible legal or management problems with tenants
■ Some tax breaks may balance income tax on rent	■ Taxable gain likely to be high when you sell
■ Potential to receive price appreciation over time	■ Tenants can cause damage to property

Pros and Cons for Selling

FOR	AGAINST
■ Less property to manage and maintain	■ May need to sell in bad local market
■ Raises cash that can be reinvested	■ Loss of property appreciation
■ Probable tax-free capital gain	■ Could be expensive to buy comparable property in future

The lesson here is that if you are facing a large taxable gain on your home, you don't want to rent it out. Simply stated, if you already have it tax-free don't change it to rental property where you will have to pay tax on the gain. Of course this situation begs the question of an obvious remedy that may work for some: Move back into the house, live there for two years, and qualify for another exemption before you again sell.

Note that for clarity our example does not take into account selling costs that can be deducted from gain, nor does it compute the depreciation you would be required to take for the time any property is rented out.

ARE YOU A DEALER OR AN INVESTOR?

To take advantage of these dramatic ways to save your tax dollars you must make sure you remain classified as a genuine investor—specifically, you want to avoid being classified under IRS rules as a "dealer." Let's take a moment and review the IRS definitions of a "dealer" and an "investor." The issue is important because first it concerns how much tax is paid and when it is paid. Second, we need to dispel the myths of who is labeled a "dealer." Put simply, an investor is someone who buys a property with the intent of holding that property for the production of income. For example, an investor buys and holds; he or she does not turn around after buying and resell.

When we sell a property as investors we are taxed at favorable capital gains rates. We also take depreciation deductions. We expect we will be allowed to exchange our property under Internal Revenue Code Section 1031. Finally, we hope to qualify for the deferral of taxable gain by using the installment sale provisions of the tax code.

In turn, one who is classified as a "dealer" is taxed at ordinary income tax rates upon sale, with no deferral and no depreciation deductions. Obviously all investors want to avoid being categorized as a dealer.

How does one get defined as a dealer? As suggested by the definition of an investor, the first yardstick is based on the *intent* of the investor. For example, if the buyer of a property bought with the intent to immediately sell within a short period of time, then he or she would be a dealer with respect to that property. However, if the property was bought with the intent to hold for income and appreciation, he or she would be an investor entitled to the full benefits as mentioned above. Therefore, it's always a good idea to represent to others—your attorney, accountant, other investors—that you intend to hold. Another solution is to create documentation that proves the segregation between property types.

It follows, then, that the standard of defining a dealer is the length of time of ownership. Specifically, properties held for less than two years are likely be treated as inventory of a dealer. Properties held longer have a better chance of being treated as investments.

Obviously, the greater the number of sales during a period of time, the more likely one might be branded as a dealer. Again, this factor by itself is not usually enough to make one a dealer. However, subdividing a land parcel and acting as a developer is a sure road to being marked as a dealer, particularly if you maintain a business office for the sale of that property.

A closely related factor is the amount of time and effort devoted to sales. Perhaps one way to mitigate dealership status as developer might be to rent out the properties once they are created. Certainly if you build and immediately sell you are likely to be marked as a dealer, at least for that particular project.

Another problem area is when one uses advertising or similar personal sales efforts to find property. These don't in themselves invalidate you as an investor but if the actions are regular they can be an element that points in the direction of being a dealer. This is especially true when combined with other elements.

In summary, number of sales, selling within two years, and extent and consistency of sales efforts all point to one being a dealer. One way to minimize dealer status is to segregate properties you buy and sell rapidly, or develop into a different ownership entity such as a corporation, from your "buy-and-hold" investment properties, which you keep in your own name or a limited liability corporation or limited partnership. Another and more common approach for the small investor is to provide good documentation that details precisely how and why each property was acquired. In this way you can remain an investor for most of your property while acting as a dealer on other property you wish to rapidly turn over.

You can act as a dealer on some property and as an investor on others, but if your actions regarding your investment property are similar to the way you treat your dealer property, the IRS may on audit reclassify your investment transactions as dealer sales. For example, if you buy and sell several houses a year as a dealer, and you also have certain properties you buy where your intent is to hold for a period of time, a problem will arise when you sell one of your investment properties in a relatively short amount of time. Regardless of the fact that you might have kept the property for more than two years, if you are buying and reselling other properties in under two years you might get your so-called investment sales reclassified into dealer sales. Obviously the IRS will look at your activities as well as your intentions.

At the risk of confusing you, one final point should be made. As an investor you might have a property you bought and resold in perhaps a year's time without having that property classified as a dealer's sale. However, if you did a number of such sales in the next year, you make the first sale the year before suspect and in danger of reclassification by the IRS.

Bear in mind that dealers are not able to use the installment sale procedure or enter into a tax-free exchange. Dealers must pay the tax on any sale in the year when the sale is completed.

THE TAX-DEFERRED "STARKER" EXCHANGE

We invest in real estate to make money. None of us wants to give money away. So wouldn't it be better to sell a property, *not* pay a tax, and reinvest into another property our equity plus the tax we normally would have paid? We can do just that. In fact, once you know the particulars it's not difficult. Many accountants and lawyers are available to help you along the way. Rules governing exchanges have become easier to follow in recent years.

We've discussed earlier in this chapter how the new tax laws benefit those of us who sell one home for another. In fact, if you sell your principal residence, and have lived there for two out of the past five years before it is sold, you can exclude up to $500,000 ($250,000 if you are single) of any gain you have made.

In contrast when we sell investment property (not our personal residence), we pay a capital gains tax. This tax is a "discount" from the tax on ordinary income, but a tax nonetheless. Here we discuss an accepted method to legally avoid paying a current tax. This is known as the Starker (named after the taxpayer who went all the way to the Supreme Court to win his point), or "deferred" like-kind, Exchange. It is under Section 1031 of the Internal Revenue Code. Here, if you exchange one property for another (like kind)—even if the replacement property is obtained at a later date—you do not have to pay tax on the current sale but can defer payment until later. Note that an exchange is not a way to escape paying the tax owed on a sale. It does, however, allow you to defer paying that tax until you sell your last investment property—and as you have seen here, if you turn your final investment into a residence, you may qualify for the personal residence exclusion and thus ultimately substantially lower your capital gains tax.

A recent Tax Court decision explains the principle of exchanging: "The primary reason that has been given for deferring recognition of gain under section 1031(a) on exchanges of like-kind property is that the exchange does not materially alter the taxpayer's economic position; the property received in the exchange is considered a continuation of the old property still unliquidated." (*Decleene v. Commissioner*, 2000 U.S. Tax Court, November 17, 2000). The actual definition in Title 26, Section 1031 of the Internal Revenue Code says, "No gain or loss shall be recognized on the exchange of property held for productive use in a trade or business or for investment if such property is exchanged solely for property of like kind which is to be held either for productive use in a trade or business or for investment."

Since the original Starker Exchange allowed a time delay in choosing the property into which you would exchange your equity, Congress refined the regulations by setting fixed time limitations. Specifically you must identify the replacement property (or properties) within 45 days from the date you sell your former or "relinquished" property, and you must take title to that property no later than 180 days from when you transfer your first property. These are critical time limitations that must not be missed when you enter into a 1031 exchange.

Note that you can defer capital-gains taxes by reinvesting in another holding of equal or greater value, but if your replacement property(ies) costs less than your old one, you may face a tax bill.

Section 1031 of the Internal Revenue Code spells out the rules for the tax-deferred exchange. Here are some of the highlights:

- An actual exchange must take place (i.e., you must sell and then purchase).
- The relinquished property and the replacement property must be "property held for productive use in a trade or business or for investment." Your principal residence cannot be one of these properties without having changed your residence into an investment beforehand.

■ The replacement property must be of "like kind." This definition is somewhat generous. Ordinarily all real estate is considered "like kind" with all other real estate. Thus, a land parcel can be exchanged for a multifamily property, a condominium unit for a commercial building, or single-family rental for industrial property.

■ A neutral party must hold the sale proceeds until the replacement property is obtained. A third-party "qualified intermediary," or "exchange accommodators" who are often affiliated with title companies, or an established escrow agent must be involved. This rule is to insure that you don't have use of these funds until they are used to purchase the property into which you are exchanging your equity. It is an unconditional requirement that the sales proceeds not be available to you as seller of the relinquished property under any circumstances. However, you will be allowed to receive interest on the escrowed funds. This interest could be a substantial amount considering that a sizable amount of money could be held up to 180 days. Once title is ready to be passed on the replacement property, you can use this interest to help purchase the property, or have it paid directly to you.

When you complete the exchange you will be computing your tax consequence quite differently than you would if you were buying and selling a property outright. In fact, your profit from the first (relinquished) property will be deferred until you sell—or exchange a second time—your second (replacement) property. When you do sell your final property you will pay, at capital gains rates, what monies you owe on your gain. Essentially you are postponing the taxes you owe now to a later time when they can be paid with cheaper, inflated dollars.

Note that the cost basis (original purchase price plus capital improvements minus depreciation) of your old property will be carried over into your new property, so that your taxable gain (net selling price minus original cost plus improvements and depreciation taken) is deferred, thereby giving you the net effect of using the taxes you owe as a larger down payment and equity into the new replacement property.

Furthermore, you don't need to be limited to identifying one property. A maximum of three may be chosen, with the limitation that their aggregate fair market value does not exceed 200% of the aggregate fair market value of all of the relinquished properties. Additionally, the replacement property or properties must be clearly described in writing with legal description, street address, or obvious name, such as "Town & Country Apartments."

There are three rules governing the identification of multiple properties:

1. *The Three-Property Rule.* The Three-Property Rule indicates that you may identify up to three replacement properties regardless of their fair market value. It is not necessary to purchase all of the identified properties. Even if you intend to buy only one replacement property, you might identify one or two alternate properties in case the first property purchase falls through. For those who are planning to identify and purchase three or fewer replacement properties, the following 200% and 95% rules will not apply.

2. *The 200% Rule.* The regulations permit the identification of more than three replacement properties but only under the following circumstances. The total fair market value of *all* of the identified properties must not exceed twice the contract price (200%) of the property sold. Exceeding the 200% limit will void the exchange. However, there is one exception to this rule, which is:

3. *The 95% Rule.* If more than three properties have been identified, and their total fair market value exceeds 200% of the value of what was sold, the exchange may still be valid if 95% of the total cost of all properties on the list are purchased. This means if there are properties costing $100,000 each on your list, then you must purchase at least $95,000 worth of each of them.

None of the rules described above are applicable if all of the acquisition properties are closed within 45 days of the close of your old property. When you are planning to acquire multiple properties, it would be wise to avoid the 200% Rule. Completing the exchange in 45 days may seem hard, but adequate planning before the exchange begins—a delayed closing on first, or relinquished property, obviously adds time—can lead to a successful close within 45 days. Normally, a considerable period of time can elapse from when a deposit is taken to when a property closes—that's extra time beyond the 45 days. Note that if you are exchanging out of multiple properties, the first property that closes will begin the 45-day identification period.

Here are some secondary points of which you need to be aware:

- If property received in a like-kind exchange between related persons is disposed of within two years of transfer, the original exchange will not qualify for nonrecognition of gain.

- According to IRS rules, the escrow agent you use cannot be your attorney or an attorney you have used on other legal matters within two years of the date of the sale of the relinquished property. Neither can your accountant, broker, or any others with whom you do business be your intermediary, nor can a parent, child, or sibling.

- Property located in the United States cannot be exchanged for property outside the United States.

- Properties must be clearly and accurately identified in writing and *must* be delivered to the qualified intermediary no later than midnight of the forty-fifth day. Deletions or substitutions of properties made during the 45 days must also be in writing. There are *no* circumstances that will allow for an extension of the identification period.

In summary, 1031 exchanges aren't projects you can do yourself. You cannot "sell" a property and then "buy" another. You must use an intermediary, who sells the property on your behalf, buys the next one, and then transfers the deed to you. Time is critical. Within 45 days of closing on your old property, you must identify up to three potential replacements by sending a written notice to the seller and your *qualified intermediary*. Then you have another 135 days to complete the purchase. Note that if the tax-filing deadline comes before you pass title you may wish to file for an extension.

You may also buy the replacement property first and then exchange (sell) the relinquished property. This is called a "reverse" Starker and is more complex. Unquestionably you must get specific guidance from your own tax advisor here.

COMBINING THE "EXCHANGE" WITH THE "EXCLUSION"

Here's an exciting way some investors can minimize their tax dollar. As explained previously in this chapter, you know that once you have established a property as your principal residence (living in it for at least two years and more than two years having elapsed since you sold your last principal residence) you can exclude up to $500,000 if you are married and you file jointly, or $250,000 if single, of the gain you have made. Let's see how this exclusion can work combined with the Starker Exchange. Assume you have found a property somewhere in the United States where you would like to live in the future, perhaps a retirement home in a warm weather clime. Now you want to exchange your current investment property into the property you have your eye on and rent it out until you decide to move.

The IRS has given little guidance on how long you have to keep your new replacement property as an investment. However, renting it out to someone for a minimum of one year is advisable before making it your residence. As you have read, once you have maintained your residence for two years the "exclusion" comes into play and you may be able to avoid the capital gains tax that normally would be due when you sold your new "replacement" property.

In conclusion, you can see that the advantage of an exchange is staggering—the deferral of a large tax bite that accompanies the sale of property in which you have a low tax basis. Now that you have an idea of how a Starker 1031 Exchange works, you should begin consulting with a qualified attorney and/or CPA to complete the deal. The regulations sound complex, but once you see past the initial intricacies, the basic requirements are pretty lucid—but they must be followed to the letter.

The rules for a Starker ("like-kind") Exchange are not complex— but must be strictly exercised. Failing to comply with these rules, you may have to pay the capital gains tax on the profit you thought you deferred, plus interest and penalties. Therefore, always obtain competent, professional financial and legal assistance before you enter into an exchange.

A FINAL NOTE

It would be hard to leave a discussion on investing without touching on our current cost of borrowing. Low mortgage rates, insufficient supply of houses, the relative safety of housing as an investment, and strong price appreciation have been fueling the demand for homes as well as investment property. The mortgage interest rate for a 30-year conventional fixed-rate loan is near a historic low. These low rates have not only made home ownership possible for a growing number of families, but have also allowed homeowners to tap into their rising home equity through mortgage refinancings. Investors in multifamily properties also benefit by being able to charge more modest rents, thereby reducing vacancy.

Ever wonder where mortgage interest rates come from? Contrary to popular myth they do not come from the "Prime Rate" (unless you are getting a home equity loan) or the "Federal Funds Rate." The Prime Rate is influenced by the Federal Funds Rate, announced periodically by the Federal Reserve. The Federal Funds Rate is what the Federal Reserve charges to banks for their interbank loans—it is common practice for banks to borrow from one another all the time. However, the Fed Funds and the Prime deal only with short-term loans. By contrast, home mortgages are long-term loans.

Here's how mortgage rates are determined: Mortgages are grouped together with other mortgages in packages of millions of dollars each and traded as "mortgage-backed securities" in the bond market. They in turn are influenced by trading in the same way stocks are (i.e., their prices change constantly). They are often traded by major investors such as Fannie Mae, Freddie Mac, Ginnie Mae, large institutions, even individuals. This trading—where buyers want lower prices and sellers try to get the highest prices—sets the prices for mortgages.

Although most mortgages are taken for 30 years, they really have a much shorter life as most people will either pay off the mortgage, by selling a home, or refinance an existing mortgage. Therefore, mortgages are often traded like 5-year and 10-year Treasury notes, but at a slightly higher rate—generally 1.5% to 2.5% higher than the Treasury notes as mortgages entail more risk and people buying mortgage-backed securities will want a higher return through higher interest rates. So this is why astute investors follow the Treasury market and their relative yields to determine what's happening in the mortgage market.

Success Is
Not about Education,
or Even Hard Work—
It's about Following Through

Have you noticed that many of the most educated people you know make far less than others with average (or below average) educations? Why is that? It's because education is not necessarily the path to financial security. Education is important, but it's valueless unless it can be used to follow through on your imagination, to invent and create opportunity—and, of course, to work hard. Otherwise, you might as well use your education to work hard at making someone else rich. So conquer your education and follow through on one of the best pathways to profit—real estate investment. Remember the old adage, "If at first you don't succeed, try, try again"—and don't give up, persist, persist!

TIPS TO REMEMBER

1. Build a team of professionals—agent, lawyer, mortgage broker, insurance specialist, inspector, property manager, contractor, handyman—with whom you can network.
2. Raise cash by refinancing or getting a home equity loan on existing property.
3. Use partners—former client, family member, or friend—for larger deals.
4. If possible, have enough units (either residential or commercial) so that if one unit is vacant it won't be a disaster
5. When the market is soft, lease out with less-than-market rents but use short-term leases so you can scale up rents as soon as the market turns.
6. Buy in the best location you can afford.
7. Pick buildings with minimal common areas.
8. Assess carefully the costs in a fixer-upper as well as operating costs in a multifamily.
9. Don't let your need to thoroughly analyze prevent you from making offers.
10. Catalog price trends annually for single- and multifamily prices in area communities.

11. Study each community's zoning laws.

12. Know the rules for local homeowner associations.

13. Keep an inventory of capital investment improvements such as new roof, remodeled bathroom, skylight, and so on for depreciation purposes.

14. Always keep an eye for when you can convert short-term capital gains to long-term.

15. The best money is tax-free. Consider using the personal exclusion gain to free up investment cash.

16. Keep cash in a reserve account for unexpected expenses.

17. Make sure your capitalization rate is more than your interest rate.

18. Leverage with the biggest mortgage for the longest period of time.

19. A good deal makes its own time, so search for bargains.

FINAL THOUGHTS

Some final thoughts for beginners on investment strategy at mid-decade:

- Get a home equity loan or otherwise refinance your present home, renting out under established guidelines (see "Tax Rules for Second-Home Ownership" in Chapter 20), and buy another "second" home in which to live and enjoy tax-free appreciation for up to three years.

- Refinance or get home equity loan on your present home and buy multifamily.

- Sell your current home and exclude the gain and buy a two- or three-family, living in one of the units.

- If you already own an investment property—rental house or condo, multifamily, commercial building, or land parcel— exchange your equity into a new investment property or properties.

- Or (tongue-in-cheek), don't do anything and wait for interest rates to go down, and selling prices to drop, or simply wait for the proper time three years from now when you can properly evaluate interest rates, current prices, and whether opportunity has been lost, because, as Edison said, it "looks like work."

INDEX

Made in the USA